Change from Within

339
43

Humanizing Social Welfare Organizations

Change from Within
Humanizing Social Welfare Organizations
Edited by Herman Resnick
and Rino J. Patti

Temple University Press *Philadelphia*

Temple University Press
© 1980 by Temple University. All rights reserved
Published 1980
Printed in the United States of America

Library of Congress Cataloging in Publication Data

Main entry under title:

Change from within.

    Includes bibliographical references and index.
    1. Social work aᵈministration—Addresses, essays,
lectures. I. Resnick, Herman, 1930–   II. Patti,
Rino J.
HV41.C44   361.3′068   80-13344
ISBN 0-87722-173-1
ISBN 0-8722-200-2 pbk.

Contents

Preface

The philosophers have only interpreted the world in different ways. The point, however, is to change it.

—Hegel

  The purpose of this book is to provide human service professionals with a set of concepts, analytic tools, and action guidelines based on small-group and organizational models that may inform their efforts to make organizations more effective and humane instruments for the delivery of services. A secondary, but no less important, purpose is to focus attention on organizational change methodology as a subject for scholarly inquiry and research. To date there has been little scholarly attention given to change efforts initiated by low-power persons in formal organizations.[1] It is the editors' hope that this volume will serve to consolidate some of the important beginning work that has been done in this field and provide a point of departure for more extensive and systematic inquiries in the future.

  The book is designed to aid individuals and groups in the human service professions, including social workers, nurses and teachers, and others who seek to effect changes in the policies and practices of the organizations that employ them. Human service practitioners at direct service, supervisory, and even management levels often find themselves implementing policy and program decisions imposed by superiors that they consider not to be in the best interests of the organization's clientele. Just as frequently, such persons must contend with administrative practices, rules, and procedures that have the effect of reducing organizational effectiveness by undermining employee morale and/or impeding the service delivery process. While these and related problems are not new to human service organizations, in recent years professionals have become increasingly sensitive to such dysfunctions and have become more actively involved in their solution.[2] So far, unfortunately, there has been little in the way of systematically developed theory, method, or research to guide such efforts. As a consequence, practitioners have been forced to rely on assumptions, analytic tools, and intervention techniques drawn largely from their clinical training or, more commonly, from personal judgment and experience. Reliance on these usually implicit sources of expertise has often resulted in practitioners' viewing agency problems as the collective expression of individual personalities, rather than as organizational phenomena per se. In the absence of explicit paradigms for organizational analysis and action, practitioners who have sought to effect changes in their agencies have often lacked a sense of clarity and confidence that derives from a well-formulated base of knowledge and expertise.

ORGANIZATION OF THE BOOK

Following the introductory chapter, the book is divided into three sections and a postscript. Part I focuses on the organizational context of service delivery. Its purpose is to provide the reader with analytic tools for assessing how organizational context influences the service delivery process. While the articles included here address a number of problems commonly encountered in human service agencies, they are less concerned with cataloguing these concerns than with understanding the organizational dynamics that give rise to them. Collectively, these articles should aid the practitioner–change agent in conducting the problem analysis described in the model of change to be outlined in the Introduction.

Part II addresses the issue of receptivity and/or resistance to change initiated from below. The articles included here provide complementary perspectives on structural, interpersonal, and individual factors in organizations that make them more or less amenable to change proposals. The analysis of resistance is critical to our model of change inasmuch as it provides the action system with critical information regarding the goals it can feasibly pursue and the resources it will need to achieve its purposes.

Part III is concerned with the practitioner–change agent in action. Many of the articles touch on the content developed in the previous section, but their principle emphasis is the process of change itself, including the formulation of goals, the development and maintenance of the action system, strategy planning, and tactical implementation.

We conclude the volume with a brief postscript that identifies selected issues and developments likely to influence organizational change practices significantly in the years ahead.

Notes

1. A beginning literature has begun to emerge. See, for example, George Brager and Stephen Holloway, *Changing Human Service Organizations* (New York: Free Press, 1978), and Harold Weissman, *Overcoming Mismanagement in the Human Services* (San Francisco: Jossey-Bass, 1973).
2. See, for example, the statement developed by the National Association of Social Workers, Ad Hoc Committee on Advocacy, "The Social Worker as Advocate: Champion of Social Victims," *Social Work* 14, no. 2 (April 1969): 16–22, and Willard Richan and Allan Mendelsohn, *Social Work: The Unloved Profession* (New York: Franklin Watts, 1973), pp. 126–162.

Foreword

Ronald Lippitt

Professor Emeritus
Sociology and Psychology
University of Michigan

In this volume editors/authors Resnick and Patti have compiled and created a very significant resourcebook for all organization change-agents, dedicated professionals, and forward-looking administrators.

Although the focus of the contributions is on influencing upward in initiating processes of change in social service agencies, the basic analyses of readiness to change, resistance to change, and strategies for change are a generic concept and technique toolkit for all change agentry.

But this volume is of unique value and support for the increasing number of direct service professionals and "middle management" supervisors in human service and educational institutions and organizations. These are the personnel who are most directly in contact with, and sensitive to, the needs and expectations of the client consumers of service. They have the best data on the neglected, unreached, and mis-served. And they also include the creators of significant service innovations that warrant attention, evaluation, and dissemination as the cutting edge of effective human service.

Resnick, Patti, and their contributor colleagues point to the dilemma, for these professionals, of coping actively and effectively with their awareness of the discrepancy between "what is" and "what ought to be"; of dealing with this sense of conflict between their "contract" to represent high standards of professional service, and their agency job contract to implement regulations, policies, and bureaucratic routines which often seem to subvert the actualization of their standards of best practice. This volume, better than any other in the human service literature, identifies, analyzes, and reports the temptations, traps, and action potentials for dedicated professionals who want to deal creatively and potently with this dilemma.

I am vividly reminded of a unit in my first group work course with my great professor, L. K. Hall, at Springfield College. He labelled this unit,

"Dealing with divine discontent." It was a "doing something about it" posture that was positive and activist. The essence of it was support for achieving the awareness and sensitivity to be discontented with the way things are without wasting energy on negative discharges of frustration, anger, and attack tactics which, as he so vividly illustrated, had the consequence of loss of personal morale and loss of significant impact on the problem we wanted to solve. The editors correctly comment (p. 111) that "low-power practitioners frequently become so intensely committed to the substance of a proposal [for change] that they fail to give sufficient attention to the factors that will impede or support its acceptance and implementation." Because a fight orientation is such a major stimulator of resistance, I would propose changing the insurgents' guideline (p. 204), "Never fight a battle if there is a chance of losing it," to "Never fight a battle if there is a chance of initiating collaborative problem-solving."

Several chapters, particularly the one by Klein (Chapter 10), point out that resistance to change is a natural predictable process, and provides important learning opportunities for the change-agent, often providing the basis for improved alternatives and the prevention of serious mistakes.

An implication of this orientation is that the professional who wants to take initiative to facilitate organizational change must work on the challenge of developing a repertoire of skills and support for change strategies comparable in technical sophistication to the professional intervention skills and values needed to work effectively with individual and group clients.

This volume takes a big step forward in spelling out conceptually and operationally such important diagnostic imperatives as the assessment of readiness for change, the assessment of one's own potential to take successful change initiation, and the deriving of appropriate alternative strategies for change efforts. Then there are very important presentations of models for taking action, and case examples of successful types of efforts to influence upwards.

I think the various authors might have pointed out more concretely that the development and implementation of successful change efforts can be more than a risk; they can also, if appropriately documented, be a source of important publication, of visibility as an innovator of professional practice, and of respect and leadership among peers.

Perhaps a bit missing from the volume is a supportive cluster of observations of current trends and future projections (e.g., Toffler's "Third Wave" analysis) that should encourage the types of initiative-taking supported in these chapters. For example, there seems to be evidence of trends toward fewer levels of organizational bureaucracy, more two-way, up and down communication in goal setting and planning, more coalition-type influence of consumers and workers, more emphasis on quality of work and service, more personalization or individualization of service and education, and more training of administrators in the values, norms, and procedures of participative management.

So this volume is not only a high quality resource for us, but in many ways it is uniquely timely for the decades ahead—because the opportunities to initiate improvements in professional and organizational practice are greater than ever, peer support is more ready, and the ears "upstairs" are more sensitive. It may appear that budget and accountability pressure are a counter-force to innovative change. This is not my observation. The need for, and the vulnerability to, meaningful improvements in professional and organizational practice seem to be activated by these pressures.

Introduction

Chapter 1   An Overview of

Organizational Change

In an era when strategies and technologies for organizational change abound, one may reasonably question why it is necessary for human service professionals to become systematically involved in modifying the policies and procedures of the agencies in which they are employed. Most practitioners are heavily involved in the business of delivering services, and one could argue that they should devote themselves to this primary responsibility and leave the job of organizational change to administrators, consultants, and the like. It is important, therefore, that the rationale for organizational change from below be explicitly set forth.

One of the major insights provided by organizational theory and research in recent years is that human service organizations, no less than other kinds of organizations, tend over time to become preoccupied with their own maintenance and survival. Social scientists have coined the term "goal displacement" to describe the phenomenon wherein the avowed social purposes of public service institutions are replaced by latent goals such as the protection of organizational jurisdiction, program continuity, employment security, and a host of other self-serving and self-aggrandizing objectives.[1] In partial response to this phenomenon, a number of accountability mechanisms, including citizen participation, program evaluation, legislative audits, and consumer protection associations, have been developed to ensure that human service organizations continue to serve the purposes for which they were officially created. Organizational change is essentially an extension of this effort to countervail the goal-displacing tendencies of formal organizations. It differs from other mechanisms in that it is an internal force for change that is an integral, albeit informal part of the administrative fabric of the agency. Its practitioners are in a position to be much more sensitive to and informed about the intricacies of agency operation and the nuances of agency culture and, therefore, potentially at least, more likely to have immediate access to the problems that are occurring and the processes that must be altered. In addition, because human service professionals, as a part of their training, usually subscribe to a set of ethics and norms regarding the primacy of client welfare, they are able to enunciate a set of standards and values against which organizational performance can be measured. In this sense, organizational change provides an additional, and potentially corrective, force to the process of goal displacement.

A second rationale for organizational change from below grows out of the recognition that, as agencies grow large and become vertically differentiated, the ability to communicate upward in the administrative hierarchy tends to become increasingly difficult.[2] Even in those instances where organizations maintain elaborate information systems whose purpose, in part, is to provide decision-makers with information about agency dysfunctions, normal processes of information attrition and distortion often tend to obscure messages as they are conveyed up the line. The greater the administrative distance—that is, the number of hierarchical levels between those who generate data about organizational performance and those who use it for decision-making—the greater, in general, is the likelihood that information will be distorted.[3] Many administrators seek to deal with this problem by creating opportunities for subordinates to bypass normal channels of communication and provide their input directly.[4] Change from below is essentially a variant of this informal approach for supplementing the formal communication process. Criticisms of agency performance, ideas about how to correct problems, proposals for the adoption of innovations, all of which can be screened out or blocked as they are communicated from subordinates to superiors, tend, in the course of an internal change effort, to be communicated directly from subordinates to decision-makers, skipping intermediate authority. Information and ideas conveyed in this manner are, if anything, more valuable to decision-makers precisely because they are initiated by subordinates who run some risk of being rejected and/or penalized for circumventing the usual process of communication.

Finally, one can argue the importance of organizational change activity in terms of its value for human service practitioners who become so engaged. Though the ultimate purpose of such efforts is to enhance agency effectiveness vis-à-vis clients, it is safe to say that the quality of services provided will be affected by the morale and work satisfaction of the service staff. Change from below is a means through which practitioners can actively influence their organizational environment. Since, as a general rule, employees who participate in influencing agency climate and structure tend to be more committed to their work, it follows that involvement in organizational change tends to promote this outcome as well.[5] There are, of course, other avenues that employees can utilize to influence agency conditions, but organizational change is particularly useful because it is a self-initiated and internally maintained expression of practitioner interest in improving organizational performance. To be sure, there are times when practitioner-initiated change efforts are unsuccessful and the participants come away more alienated and more resigned to the status quo as a result. This is perhaps inevitable in some instances, but it is our belief that as practitioners become more skilled and knowledgeable about organizations and the art of changing them, they will not only be more realistic about what they can hope to change but more consistently effective in doing so.

In setting forth this rationale for change from below we do not wish to imply that low-power practitioners are necessarily more committed to improving human service agencies than their superiors. Nor do we wish to suggest that only those changes emanating from below are virtuous, progressive, and the like. Clearly, many innovative ideas for improving social services are initiated by upper-level administrators. It serves no purpose to deny this reality or to obscure the central role that agency management can play in promoting constructive organizational change. Rather, our intent here is to argue that the perspectives of low-power people, perspectives that grow out of day-to-day experience with program implementation and a familiarity with client need, should be actively promulgated in the administrative decision-making process. To be sure, some of the proposals for change coming from below will be ill-informed, unrealistic, and even, on occasion, prompted by parochial interests unrelated to client need. Still, on balance, subordinate-initiated change can provide agency administrators with a valuable source of unfiltered feedback regarding the consequences of their actions and, at the same time, augment the body of information and alternatives they draw from in making decisions. Perhaps as important, however, involvement in change from below is the crucible on which organizational citizenship is forged. If human service professionals are to be more than mere technicians, they must concern themselves with the social issues that form the context of their work. Change from below is, if nothing else, a vehicle for enabling practitioners to see the important relationship between human service technology and social purpose.

ORGANIZATIONAL CHANGE FOR WHAT?

As we have suggested, organizational change from below is not an end in itself, but a means of enhancing the effectiveness of human service organizations in their relations with clients. Because of this, it is essential that the practitioner–change agent have a well-formulated conception of organizational effectiveness that transcends the particular issue or problem with which he or she is concerned and the concrete recommendations being promulgated. Without this larger conception of what the agency should be, a change objective, no matter how important in the short term, may have little relevance or utility for long-term organizational development. Under the worst circumstances, change efforts conducted in a vacuum, divorced from some normative model of agency functioning, run the risk of generating unanticipated consequences that are more detrimental to agency effectiveness than was the original problem. Finally, organizational change that is grounded in a broad, explicit conception of agency functioning is less likely to be subject to the vagaries of expedience and self-interest, which in the heat of change can sometimes divert the action system's attention from its substantive purpose.

What then are the characteristics of an effective organization in the human services that change agents should seek to promote through their efforts? Or, more specifically, what agency conditions and processes are most likely to result in services that are responsive to client need, that are skillfully and efficiently delivered, and that are technically advanced and humanely administered? Theory and research suggest the dimensions of an organizational model that is conducive to these outcomes. The model, which is variously referred to as "organic" or "dynamic," is best suited to those situations in which an organization operates in a rapidly changing and unstable environment, where its tasks and functions are varied and nonroutine, where the service goals are difficult to specify, and where heavy reliance is placed on the cognitive and interpersonal skills of staff to solve problems.[6] Clearly, these are conditions that obtain in most human service organizations.

The organic or dynamic organizational model incorporates the following dimensions:

1. A division of labor and task assignment based on an assessment of how the knowledge, skills, and experiences of staff can be flexibly utilized to accomplish the work required.
2. A relatively shallow hierarchy of authority—that is, minimal stratification—where superiors have general authority and responsibility for coordinating the work of subordinates, but tend to rely on the judgment and discretion of staff in carrying out day-to-day operations.
3. A decision-making process that allows for participation by members at all administrative levels who have knowledge and information relevant to the decision being made.

4. Rules and procedures that provide guidelines for worker performance, but allow sufficient latitude for the worker to flexibly adapt his or her behavior to the needs of the situation.
5. Communication processes that allow for, and facilitate, the flow of information up and down the hierarchy as well as diagonally among persons in different departments and at different levels.
6. A high value placed on subordinates' understanding and developing commitment to the organization's goals and objectives, rather than obedience for its own sake or blind compliance with the dictates of those in authority.
7. A climate that is supportive of professional growth and development, where employees are seen as an expanding and renewable resource rather than a fixed pool of capabilities to be impersonally exploited.
8. A style of leadership that depends heavily on consultation with subordinates, individually and in groups, rather than on unilateral administrative action.

This is, of course, only a skeletal outline of the dimensions of the organic organization. The central point is that there is a growing body of empirical evidence to suggest that human service organizations that approximate the conditions and processes listed above are likely to be more effective instruments for service delivery.[7] Among other things, such agencies are found to be more responsive to changes in their environment and more capable of changing their programs to incorporate service innovations. Professional employees in such organizations are likely to be less alienated from their work and from peers, more satisfied with their jobs, and more productive.

The organic model is after all an ideal-typical construct that is seldom fully actualized. For the organizational change practitioner, it should serve not so much as a set of objectives to be immediately accomplished, since this is seldom possible, but rather as an agenda for long-range organizational development that can serve to inform the immediate change efforts being attempted. In this way, organizational change efforts are not just ad hoc actions devoted to modifying a single aspect of agency practice, but instead become an integral part of the long-term plan, whose purpose it is to effect more fundamental and lasting changes in the organization environment.

WHAT IS ORGANIZATIONAL CHANGE?

Organizational change is a set of interrelated activities engaged in by human service practitioners, in their roles as professional employees, for the purpose of modifying the formal policies, programs, procedures, or management practices of the agencies that employ them. The primary intended outcomes of such change efforts are to increase the effectiveness of the services provided and/or to remove organizational conditions that are deleterious to the client population served.[8]

Unlike many forms of planned change, organizational change from below, as we define it, is initiated in the lower reaches of the administrative hierarchy, a reversal of the direction in which influence normally flows in agencies. The change agent, which may be an individual, an ad hoc group brought together for purposes of addressing a particular issue, or a formal subunit of an organization, assumes responsibility for identifying and defining an organizational problem, developing a proposal for change, and gaining the approval of appropriate decision-makers. Specific change efforts may include attempts to gain entitlements for clients as individuals or in groups who are denied services because of inflexible, arbitrary, or unfair administrative procedures; to establish mechanisms to promote service coordination between departments in an agency; to add clients to an agency board to achieve greater community representation in the policy-making process; or to create a new service or program to deal with a previously unmet need.

A distinctive feature of organizational change is that its practitioners are not usually legitimated by their organizations as change agents—that is, their source of legitimation for this activity is derived more from their professional purposes and commitments than from their agency job descriptions, which very rarely include this function. This has two important implications: First, change efforts are normally undertaken as an additional, self-imposed responsibility that the practitioner (group or unit) must reconcile with the demands and expectations of his or her (or their) primary assignment. Second, in some sense, such efforts are likely to be seen as a violation of the employee-employer contract, particularly if they threaten to alter the balance of power or to disrupt routine in the agency. Both these factors make the role of the change agent stressful.

The intervention model for organizational change from below has not as yet been fully articulated, nor has its efficacy as an approach to changing agency behavior been systematically evaluated. Experience and a limited number of case studies seem to suggest, however, that organizational change consists of the following interrelated analytic and inter-actional activities (see Figure 1-1):

Problem Analysis. Organizational change begins when human service staff members decide that some agency program, policy, procedure, or condition is adversely affecting the delivery of client service and that something needs to be done about it. A typical next step is to convene informally a like-minded staff group to consider (and analyze) the problem and commit themselves to some activity to remedy or reduce the problem.

Goal Formulation and Analysis of Resistance. Specification of the goals and concrete recommendations for altering the condition in question are required. As the problem is discussed and reworked, the staff group (now properly called an action system) comes to some tentative agreement as to what it hopes to achieve as a result of this activity—that is, some specific alteration of a policy, procedure, or agency condition. This discussion considers not only the staff action system's wishes for a desirable outcome but the potential organizational obstacles to the change goal as well. In the face of these, the action system may choose to modify its original goals, particularly as it confronts the limitations of its resources (size of the group, amount of time and energy it has, force of the community support, and so on).

Action System Development and Maintenance. As the action system comes to some tentative agreements on what problems it is focusing on and what goals might conceivably reduce these problems, it is at the same time implicitly or explicitly developing some group conditions that will influence, if not determine, its effectiveness. To facilitate or inhibit the development of openness, it will establish leadership, group norms, and operating procedures—three conditions needed in an action system for effective organizational change. A key activity in the early stages is the selection of staff members both to swell the ranks of the action system and to provide it with persons who have the necessary knowledge, skills, experience, and prestige to do its work.

Formulation of a Plan of Action. At a critical point in its deliberations, the action system tends to converge on an overall tentative strategy that reflects the desires of the action system members as well as their "real-politic" assessment of the potential resistance to such a strategy. This assessment is based on a realistic appraisal of the resources and influence necessary to obtain a favorable action on the change proposal from

FIGURE 1-1 *Organizational Change Process*

Problem Analysis	Goal Formulation and Analysis of Resistance	Action System Development and Maintenance	Formulation and Implementation of Plan of Action	Implementation Assessment of Decision	Retrieval and Transmission of Learning
Practitioner perceives a problem in agency functioning.	Action system develops goal with specific recommendation.	Action system is expanded to include persons with desired skills, power, etc.	Action system formulates plan of action (i.e., when to surface proposal, in what context, by whom), general strategy (i.e., collaborative or adversary), and tactics.	Change proposal is accepted by decision-makers in whole or in some acceptable modified version.	Action system members specify learnings from change activities and communicate to colleagues within organization.
Practitioner acts as catalyst to sensitize potential colleague allies to perceived problem.	Action system identifies potential sources of resistance to proposed change goals.	Leadership, norms, patterns of communication, decision-making processes emerge as the action system develops mechanisms for internal maintenance.	Proposal is introduced to decision-maker in accordance with plan of action.	Action system disbands.	Members of action system monitor and assess implementation of change proposal to determine impact on problem initially perceived.
Practitioner and colleagues further define and analyze problem and decide to initiate corrective action. The action system is formed.	Action system redefines goals in light of anticipated resistance and analysis of own resources.	Action system moves to develop support for proposal outside action system, e.g., sympathetic members of administration, external groups, professional associations.	Support and/or resistance to proposal by decision-makers is assessed.	Action system remains intact.	
As goals are more sharply defined, some members drop out or become marginal to the action system.		Goals are modified to reflect changes in action system composition and preferences of external support group.	Plan of action and/or proposal is modified to reflect new analysis of what will be required to obtain approval from decision-makers. (This may occur several times.)	Change proposal is accepted by decision-makers in some acceptable modified version.	
				Action system reassesses plan of action proposal and decides whether to persist or disband.	
				Change proposal is rejected by decision-makers, with no counter.	
				Action system negotiates with decision-makers to achieve most favorable outcome possible.	
				Change proposal is rejected and substitute proposal is made.	
				A compromise version of the change proposal is accepted and approved by decision-makers.	

decision-makers. The action system must decide at this juncture whether its overall strategy will be collaborative—that is, will work with the system and try to improve it—or adversary—work more against the system in order to improve it. Tactical issues that flow from these early basic decisions will include: Who will contact whom? When should decision-making meetings take place? What kind of climate should prevail at such meetings? A guideline for both strategy and tactical decisions is to take those actions that have the greatest possibility of goal achievement.

Implementation of the Plan of Action. Once a preliminary overall plan with a set of tactics is agreed to, the next steps occur quickly: contacting inside and outside supports for further information and leverage, and meeting with the decision-making administrators. As action system members move from thinking and planning to action, they frequently encounter obstacles to their contemplated changes. These obstacles may not deter action, but rather serve to redirect it in ways that will increase the possibility of obtaining the members' original goals (though perhaps in revised form). For example, administrators sometimes reject part of the change suggestion and/or add their own ideas to it. An action system may welcome this (even though it modifies the change goal) because the administrators' modification often signals a commitment to the change, and a willingness to later support the diffusion of the proposal throughout the system.

Assessment of Decision Implementation. After some affirmative decision has been reached by the administration vis-à-vis the change proposal (or its parts), the action system still has work to do in order to ensure that desired changes in fact occur and such changes are maintained. Even though the administration has agreed to the change suggestion at some level of commitment, it is necessary that the action system monitor the change proposal as it is implanted throughout the system. Not only might top echelon decision-makers resist, but colleagues and other role groups (such as clerical and paraprofessional employees) not actively involved in the change project might themselves become an obstacle to the successful internalization of the change process. Their interest and needs must also be considered if the change is to be successfully implemented.

Retrieval and Transmission of Learning. A final step for the action system is conceptualizing and communicating what they have learned from this experience. This process will not only serve to make action system members more effective in future change efforts, but will also help them to transmit the results of their experience to colleagues within the agency and to the larger professional community.

Conceptually, these components of the organizational change process can be treated as distinct entities linked together in some linear fashion. In practice, however, the components are highly interdependent so that, as each phase of the process unfolds, it normally has significant implications for the work that has gone before, as well as the work still to be done. Figure 1-1 is a crude attempt to represent the interaction between steps in the change process. For example, an examination of the figure will indicate that goal formulation and action system development and maintenance are highly interdependent phases of the change process. The nature of the goals originally selected by the action system influence its recruitment processes, while, in turn, the eventual composition and nature of the action system almost inevitably result in some refinement and/or reformation of the original change goals.

RISK AND ORGANIZATIONAL CHANGE[9]

Even this brief look at the parameters of organizational change from below suggests that there may be occupational risks associated with such efforts. At least three kinds of risk can be identified: job loss, restricted upward mobility, and strained work relationships. Each of these is discussed below, followed by some suggestions for how risk can be minimized.

It is perhaps belaboring the obvious to state that the most immediate impediment to organizational change is the fear of losing one's job. To the extent that change from below involves dissent from organizational policies, the violation of group norms, and/or open conflict with the executive or board, job loss is of course a possibility. While dismissal is not often employed to neutralize advocacy efforts, virtually everyone has heard of such instances, and in a tight job market the exceptional case has a way of appearing to be a statistically significant trend.

On the face of it, dismissal from a job can involve such obviously undesirable consequences as inconvenience, possible embarassment with friends and family, income loss, relocation, and the burden of explaining negative job references. Perhaps just as significant is the loss of professional identity that can occur when one is dismissed from an agency. In the absence of strong societal approval, the social worker's status is defined as much by place of employment as by professional qualifications.

The phrase "I am a social worker" takes on shape and substance even for the relatively informed layman, only when it is followed by an explanation about where one works, one's duties, the clients with whom one works, and so on. One indication of this is the fact, long observed in professional circles, that a social worker's status in the eyes of the community (indeed, among colleagues as well) tends to be associated with where he or she is employed. Under these circumstances, dismissal takes on important implications for the social worker's public identity.

Among those who would promote organizational change there seem to be three general approaches to dealing with the threat of job loss. The first is to treat it as a red herring, a false spectre that need not be a real constraint if the social worker will only exercise the rights and utilize the discretion that are available to him or her as an employee. The implication here is that the problem is really the practitioner's lack of commitment to client welfare and timidity in the face of authority. A second reaction is to argue that job loss is the price a professional should be prepared to pay in the interest of keeping the welfare bureaucracy responsive to client needs. Indeed, in this view, the change agent is probably being most successful when his or her job is being threatened. Finally, there is a position that holds that, while there is inevitably some risk associated with change, the practitioner should not be expected to assume this burden alone. If change from below is to be widely practiced, it must be buttressed with institutionalized supports that can be called upon when the agency utilizes punitive measures to curtail ethically sound change efforts. This position promises the most realistic long-range solution to the threat of job loss. Mechanisms developed by the National Association of Social Workers in recent years to assist workers subjected to arbitrary dismissals are a promising step in this direction.

Involvement in organizational change can also have implications for upward mobility in an agency. In the absence of a career path and a reward structure for those who wish to remain in direct practice, the practitioner who desires more money, status, and recognition must usually seek advancement through the administrative hierarchy. This fact alone often creates disincentives to become involved in change efforts, especially those in which there is a potential for conflict, because promotion is very likely to be contingent upon behavioral evidences of loyalty to the organization. This is not to say that intellect and skill are irrelevant to the selection process, because clearly an agency's administrative hierarchy is usually seeking to bolster its capability. Still, a central task of administration is to maintain organizational stability and continuity, and one of the most important ways to do this is to ensure that people brought into positions of leadership are committed to the agency's normative structure.

These preconditions for advancement are not likely to escape the notice of practitioners. The young worker may not feel overly constrained, since lateral mobility is still a viable option, if not a necessity. At some point, however, when career aspirations start to crystallize and considerations of security and status become salient motivators, the potential costs associated with change from below may begin to rise dramatically. At this juncture administrative approval becomes an important occupational asset.

A third potential risk is the strain that can sometimes occur in relationships with colleagues and/or superiors. Indeed, our observation suggests that fear of losing the support and good will of co-workers is often a more compelling consideration for practitioners entertaining a change effort than either dismissal or upward mobility. This is not too surprising. The delivery of services to troubled and often dependent clients is, after all, an energy-depleting, lonely activity. Human service workers generally rely heavily on fellow employees for consultation, advice, and approval. To the extent that a change is controversial and generates conflict, the practitioner–change agent may experience some temporary strain and loss of support in relationships with colleagues.

These and related risks will ordinarily be considered by a practitioner who is deciding whether to become involved in a change effort. Whether they are considered acceptable risks will depend ultimately on his or her estimate of the severity and magnitude of the problem, personal inclination, and personal circumstances. In addition, however, the assessment of risk should also be grounded in an understanding of whether the conditions necessary to sustain a change effort and minimize risk are present. Three conditions that seem particularly important are organizational legitimacy, professional credibility, and colleague support.

Organizational Legitimacy

The basic source of legitimacy for the change agent, as we mentioned earlier, is his or her ethical obligation to the primacy of client welfare. Where this obligation conflicts with loyalty to the employing organization's policies and procedures, the professional practitioner is committed to give precedence to client interests. This ethical prescript is the cornerstone of change efforts and provides the practitioner with an essential rationale for assuming this role. As important as this is, however, it will probably not be sufficient to justify the worker's change efforts in the eyes of his or her administrative superiors since, as our earlier discussion suggested, the worker has not been vested with formal authority to perform this role. In this situation, the change agent, who is acting in accordance with a professionally prescribed code of conduct, may find that his or her behavior is defined as organizationally irresponsible. To establish organizational legitimacy for the advocacy role, then, the practitioner must seek to justify his or her activity in terms that have some relevance to the social economy of the employing agency. Generally, there appear to be four ways in which this can be done.

1. The practitioner can claim legitimacy on the basis of substantive knowledge regarding the problem at hand. That is to say, the change agent can argue that, by virtue of some special knowledge or skill, he or she can assist the organization in coming to a more rational and effective solution than has heretofore been available for dealing with the issue in question. Such an assertion cannot be made in the abstract, but must be buttressed with some visible evidence of competence—for example, a thorough knowledge of the problem, an understanding of those factors that condition the organization's response, a well-documented plan for action.

2. The worker can seek to justify his or her role as a preserver of organizational values. The argument here is that change is a way of keeping the organization's performance consonant with its own formally stated objectives, to ensure that client rights and entitlements are honored and that organizational convenience does not replace client welfare as the criterion for action. The change agent's particular contribution is to help the organization avoid the danger of consensually validating itself.

3. The practitioner can also seek to legitimate his or her role on the grounds that organizational change is a necessary supplement to the communication processes in an organization. The normal processes of communication up through an administrative hierarchy, as previously mentioned, often result in information loss or distortion that can, over time, deprive administrators of the data they need to assess the effects of the agency's programs and procedures accurately. The practitioner can argue that organizational change provides undigested timely information to decision makers regarding matters of crucial importance.

4. Finally, the change agent can attempt to justify his or her action on the basis of political self-interest. This approach is more likely to be effective when employed by a group (for example, a union) or formal unit of the organization that has some ability to withhold needed services or otherwise disrupt the organization's normal operations. In this instance, the action system seeks to establish the right to have its interests formally represented in the decision-making process on the grounds that its values and needs will not otherwise be adequately reflected.

Any of these bases for establishing organizational legitimacy may be rejected by administrative superiors as an insufficient rationale for deviating from official role prescriptions. Nevertheless, it seems almost certain that unless the practitioner has a clear conception in which to anchor his or her claim to legitimacy and the ability to give substance to that conception in dealings with agency leadership, change efforts will be difficult to sustain.

Professional Credibility

The risks associated with change from below also seem to be very much related to whether the practitioner possesses certain attributes that decrease his or her vulnerability to administrative reprisals. Three attributes constitute important sources of professional credibility and influence that can be drawn upon in an advocacy effort: membership in the system, technical competence, and special expertise.

By membership in the system, we refer not simply to a formal status, but rather to whether the practitioner is perceived by others as being an integral part of the group life of the institution. Tenure is an important precondition to achieving membership, but it is hardly sufficient. Membership is more crucially dependent upon an incumbent's understanding of the organization's normative structure, both formal and informal, its ideology, and its vested interests. It is rooted in having experienced and struggled with problems growing out of limited resources, community pressures, interdepartmental rivalries, idiosyncratic personalities, and the like. It becomes established as one identifies with the frustrations and accomplishments of one's colleagues and superiors and comes to understand compassionately the magnitude of their investment in the existing order of things. Perhaps most importantly, membership is achieved when one becomes sensitive to the personal costs entailed in organizational change. Until the practitioner has acquired this perspective, he or she is likely to be seen as something of an organizational transient, with all the vulnerability that this normally implies.

Technical competence in one's primary role assignment is also an important, risk-reducing attribute for the change agent. Essentially this means being thorough and technically proficient in the performance of one's duties. Where these standards of performance have not been met, it becomes all too easy for the organization to discredit the cause being advocated by attacking the credibility of the practitioner. The worker whose performance has been shoddy or irresponsible makes an excellent target for those who are threatened or inconvenienced by the changes proposed.

Beyond the competent performance of one's organizationally defined role, it is also useful to possess some special expertise that contributes to agency maintenance or development. This expertise can take many forms, including grantsmanship, relationships with an ethnic community, or substantive knowledge of a problem area that is of concern to the agency. Whatever the nature of this expertise, it is important that one's administrative superiors recognize it as a special contribution, above and beyond that which is normally expected of someone in the practitioner role.

In sum, then, the risks associated with change are usually relative to the presence or absence of certain worker attributes. The more a practitioner is perceived by superiors as having one or more of the attributes discussed above, the less vulnerable he or she is likely to be to the risks mentioned earlier. All this suggests that one of the change agent's first tasks should be to assess his or her organizational strengths and weaknesses dispassionately. In the absence of one or more of the attributes discussed above, the practitioner may find the risks unacceptably high.

Colleague Support

One of the most important requirements of a sustained change effort is the presence of support from colleagues and peers. Notwithstanding the occasional dramatic case in which a low-power person single-handedly challenges an organization's policies, most practitioners find it necessary to seek the help of their fellow workers. This is true not only because there is power in numbers but, more importantly, because group support helps mitigate the vulnerability and uncertainty attendant to change. Generally, two kinds of colleague support are necessary: task and expressive.

The energy, time and skill required in most change efforts are often more than even the most dedicated individual practitioner can command. It is not unusual, for example, in situations involving substantive organizational changes, for an intervention to consist of a number of data-gathering interviews with people in several departments, access to and analysis of records and reports, personal contacts with representatives of standard-setting, funding, and community-based groups, proposal writing, lengthy problem-solving or negotiating sessions, and so on. The change agent who must continue to perform his or her regular duties is seldom able to carry this burden alone. But, even if one were able to do so, it would probably not be desirable, since the individual practitioner is unlikely to have the range of knowledge and skills required by these diverse tasks. A skillful handling of these tasks is usually better achieved by drawing upon the various talents and aptitudes of fellow workers.

Just as important, the change agent also requires expressive support from colleagues or peers in order to maintain morale and perspective.

TABLE 1-1
Approaches to Organizational Change

Critical Intervention Variables	Administrative Change	Organizational Development	Organizational Change from Below
Change Agent / Action System	Arministrative personnel with officially prescribed authority to initiate changes (including policy board)	Outside consultant retained by agency administration to facilitate problem resolution	Employees of agencies with no formally prescribed authority or responsibility to initiate change
Primary Sources of Legitimacy	Legislative mandate, executive order, administrative rules and regulations, agency policies	Contract with agency administration, authority to intervene delegated by administrative official	Professional ethics and values, employee associations (e.g., unions)
Primary Sources of Power	Control over resources, information	Expertise (knowledge and skill regarding change processes)	Other workers, knowledge of problem, professional expertise
Scope of Concern	Entire organization: structure, policy, program, technology,	Organization units: departments, work teams; primary interest in	Organization units: departments, work teams; primary interest in

	personnel, inter-personal processes, cultural norms, decision-making processes, etc.	altering interpersonal processes and group norms	changing policies, programs, decision processes, and work procedures
Common Tactics	Directives, budgetary control, personnel changes, consensus-building through staff participation	Data feedback, team-building, staff development, group process	Participation on agency committees, fact-finding, building internal support through education and persuasion
Major Constraints and Sources of Resistance	Subordinate inertia stemming from fear, entrenched interests, scarce resources, lack of external support, inability to control implementation processes	Limited time involvement, lack of administrative support, employee distrust of outsider	Superior's disagreement insufficient time, energy, and knowledge, uncertain legitimacy, fear of reprisal and disapproval, job insecurity

Since the practitioner often operates in largely uncharted waters, without clear precedents or previous experience, stress and confusion are not uncommon. In this context, it becomes crucial to have regular access to one or more peers who, in the context of a trusting relationship, will challenge assumptions, question the choice of tactics, and provide a balancing perspective on the motivations of administrative superiors. Such supportive relationships can also provide the worker with an opportunity to ventilate feelings of anger, frustration, fear, and self-doubt that often occur in a change scenario.

It is our contention, then, that without the kinds of support discussed above the difficulties normally associated with change from below become compounded. The practitioner who does not attend to this need runs a high risk of being forced to withdraw prematurely or become exhausted. In either case, cynicism and alienation are often the unfortunate aftermath.

CONTRASTING APPROACHES TO ORGANIZATIONAL CHANGE

Change from below, as we have defined it in the preceding pages, is only one of many types of change that occur in human service agencies. Planned change efforts initiated by administrators and by organizational development consultants are two other approaches that have received extensive discussion in the literature.[10] It is not our intent to deal with these approaches in the following chapters, but for purposes of defining our subject more sharply it may be instructive to compare them with change from below. Table 1-1 highlights some of the differences and similarities in these approaches. Several points are worth noting.

1. The practitioner–change agent has little official vested legitimacy as a change agent when compared to the administrator or the organizational consultant. Such legitimacy as he or she possesses at the outset derives largely from the internalized professional norms and values that may or may not be recognized as legitimate by the organization.

2. The practitioner–change agent relies basically on symbolic power and interpersonal power. In this sense, change from below resembles organizational development. Although the worker may be able to develop power that is effectively coercive, this is seldom possible unless he or she can become allied with significant external groups and/or can command the allegiance of a large portion of the organization's work force. Mobilizing this kind of power base is ordinarily difficult for the low-

power person to achieve. Administrators, by contrast, frequently have access to coercive power that can be employed to effect change.

3. The practitioner–change agent generally has a somewhat narrower scope of concern than the administrator or external consultant. For the most part, subordinates are concerned with altering conditions that affect their ability to deliver services. This is often a source of strain, since their proposals for change grow out of firsthand experience with the problem. At the same time, a specific focus or concern can obscure the broader organization implications of a proposed change.

4. The tactics most often employed by practitioner–change agents are often similar to those utilized by consultants. In both cases, the range of tactics is somewhat circumscribed by the sources of power upon which they can draw. While change from below can involve the use of more strident tactics, successful implementation requires access to a broad power base. The range of tactics available to administrative change agents, on the other hand, is theoretically the largest, but in practice tends to be limited by the actor's management style, by his or her assumptions about how people change, and/or by his or her estimation of secondary undesirable consequences.

All change processes involve significant resistance. The administrative change agent usually has somewhat more ability to deal with resistance because of his or her access to sources of power. The practitioner–change agent has both the greatest number of constraints and the most potentially formidable resistance, and at the same time the least power upon which to draw.

Notes

1. For a general discussion, see Peter Blau and W. Richard Scott, *Formal Organizations* (San Francisco: Chandler, 1962), pp. 228–231.
2. See Anthony Downs, *Inside Bureaucracy* (Boston: Little, Brown, 1967), pp. 116–118.
3. Downs, *Inside Bureaucracy,* pp. 116–118, and Everett Rogers and Rekha Agarwala-Rogers, *Communication in Organizations* (New York: Free Press, 1976), pp. 89–99.
4. Rogers and Agarwala-Rogers, *Communication in Organizations,* pp. 94–95.
5. See, for example, a summary of research on this topic in Jack Rothman, *Planning and Organizing for Social Change* (New York: Columbia University Press, 1974), pp. 171–174.
6. See Wendell French and Cecil Bell, *Organizational Development* (Englewood Cliffs, N.J.: Prentice-Hall, 1973), pp. 182–191, and Jerald Hage and Michael Aiken, *Social Change in Complex Organizations* (New York: Random House, 1970), pp. 62–82.

7. Joseph Olmstead and Harold Christensen, *Effects of Agency Work Contexts: An Intensive Field Study* (National Study of Welfare and Rehabilitation Workers, Work and Organizational Contexts, vol. 1; Washington, D.C.: U.S. Department of Health, Education and Welfare, 1973); Hage and Aiken, *Social Change in Complex Organizations,* pp. 30–61; Paul Weinberger, "Job Satisfaction and Staff Retention in Social Work," in *Perspectives on Social Welfare,* ed. Weinberger (New York: Macmillan, 1974), pp. 478–479; and Edward E. Schwartz and William C. Sample, "First Findings from Midway," *Social Service Review* 41, no. 2 (1967): 113–151.

8. This definition draws from that originally set forth in Rino Patti, "Limitations and Prospects of Internal Advocacy," *Social Casework* 55, no. 9 (Nov. 1974): 537–538.

9. This section is based largely on Rino Patti, "Limitations and Prospects," pp. 538–545.

10. See, for example, Paul Hershey and Kenneth Blanchard, *Management of Organizational Behavior* (Englewood Cliffs, N.J.: Prentice-Hall, 1977), pp. 273–306, and French and Bell, *Organizational Development.*

Part I   The Organizational Context of
Service Delivery

Most professional practitioners in human service agencies can readily describe in detail the organizational problems that constrain or impede the delivery of service to clients. Lack of time, excessive caseloads, poor coordination, restrictive eligibility requirements, burdensome paperwork, and seemingly arbitrary rules are only a few of the many constraints that workers commonly encounter in their day-to-day work. It is often more difficult, however, for practitioners to explain the organizational dynamics that give rise to and perpetuate these and similar problems. At this level of analysis, they often resort to conventional explanations about the insensitivity of large organizations and "mindless bureaucrats." Just as frequent is the tendency to attribute such agency dysfunctions to the personal inadequacies or destructive intentions of superiors. Such explanations may have cathartic value, but they are not likely to add much to the practitioner's understanding of the problems that interfere with service delivery. This deficit is more than academic, because unless practitioners have some perspective on the institutional dynamics that underlie the problems at issue, both the goals they seek and the strategies they employ to achieve them may be misplaced.

Part I seeks to provide several theoretical perspectives on how organizational context influences (constrains and facilitates) the service delivery process. By "context" we refer to structural arrangements and organizational processes that collectively do much to determine the nature and effectiveness of relationships between subordinates and superiors and practitioners and clients in social agencies. A major theme running throughout this section is that many of the problems that interfere with the delivery of services are not the result of individual choices and/or personal competencies, but rather grow out of and are perpetuated by systemic forces. This is not to say that individuals passively reflect the organizational environment, nor that they need ultimately be controlled by it. To take such an extreme, deterministic stance would run counter to the basic argument presented in this volume, namely, that practitioners can help to shape the service delivery systems in which they operate. At the same time, it seems apparent that, unless professionals are alert to how they and clients are affected by the organizational context, their ability to assess the problems they encounter and thus to engage in purposeful change efforts will be greatly diminished.

The six chapters that follow are broadly concerned with analyzing the effects of organizational context on selected aspects of behavior in social agencies. The first three chapters define a number of important contextual variables and present analytic schema that may be useful in helping practitioners understand the relationships between structure and behavior. The remaining three selections focus on specific problems encountered by clients and workers in social agencies that interfere with the provision of services.

In Chapter 2, Resnick addresses a phenomenon that is pervasive yet seldom explicitly recognized in human service organizations—that is, the strain that arises from attempting to reconcile the conflicting demands of primary and secondary systems of relationships. Though these conflicts are experienced in family and community settings as well, they are perhaps nowhere more acute than in social agencies, where professional norms encourage the development of primary group relationships among peers and with clients. At the same time, however, such agencies must, as Resnick points out, avoid operating consistently by primary group norms lest they develop problems with favoritism, diffuseness of purpose, and the like. On the other hand, to operate social agencies strictly in accordance with the impersonal and universalistic norms of secondary systems would itself prove problematic since such organizations by virtue of their mission must be prepared to provide highly individualized services in the context of intimate therapeutic relationships. In the last analysis, there is no permanent solution to the strain that is inherent in attempts to balance the requirements of primary and secondary systems. Nevertheless, change agents may find this framework useful for analyzing agency problems and consciously mapping the intended consequences of proposed changes.

In addition to understanding the interplay of primary and secondary system norms and the strains that emerge from them, the practitioner can also gain insights into organizational behavior by examining the formal structure of the agency. Important among these structural characteristics are the size of the organization, its goals, how authority is distributed, and patterns of communication. In Chapter 3, Patti focuses on these contextual variables and, drawing upon recent empirical research, traces their impact on social workers' satisfaction with and performance in their jobs. While the variables addressed in this chapter do not exhaust those that have a bearing on worker satisfaction and performance, the analysis nevertheless points to the critical relationships between structure and practitioner behavior. Human service workers increasingly find themselves in large formalized agencies, with authority concentrated at the apex of the organizational pyramid. Moreover, the growing emphasis on tightly formulated goals, and the development of ever more elaborate management systems to monitor and control what occurs in the service delivery process, suggests that organizational context will increasingly impose itself on workers and influence, for better or worse, how they perform their jobs. The analytic framework offered in Chapter 3 may be useful as a guide for assessing agency structure and understanding its implications for practitioners.

In contrast to the Resnick and Patti chapters, which address internal agency dynamics, the chapter by Greenley and Kirk focuses attention on the organization's interface with potential clients. In the day-to-day concern with meeting needs of clients in service, practitioners sometimes lose sight of how clients are selected for, or diverted from, service in the first place. Employing the concepts of boundary control and agency domain, the authors suggest that agencies will vary greatly in how selective they are in choosing clients for service and, relatedly, in the frequency with which they refer applicants to other agencies. Given the tendency of some agencies to narrow the range of clients they are publicly committed to serve in order to deal with those who are more attractive or amenable to prevailing methods of treatment, practitioners would do well to understand the circumstances under which this selection process is likely to occur. Chapter 4 offers a conceptual framework for such an analysis.

The last three chapters address specific problems and concerns confronting social workers in social agencies. Few such issues have received as much attention in professional circles as the organizational constraints imposed on front-line practitioners in large social welfare bureaucracies. Among other things, these constraints are thought to undermine professionals' ability to perform in accordance with the norms and principles considered necessary for effective practice. Of particular concern has been the tendency of social welfare organizations to prescribe employee behavior through elaborate sets of rules and procedures, thereby limiting the exercise of discretion by front-line workers. In Chapter 5, Finch critically examines this issue and concludes that organizationally imposed limitations on direct service workers may not be as widespread as has commonly been assumed. In any case, he suggests, the proscription of professional discretion may derive less from explicit attempts at bureaucratic control than from the increasingly specialized nature of social services in agencies. In this emerging scenario, services to clients are divided among units, each of which serves a limited and specialized function. This compartmentalization of client and function, according to Finch, may do more to constrict professional autonomy and undermine services than the more overt forms of organizational control (for example, rules, regulations) that have typically been the object of social workers' criticisms.

Wasserman's chapter, which can profitably be read in conjunction with the Finch and Patti chapters, provides a graphic picture of the long-term effects that rigid, impersonal bureaucracies can have on professional practitioners. The findings reported in this study, supported by a growing body of research literature (see, for example, Aiken and Hage, "Organizational Alienation," and Olmstead and Christensen, *Effects of Agency Work Contexts*), point to the conclusion that the structure and climate in social agencies has rather marked effects on social workers' sense of efficacy, their attitudes toward work, and their relationships with colleagues. While the ultimate purpose of agencies is the provision of services to clients and not the development and nurturance of practitioners, Chapter 6 and other studies suggest the interdependence of these outcomes. At the very least, such research underlines the importance of practitioners' being alert to agency conditions that may detract from their ability to develop and fully utilize their capabilities. In this context, efforts to promote a more responsive and humane agency climate are not to be seen as self-serving but rather as attempts to enhance organizational effectiveness.

There is no tenet of faith in social welfare so strongly held as the notion that agencies should continually strive, within their respective domains, to be responsive to the needs of those who are most urgently in need of service. Yet all but the most idealistic realize that there is frequently a lag between evident client needs and the provision of appropriate services. There are many reasons why this occurs, including different assessments of service priorities, funding limitations, and the like. In Chapter 7, Scott addresses this general problem in one field, services for the blind, and presents persuasive data to show how the prevailing biases and priorities of support and funding groups interact with organizational needs to maintain existing patterns of service and result in systematic inattention to the problems of an already largely neglected client group. Others have observed a similar phenomenon in the family service field (see Cloward and Epstein, "Private Social Welfare's Disengagement"). Indeed, as Scott himself points out, there is no reason to believe that the problem he identifies is any less common in human service agencies than in other types of complex organizations. The practitioner–change agent who would undertake to change the program configuration and service priorities of his or her agency should be aware of the substantial array of forces that constrain agencies to pursue their existing policies even in the face of compelling evidence of the need to redirect agency priorities.

Suppplementary References

Aiken, Michael, and Jerald Hage. "Organizational Alienation: A Comparative Analysis," in *The Sociology of Organizations: Basic Studies,* ed. Oscar Grusky and George Miller, pp. 517–526. New York: Free Press, 1970.

Cloward, Richard, and Irwin Epstein. "Private Social Welfare's Disengagement from the Poor: The Case of Family Adjustment Agencies," in *Social Welfare Institutions,* ed. Mayer Zald, pp. 623–644. New York: John Wiley, 1965.

Green, A. D. "The Professional Worker in the Bureaucracy," *Social Service Review* 40, no. 1 (March 1966): 74–83.

Hasenfeld, Yeheskel, and Richard English, eds. *Human Service Organizations.* Ann Arbor: University of Michigan Press, 1974.

Olmstead, Joseph, and Harold Christensen. *Effects of Agency Work Contexts: An Intensive Field Study.* National Study of Social Welfare and Rehabilitation Workers, Work and Organizational Contexts, vol. 1. Washington, D.C.: U.S. Department of Health, Education and Welfare, 1973.

Rothman, Jack. *Planning and Organizing for Social Change.* New York: Columbia University Press, 1974.

Toren, Nina. "Semi-Professionalism and Social Work: A Theoretical Perspective," in *The Semi-Professions and Their Organization,* ed. Amitai Etzioni, pp. 169–184. New York: Free Press, 1969.

Vinter, Robert. "The Social Structure of Service," in *Issues in American Social Work,* ed. Alfred Kahn, pp. 242–269. New York: Columbia University Press, 1959.

Chapter 2 A Social System View of Strain

Herman Resnick

Individuals often find themselves in organizational and other situations where strain and confusion result from conflicting demands.[1] For example, professional helpers are frequently caught between the opposing expectations of their clients and their bureaucratically administered organizations, or children often have to struggle to reconcile the "fun" norms of their peer group and the academic requirements of their school. Human service workers often perceive these dilemmas from an intrapsychic or interpersonal viewpoint. But the problems falling within the scope of the human service worker may also be viewed through the perspective of a social system framework.

This chapter provides human service personnel with a model for analysis that offers a macro-view of the problems encountered in practice, a model that suggests that it is the very nature of the social systems in which they and their clients participate that creates (or is a potential source of) these problems.[2] This model is not intended to be a guide for intervention, but a means to help practitioners increase their awareness of the social system roots of both worker and client strain.

CONCEPT DEFINITION

Two major formulations from the sociological literature, *primary and secondary systems* and the *pattern variables,* are combined to form a frame of reference for analysis.[3] Let us begin by briefly reviewing these two major formulations.

It might also be useful to make clear how other concepts are used in this chapter. "Social systems," for example, will be used synonymously

Reprinted from *Administration in Mental Health* 7, no. 1 (Fall 1979): 43–57, with the permission of Human Sciences Press, 72 Fifth Avenue, N.Y., N.Y. © 1979 Human Sciences Press. All rights reserved.

with groups, families, organizations, communities, and societies. "Strain," "problem," and "dysfunction" will also be used interchangeably, to mean a state of tension experienced within an individual or between social systems.

Primary and Secondary Social Systems

One may describe industrial society as consisting of two types of social systems. The first, the primary social system, is

> characterised by intimate face-to-face association and coopera-
> tion. . . . It is fundamental in forming the social nature and ideals
> of the individual. The result of intimate association, psycho-
> logically, is a certain *fusion* of individualities in a common whole,
> so that one's *self,* for many purposes at least, is the common life
> and purpose of the group. Perhaps the simplest way of describing
> this wholeness is by saying that it is a *"we"*; it involves the sort of
> sympathy and mutual identification for which "we" is the natural
> expression. One lives in the feeling of the whole and finds the
> chief aims of his will in that feeling.[4]

The family, the neighborhood, peer groups, and religious and racial groups are illustrations of primary systems.

The secondary social system, by contrast, has characteristics that

> are the opposite or complement of those of the primary group.
> Relations among members are "cool," impersonal, rational, con-
> tractual, and formal. People participate not as whole personalities
> but only in delimited and special capacities; the group is not an end
> in itself but a means to other ends. Secondary groups are typically
> large and members have usually only intermittent contacts, often
> indirectly through the written rather than the spoken word.
> Examples range from the professional association to the large
> bureaucratic corporation to the national state itself.[5]

In secondary systems, then, individuals do not act freely, but perform some organizational function. Roles are the major vehicle for mediating interaction, and personal relations tend to be at a minimum. In primary systems, it is the emotional bond that organizes existence and unifies members. These are, of course, ideal types; primary orientations may intrude into secondary systems, and vice versa. Indeed, these intrusive elements will be crucial to our notion of strain in systems.

Pattern Variables

It might now be helpful to review primary and secondary systems as they relate to a well-known sociological tool, Parsons' four pattern variables (emotions, standard-setting, scope of interest, and status) (see Table 2-1).

EMOTIONS: AFFECTIVITY VS. AFFECTIVE NEUTRALITY

The emotions variable has to do with the extent to which the norms of a system require one to live and relate emotionally. In a primary group, the expression of emotion is allowed, even encouraged. In a family, for example, husband, wife, and children can exchange insults, hug and kiss, and share feelings about events. Long-time neighbors and members of ethnic groups may do the same. The norms in primary groups are in the direction of affect expression. In secondary systems, another norm is operative, affective neutrality, which typically results in the suppression of emotions in interaction. Supervisors are expected to relate in emotionally disciplined ways to subordinates, and colleagues are expected to relate impersonally to other colleagues. Professional helpers are socialized to manage their feelings and behaviors consciously and purposively in the service of client needs, not their own needs. In general, organizational and professional relationships are expected to be limited and controlled.

STANDARD-SETTING: PARTICULARISM VS. UNIVERSALISM

The standard-setting variable refers to claims to equal treatment for all persons in a given population (universalism) and claims to special treatment for certain persons (particularism).

In primary systems, standards are usually set in a particularistic way, based on individual needs, kinship relations, or friendship: the uniqueness of the individual member in a system is recognized.[6] Thus a mother will treat one child differently from another, depending on the child's needs or interests. Or a member of a religious or racial group might look more favorably on a new neighbor with a similar background. In other words, in primary systems members are positively expected to appraise and react to one another particularistically.

In secondary systems, standards are set universalistically; for example, all social workers in grades 1, 2, and 3 within a given organization are required to report to work at 8 A.M. and leave at 5 P.M., receive a certain salary, and perform certain specific functions. Or, all clients in a given category are required to receive similar payment allowances. The principle undergirding these illustrations is that standards for treatment of members of a given group be the same for all members of that group, regardless of other considerations.

SCOPE OF INTEREST: DIFFUSENESS VS. SPECIFICITY[7]

The third variable poses the question of the breadth and depth of persons' interest in each other. In primary groups, parents are encouraged to know about each other and their children deeply and fully. Friends and neighbors confide intimacies and hopes and worries to each other. Their interest is diffuse, and their reaction is to the other individual as a total person, not to a part of that person.

In secondary groups, however, scope of interest is more specific and related to the purposes of the social system in which the individuals participate. For example, the factory owner is oriented toward the productivity of the workers, not toward their personal lives. Many professors see their teaching roles as limited to helping their students learn the subject matter of the course, not to getting to know them more fully. In general, transactions in secondary systems can often be effectively accomplished without the members of those transactions knowing each other personally; that is, the roles of these members facilitate transactions adequately so that the purposes of such transactions can be achieved.

STATUS: ASCRIPTION VS. ACHIEVEMENT

Every social system has some basis for awarding opportunity and material goods to its members. In primary groups, status is allocated on the basis of ascriptive criteria; if persons are of a certain sex, race, or class, they will, because of this culturally standardized identity, have more or less opportunity and more or fewer rewards.[8] In secondary systems, *"achievement* standards are employed and statuses or rewards are allocated to persons on the basis of performance."[9] Competence becomes a major criterion for determining opportunity: "What a man *is* does not matter; it is what he can *do* that should determine his fate."

TABLE 2-1
Overview of Frame of Reference

Type of Strain (Pattern Variables)	Primary Orientations		Secondary Orientations	
	Secondary Systems (as related to:)	Primary Systems (as related to:)	Secondary Systems (as related to:)	Primary Systems (as related to:)
Emotions: Norms regarding expression of emotion. Primary—affectivity. Secondary—affective neutrality.	*Neutrality:* Cool interpersonal relations do not meet some basic needs of populations who are emotionally needy because of age, problematic conditions, etc. Strain is experienced by recipients, consumers, and practitioners.	*Affectivity:* Expression of and reliance upon emotions may lead, in extreme cases, to violence, incest, etc. Threat to durability and stability of social system.	*Affectivity:* Expressing anger at a staff meeting or affective to a subordinate is a violation of organizational norms and causes strain for system.	*Neutrality:* Relating to members of a family in an impersonal manner or showing emotion only at certain times of the day, etc., may cause family members feel rejection of their legitimate socioemotional needs.
Standard-setting: Criteria for establishing and administering standards. Primary—particularism. Secondary—universalism.	*Universalism:* Often cannot take individual variations into account.	*Particularism:* Special arrangements for special needs may lead to individual reactions of jealousy, and reduction of commitment to organization and its purposes.	*Particularism:* Making special arrangements for a youth may lead to all youths wanting special arrangements with strain resulting when they are refused.	*Universalism:* One rule for residential treatment institution for all children, regardless of capacity, maturity, or circumstance leads to rigidity and unresponsiveness of system to participants.

Scope of interest:
Range of interest possible in another. Primary—diffuseness. Secondary—specificity.

Status:
Basis for awarding opportunity and prestige. Primary—ascription. Secondary—achievement.

Specificity:
Participants in and recipients of organizations often feel it is not interested in them as people, but as mere objects or means to the organization's end.

Achievement:
Participants have to continually produce to achieve opportunities and rewards.

Diffuseness:
If too extensive, individuals experience a sense of loss of privacy, and systems experience a reduction of deviance.

Ascription:
Participants are "frozen" into roles and status—minimal opportunities for change.

Diffuseness:
Questions about political or personal activities are outside legitimate employer inquiry.

Ascription:
When organization gives promotions and opportunities to persons based on who they are, rather than what they do, efficiency in the organization is impaired.

Specificity:
Narrow scope of interest for family members regarding each other is regarded as a violation of reasonable expectations that primary group members should have for each other.

Achievement:
When parents relate to children based on a specific skill accomplishment rather than parent/child basis, relationship is seen and experienced as instrumental and not appropriate to family life.

EXTREMISM AND INTERPENETRATION STRAINS

On the basis of this review of the two sets of sociological concepts basic to the thesis of this chapter, we can now turn to our major emphasis, which is an analysis of the different types of strain experienced by individuals in primary and secondary systems through the perspective provided by the pattern variables. In the sections that follow, strain will be viewed as emerging from *interpenetration* of one system's norms by another and from extreme responses to norms in a system (*extremism*). The four pattern variables will be used to illustrate and analyze these two basic types of strain.

Emotions: Affectivity vs. Affective Neutrality

EXTREMISM STRAINS

Affective Neutrality in Secondary Systems

As we noted, in secondary systems impersonality typically characterizes relationships. Given human needs for affective relationships, however, many participants in secondary organizations find the lack of emotional outlet frustrating. This is especially true of participants who, for reasons of age or physical condition, have intense emotional needs.

Nursery and grade-school children, for example, experience such needs, which are appropriate for their age group but may be met only minimally by teachers, whose interactions reflect the affectively neutral orientation characteristic of the school setting as a secondary system. The same is true of institutionalized persons who have emotional problems, such as patients in mental hospitals and residents in nursing homes. These populations may find it particularly stressful to regulate their feelings along the lines required by the secondary systems in which they find themselves. For this group, service systems based on secondary orientations can have dysfunctional consequences. Indeed, their problems may be exacerbated by their experiences within such systems.[10]

Affectivity in Primary Systems

Primary systems often encourage the expression of emotions. Despite the obvious face value of such a norm, there are potential problems embedded in this freedom. For example, when members of a family or friendship group begin a quarrel, it may start with insults and teasing, but, because of the deep-rooted emotions involved, vindictive spirals may escalate the quarrel to destructive physical violence. This extreme manifestation of anger is surprisingly frequent in family life.[11] The affectivity norm may establish conditions or processes in primary groups that make extreme reactions difficult to control.

INTERPENETRATION STRAINS

Affectivity in Secondary Systems

When participants in secondary organizations respond to events or relationships in an emotional way, strain occurs. For example, when a supervisor explodes angrily at his colleagues at a staff meeting, the reactions he experiences from others and within himself indicate to him that he has violated some fundamental norms of the organization. The administrator of his department slaps his wrist gently for "letting the boys get to him." His friends in the department express surprise. His enemies kid him that "he can dish it out okay, but he can't take it." All these reactions serve to remind him of his deviance and increase his anxiety (personal communication).[12] Manifestation of strong feelings threatens the secondary system's reliance on coolness of interaction and relationship.

Similarly, when supervisors date their subordinates, this disturbs the stability of an organization, because it threatens the secondary system's formal reliance on one of the cornerstones of secondary systems—job performance as a criterion for raises and promotions.[13] Other subordinates suspect that they will receive less than equal treatment when promotions or raises occur and may conclude that emotional attachments rather than task performance will become more important to such a department in the future. Such a conclusion on the part of staff could severely limit organizational efficiency or effectiveness.

Affective Neutrality in Primary Systems

Emotional neutrality in primary groups can be equally destructive. In "The Sound of Music," for example, the captain of a naval vessel tries to raise his family as he administers his ship. He is impersonal and affectively neutral with all his children, including the little toddler who yearns to be hugged and kissed by him. The children respond to strain by transferring their loyalties to a governess who fills their needs for affectivity.

Less happy outcomes occur when more problematic family systems experience this type of strain. Children of these families may experience parental affective neutrality as rejection or indifference to their needs and respond with a wide range of symptoms: running away from home, becoming pregnant, getting in trouble with the law, and similar kinds of acting-out behavior.

Standard-Setting: Particularism vs. Universalism

EXTREMISM STRAINS

Universalism in Secondary Systems

Probably the strongest criticism leveled at secondary systems is their overreliance on rules. These rules or standards governing the conduct of personnel within organizations and that of clients are developed to ensure uniform practices and are usually based on notions of fairness or efficiency, that is, universalistic standards. The rules are directives for general situations, however, and do not cover specific cases; therein lies the difficulty. Individuals coming to organizations for services or goods have unique concerns or needs that often require individualized response from the secondary system.

For example, in a camp for delinquent boys, a rule exists that all children should be at the mess hall for breakfast at 7:30 A.M. But some of the boys have frightening dreams and embarrassing bed-wetting each night, which makes it difficult for them to follow the rule. Adherence to the rule would increase the efficiency and improve the morale of the kitchen staff, but it places an enormous strain on the disturbed boys and the program staff who have to live with it. The rule (though reasonable on face value), when put into operation, has the effect of reducing the organization's commitment to its purpose, that is, treating boys in a therapeutic (particularistic) manner. Universalism in organizations may serve to make the organization more predictable and therefore more stable, but an individual's immediate needs are sometimes very cruelly subordinated to this orientation.

Particularism in Primary Systems

Particularism does allow a primary system to be responsive to its participants, but, in extreme cases, particularism can also be dysfunctional. For example, when a mother of three children consistently favors one of them in limit-setting or affection, her favoritism may give rise to strong sibling rivalry and squabbling and/or to guilt in the favored child and low self-esteem in the other two. Further, the favored child is prepared poorly for more universalistically oriented systems outside the family, such as schools and the job market.

INTERPENETRATION STRAINS

Particularism in Secondary Systems

Secondary systems seek to achieve the goal of efficiency by utilizing regulations based on universalistic standards for all members. Because of their unique needs, however, individuals often seek particularistic arrangements that both result from and lead to strain. When the administrator allows one secretary a longer lunch even if the reason for this is "valid" (for example, a sick mother), then the universalistic standard of "one hour for lunch" has been broken, and the boss is susceptible to accusations of favoritism.

Or, a child care worker in a residential treatment institution might allow a troubled youngster to go out for a stroll after hours in order to talk out his problems. The worker is bending a rule for this upset child, and he may find that the reactions of the other children, and even his colleagues and supervisor, will discourage him from continuing that flexibility in the future. As another example, we can take the dilemma often portrayed in Jimmy Cagney's or Pat O'Brien's films, where the police officer who discovers that his best friend (or kid brother) is a criminal has to decide whether he will arrest him (universalistic criteria) or not (particularistic criteria). Either decision places strain on the officer.

In a societal context, the problem, as Broom and Selznick point out, arises even more seriously for judges and other government officials. The long historic effort to achieve a government of laws and not men reflects the social value of nonprimary relations in situations where objectivity is of paramount importance."[14] Organizations need some flexibility, but where practitioners and administrators allow modification of rules for some, they become subject to the charge of favoritism if they do not bend the rules for all. This charge, if widespread enough among the staff and believed by them, can lead to morale problems, with all their implication for poor service delivery.

Universalism in Primary Systems

Still another source of strain in social systems results from attempts to conduct primary group relationships on secondary group principles. Some studies suggest that fathers transfer norms and expectations learned at the factory or office to their families, and problems result from this intrusion.[15] The organization man, unable to recognize the different nature of these two worlds, becomes oriented to his family as he is to his organization. Rarely are special arrangements allowed for his children (even if age, sex, or ability are realistic factors), because of the fear that this will weaken discipline, which is usually viewed implicitly, at least by such parents, as undermining the stability or even identity of the family system.

Scope of Interest: Diffuseness vs. Specificity

EXTREMISM STRAINS

Specificity in Secondary Systems

It is now a byword of our culture that secondary systems demean their staffs as well as the recipients of their services by interacting with them as if they were objects, not humans important in their own right. Students, workers, and clients alike react to such nonhuman climates in a variety of ways, sometimes dysfunctional both to themselves and to the organization. Anger, depression, and confusion are only some of the negative feelings reported. High turnover rates, absenteeism, and counterproductive informal interaction also result.[16] Humans are social beings, and strain may occur when the scope of interest of their secondary system is too narrow.

Diffuseness in Primary Systems

Although a diffuse scope of interest is indeed a central characteristic of primary groups, individuals do have privacy limits. An example of this is the mother who is too eager to hear about her daughter's experiences and who has developed techniques to elicit such information from her, leaving her daughter with no secrets or private self of her own. Younger children are willing and eager to share their experiences, but, as they mature into teenagers, they are less ready to share personal information with parents. Parents find this shift from a diffuse relationship to a more specific one distressing and difficult to achieve gracefully. They often experience it as a rejection of themselves and as an indication of their failure as parents.

An illustration from another system that might be called primary, a small village, reveals some systemwide negative consequences of a diffuse scope of interest. Because villages are usually small and stable over time, interaction is frequent and varied; that is, residents of the town are in touch with each other frequently while shopping, working, recreating, politicking, or participating in church activities. Both public and private behaviors become part of village gossip. This network of shared information may serve to reduce unpopular or deviant views; if *everyone* knows everything about everybody this might be a sufficient condition to reduce one's inclination to violate norms. In addition, this comprehensive knowledge of each other adversely affects individuals' sense of privacy.

One of the consequences of these conditions is a homogeneous style of life containing few attractions for modern young people, who typically and increasingly value variety, freedom to choose their own lifestyles, and increased opportunity for mobility and deviance. Young people in villages have traditionally moved away in large numbers to the city, where the scope of interest is much more specific. The interesting dilemma is that if the village seeks to expand opportunity, increase size, and encourage or tolerate a more cosmopolitan life in order to maintain its young people, it loses its identity.

INTERPENETRATION STRAINS

Diffuseness in Secondary Systems

When an employer learns about an employee's personal or family problems, strain can occur, since that information encourages the employer to react affectively and in a particularistic manner to that employee. Both actions may be dysfunctional for the employer and for organizational stability, so employers typically maintain some distance between themselves and their employees. Similarly, when employers inquire into the political views of their employees, they are violating the personal lives of their employees by intruding a diffuse scope of interest: an orientation acceptable in primary systems but not in secondary systems. Employees' political beliefs are outside the job and therefore outside the employer's legitimate scope of interest.[17]

Specificity in Primary Systems

A specific scope of interest in primary groups causes strain in that it violates group members' expectations of each other as well as community expectations. For example, a public service announcement on the radio a few years ago asked parents in an accusing tone if they knew where their adolescent children were that night. The clear implication was of that parents are inadequate if they do not interest themselves in their children's social lives and evening activities. Primary group life requires a diffuse, or broad, scope of interest, and parents who do not function that way may stand accused of indifference to the legitimate needs or interests of their children. Members of a family who only occasionally visit their old grandparents in nursing homes are also manifesting a specific scope of interest. Still another example is the wife who sees her husband merely as an income-producing mate, or the husband who views his wife only as a housekeeper or sex object.

Status: Ascription vs. Achievement

EXTREMISM STRAINS

Achievement in Secondary Systems

In one sense, the increasing use of achievement as a criterion for allocating rewards and opportunities can be viewed as a force that advances the attainment of democratic ideals in Western civilization. It allows individuals the opportunity to achieve a wide range of rewards and statuses on the basis of their own behaviors. With achievement as a standard for rewards, people are freer to strive to improve their condition or position. Nonetheless, continued participation in a work-centered world with little sense of acceptance aside from what achievements or accomplishments can bring can be a very hollow existence for most workers.

Ascription in Primary Systems

As we saw, members of primary groups receive opportunities, rewards, and status based on certain qualities, positions, and circumstances to which a social system has assigned a certain value and over which these members have little control. An example is ordinal position. The youngest child in a family is often called the "baby," even in adulthood, and often finds it difficult to vacate that role, despite real achievements outside the family. Conversely, the oldest son in some primary groups is seen as the next in line for authority and responsibility when the parents are gone, regardless of ability to handle such a role. In *The Godfather*, Sonny is seen as an incompetent potential leader by family members, but he accepts that role because he is the eldest son. The family fortunes declined at that point and do not revive until he is killed, and a more competent leader, the youngest son, becomes leader. When primary groups such as Mafia families compete with each other (or with law enforcement agencies), their use of ascriptive criteria for allocating status and roles can lead to strains that result in weakening or even destruction of these primary groups.[18]

INTERPENETRATION STRAINS

Ascription in Secondary Systems

Secondary systems, because they are goal-directed, require conditions and norms to help achieve these goals. Rewards are distributed to maximize production and efficient operation. When financial and promotional rewards are distributed to members of organizations on the basis of demonstrated competence, the organization may be said to be using achievement criteria to allocate status. This system is clearly functional to "organization goal attainment." For a variety of reasons, however, some organizations use ascriptive criteria for allocating rewards such as positions of influence or increases in salary. Some of the Southeast Asian armies are examples of military systems that are secondary in nature and structure but that utilize ascriptive criteria in assigning members of the royal or ruling families to command positions in the armed forces. Feudal armies, of course, were often guilty of this practice. Consequences of this practice may be quite severe and can threaten the very survival of the system. Armies that select top commanders based on achievement criteria (that is, competence) will obviously be more effective.

Achievement in Primary Systems

When achievement criteria are transferred into primary groups, problems may occur. Children should be loved, for example, "because they are one's children and not because of their accomplishments or deeds."[19] If a father can only love his son when the boy does well in a baseball game, or receives high grades in school, for example, that father is intruding a set of judgments from his secondary system to the primary system of his own family. A great deal of strain for the child results from this kind of treatment.

APPLICATION TO HUMAN SERVICE SETTINGS

We have now seen how interpenetration and extremism strains result in primary and secondary systems when emotions, standard-setting, scope-of-interest, and status variables are either adhered to in the extreme or are intruded into a system with opposing norms. We will now illustrate the application of this frame of reference to a specific situation in a human service organization.

A young assistant director of a small drug abuse program felt he was being torn apart by the opposing orientations of his small, young, close-knit staff and his executive director. His staff interacted with a young and demanding drug-abusing population. Their job required a great deal of time and energy and was emotionally extremely involving. The agency (originally administered and staffed by volunteers) organized itself to meet these demands around the clock. The assistant director not only shared the one clinic office with half of his staff, but handled a partial caseload and was part of the flying squad for emergencies. In addition, he and the staff went to the same parties, visited at each others' homes, and ate lunch together. In short, they were all in the same primary system. The staff placed demands on him for more funds, more service, and minimal paperwork pressure.

The executive, whose office was in the county building a mile away, saw herself as trying to represent the board and the various funding sources that supported the agency and improve the efficiency and effectiveness of the service. She placed demands on the assistant director for accountability of service, more effective operation of the program, and meeting of deadlines for reports.

The expectations from the two systems within the one organization can be analyzed by using the frame of reference illustrated in Figure 2-1.

It is evident from the figure that the strains experienced by the assistant director are real, systemwide in nature and scope, and caused by the varying reference groups to which the staff and executive systems must give allegiance. Solutions for the assistant director without third-party intervention are hard to come by in this situation and include: quitting, which does not solve the agency problem, or his problem; shifting his allegiance to the executive and her policies, which would lose him his self-respect and the respect of his staff; or playing a more pro-active and conscious mediating role between the two systems, educating each to the necessities of the other, and hoping thereby to reduce the extreme demands of both on himself and the agency. Strain will not be eliminated but merely reduced in this situation. It will return to be resolved again, leading to new conditions that create new strain.

This dynamic tension in organizational life is inevitable. It may even be seen as positive (although debilitating), since it ultimately serves to "educate" secondary-oriented persons and systems to the needs or requirements of primary systems, and vice versa. It is hoped that this chapter, by explicating the social systems nature (and not the intra- or interpersonal nature) of such dilemmas, may help raise social workers' consciousness regarding the systemic nature of many organizational problems and thereby contribute to more effective service delivery and organizational functioning.

FIGURE 2-1.
To Be More Effective

	Staff Orientation toward Assistant Director	Executive Director's Orientation toward Assistant Director
Emotion	*Affectivity*: Develop close and abiding relationships with staff.	*Affective Neutrality*: Keep cool and impersonal in relations with staff, otherwise danger of over-involvement, and loss of objectivity.
Standard-Setting	*Particularistic*: Legitimate and advisable to make special arrangements for staff based on individual needs—allow some to leave earlier and come in later, etc.	*Universalistic*: Treat all staff equally, otherwise will be manipulated and/or start playing favorites.
Scope of Interest	*Diffuseness*: Know staff personally as well as professionally.	*Specificity*: Stay out of personal lives of staff to prevent subjective evaluations of staff performance.
Status	*Ascription*: Once hired, staff needs to be worked with and developed in order to have most competent staff—incompetents are helped to improve themselves.	*Achievement*: Assess staff on the basis of competence—fire those who are incompetent.

Notes

1. See A. Mause and R. Lewis. *Professional People in England* (Cambridge, Mass.: Harvard University Press, 1953); W. Kornhauser, *Scientists in Industry: Conflict and Accommodation* (Berkeley and Los Angeles: University of California Press, 1962); Richard Hall, "Professionalization and Bureaucratization," *American Sociological Review* 33 (Feb. 1968): 92–104. See also Fred H. Goldner and R. R. Ritti, "Professionalization as Career Immobility," *American Journal of Sociology* 72 (March 1967): 489–502, and J. Ben-David, "The Professional Role of the Physician: Bureaucratized Medicine, a Study in Role Conflict," *Human Relation* 2 (Aug. 1958): 901–911. See also Irving Pilivan, "Restructuring the Provision of Social Services," *Social Work* 1, no. 1 (Jan. 1965): 34–36; W. R. Scott, "Professionals in Bureaucracies: Areas of Conflict," in H. Vollmer and D. Olills, *Professionalization,* (Englewood Cliffs, N.J.: Prentice-Hall, 1966). For an empirical study that suggests that moderate degrees of bureaucracy are not necessarily stressful for the professional and may indeed facilitate his or her functioning as an autonomous professional, see G. Engel, "The Effects of Bureaucracy on the Professional Autonomy of the Physician," *Journal of Health and Social Behavior* 10 (March 1969): 30–41.

2. A similar approach, focused on the linkages between social systems, is found in Marvin Sussman, "Cross National Family Studies: Some Conceptual Issues in Family Organizational Linkages," paper presented at the Session on Family Bureaucracies, 64th meeting of the American Sociological Association, Sept. 1, 1964, San Francisco, Calif.

3. See Talcott Parsons, *The Social System* (New York: Free Press, 1964), for a complete statement of the conceptual scheme from which the frame of reference was adapted. See also E. Devereux, "Parsons' Sociological Theory," in *The Social Theories of Talcott Parsons: A Critical Examination,* ed. M. Black (Englewood Cliffs, N.J.: Prentice-Hall: 1961), pp. 38–48. For early formulations of primary-secondary groups, see F. Tönnies, "Gemeinschaft and Gesellschaft," in *Fundamental Concepts of Sociology,* ed. C. P. Loomis. (New York: American Book Co., 1940), and R. Park, *Human Communities* (Glencoe, Ill.: Free Press, 1952), or G. Simpson, tr., *Emil Durkheim on the Division of Values in Society* (New York: Macmillan, 1933).

4. See C. H. Cooley, *Social Organization* (New York: Scribner's, 1909), p. 23. The term primary group was probably first used by Cooley.

5. See M. S. Olmstead, *The Small Group* (New York: Random House, 1966), pp. 18–19.

6. It should be noted that Parsons in his usage and definition of particularism emphasizes the latter two criteria—that is, the special or particular relationship that exists between persons that influences or determines the standards established. The conception of particularism used in this paper is adapted from L. Broom and Philip Zelznik, *Sociology* (Harper & Row, 1963), p. 25.

7. See Broom and Selznik, *Sociology,* p. 135, for their formulation of this variable: "Entering a primary relation presumes acceptance of a whole person. This is recognized in the relation between husband and wife which is understood to be not a contract but an unlimited commitment one to the other, where each assumes full responsibility for the other's well-being. In contrast non-primary relations (often called secondary) usually entail only limited responsibility of one individual to another, for example, the relation between employers and employees."

8. See Alvin Gouldner, *The Coming Crisis of Western Sociology* (New York: Basic Books, 1970).

9. Ibid.

10. See Erving Goffman, *Asylums* (New York: Doubleday-Anchor, 1961), for a comprehensive and now well-known document describing in detail the processes and mechanisms of institutionalization in closed systems. See also David Wineman and Adrienne James, "The Advocacy Challenge to Schools of Social Work," *Social Work* 14, no. 2 (April 1966), for a particularly vivid statement about the adverse effects of institutions upon individuals.

11. See Home Office Unit Report, *Murder* (London: 1961), for a British profile of the murderer's relationship to his victims: "Half the murderers killed wives, children and other relatives (usually parents). Less than 10% killed girl friends, and 12% killed acquaintances; [only] a quarter killed strangers." Also see S. Steinmetz, *Cycle of Violence* (New York: Praeger, 1977).

12. This experience was related to me by a professional social worker in a large public agency.

13. See above for a discussion of job performance as it relates to the variable called "status."
14. See Broom and Selznick, *Sociology*.
15. See A. D. Berle and K. Naegele for their study, "Middle-Class Fathers: Occupational Role and Attitudes towards Children," in *The Family,* ed. N. Bell and E. Vogel (New York: Free Press, 1960).
16. See Robert Somers and Jan Howard "Resisting Institutional Evil from Within," in *Sanctions for Evil,* ed. N. Sandford (Boston: Beacon, 1972), for a particularly strong account of large institutions and their destructive effect on inhabitants of these institutions.
17. For an excellent discussion of this source of strain (diffuseness) in secondary groups as it applies to working with handicapped clients for both rehabilitative and economic purposes, see C. Gersand and Mark Lefton, "Service and Servitude in the Sheltered Workshop," *Social Work* 15, no. 3 (July 1970): 74–81.
18. See H. Lewis, *Honored Society: The History of the Mafia* (New York: Penguin, 1972).
19. See Berle and Naegele, "Middle-Class Fathers."

Chapter 3   **Social Work Practice:**

Organizational Environment

Rino J. Patti

Social work is a profession whose members depend on the formal organizations (social agencies) in which they work for much of their legitimacy as professionals, the resources necessary to deliver services, the clientele for whom services are provided, and, in large part, the developmental opportunities that are necessary for professional growth. Yet, despite the fundamental nature of the relationship between social workers and the agencies that employ them, little attention has been given to how the internal organizational environment impinges on the practitioner as he engages in service delivery.

The primary purpose of this chapter is to identify and describe certain conditions and processes found in social welfare organizations and to examine how they variously bear on the job satisfaction and performance of practitioners. Particular attention will be given to what theory and research have to say about the relationships between selected elements of the structure of social agencies and workers' attitudes toward work and the work setting, orientation to clients, and the quantity and quality of their performance. A second purpose is to suggest the action alternatives available to practitioners who encounter organizational conditions or practices that impede service delivery.

CONTEXT OF PRACTICE

The range and diversity of organizations in which social workers practice make it impossible to speak of the agency context as a uniform phenom-

Reprinted from the *Encyclopedia of Social Work,* Vol. II (Washington, D.C.: National Association of Social Workers, 1977), pp. 1534–1541, with the permission of the publisher.

enon. There are similarities among social welfare agencies as a class, but the closer one looks at the array of organizations, the more difficult it is to generalize about their internal dynamics.[1] For purposes of analysis, therefore, it is more useful to identify those variables that appear to account for many of the differences observed in the structure and climate of social agencies. Among those variables that seem most salient in this respect are the size of the organization, its goals, the nature of authority relations, and patterns of communication. These by no means exhaust the list of relevant factors (others would include informal organization, division of labor, size of workload, salaries, and physical amenities), but they provide a useful point of departure.

Before addressing each of these variables, it is necessary to observe that what transpires within an agency's walls is vitally affected by outside forces. The institutions, groups, policies, and socioeconomic conditions that comprise an agency's external environment influence, among other things, the degree of autonomy the agency can exercise in determining its goals, the continuity of its programs, the nature of the services it offers, and the internal control mechanisms it utilizes to monitor and evaluate staff. This is not to say that a social agency is merely the passive reflection of external forces because there are invariably significant areas in which choice, discretion, and initiative can be exercised; nevertheless, these forces do reach into the social welfare organization to influence, for good or ill, the immediate context for practice. This is important to bear in mind because much that occurs within organizations can only be understood as a reaction to pressures, constraints, and opportunities that come from the outside world.

Furthermore, this discussion of the agency environment will not explicitly address the manner in which practitioners with different social, psychological, educational, and cultural attributes contribute to internal agency dynamics or how they react to various conditions and processes. Suffice it to say that while the intraorganizational environment can exert a profound influence on practitioners, such influence is never unilateral nor are its effects uniform.

AGENCY SIZE

The size of an agency—the number of paid employees it retains—is often considered an important determinant of both organizational structure and climate.[2] As the number of persons employed in an agency grows, several processes are normally set in motion. These include increased specialization of roles and tasks; more elaborate rules and procedures; an expansion in the number of administrative levels, with an accompanying growth in the number of supervisory and management personnel; and greater reliance on formal communication and accountability. In short, size tends to accentuate the bureaucratic features of social welfare organizations.

Conventional wisdom suggests that such features are associated with problems of poor communication, inflexible programs, and centralized authority, all of which tend to impede the delivery of services and produce lowered employee morale. On the face of it, however, large agencies need not be inherently less desirable places to work. They may, for example, offer the practitioner certain advantages that are not as readily available in smaller agencies, including opportunities for promotion, interaction with a variety of experts and professionals, an opportunity to develop highly specialized skills, and diversity of work experience.

Nevertheless, there is some evidence that size may be negatively correlated with certain aspects of practitioner performance and satisfaction. Support for this assertion can be found in a study conducted by Edwin Thomas, which investigated various aspects of roles and role performance of workers in public assistance settings of various sizes. Thomas concluded:

> Workers' conceptions of their roles differed according to the size of the welfare office. In smaller bureaus there was found to be greater role consensus between the worker and his supervisor about the importance of functions that workers perform, greater breadth of role conception and higher ethical commitment. . . . The size of the administrative unit was [also] found to be associated with all indicators of the quality of the workers' performance.[3]

In interpreting these findings Thomas pointed out that the apparent effects of size may have been attributable to that fact that the smaller agencies were located in less populous communities and, therefore, drew employees whose characteristics differed from those in larger communities.[4] If so, differences in performance may have been due more to the personal characteristics of the workers than to the effects of agency size.

Paul Weinberger's study of job satisfaction in child welfare agencies also indicated that practitioners in small agencies were generally more satisfied with their jobs.[5] However, since all larger agencies in this study were public organizations and all smaller agencies voluntary, it is unclear whether size, auspice, or the interaction of these variables was critical in influencing the satisfaction of workers. A recent empirical investigation of workers in thirty-one social welfare and rehabilitation agencies revealed that although size itself had no direct effect on worker satisfaction or performance, there was significant positive correlation between the size of an agency and absenteeism.[6]

Thus research evidence suggests that increased agency size may have an adverse effect on the satisfaction and performance of workers. At the same time, however, this relationship may be mediated by such factors as the characteristics of workers, their perceptions of the agency's purpose, and the auspices of the organization. It also seems probable that the potentially negative effects of size can be neutralized by purposeful administrative efforts to facilitate communication among and participation of workers and to maintain the program's flexibility.[7]

GOALS

Social welfare agencies, like other organizations, pursue a multiplicity of goals. There are the official statements derived from externally imposed mandates (law, executive order, articles of incorporation) that serve as a framework for designing the agency, mobilizing necessary resources, and, ultimately, as a set of criteria against which to measure performance. In addition, however, there are other goals that may have even greater importance for the practitioners. These include production objectives formulated by management; the output or performance expectations held by organized client groups, professional associations, and so on; preferences enunciated by management and supervisory personnel regarding the manner in which the agency should operate, sometimes referred to as systems goals; and goals of both a formal and informal nature that are pursued by staff groups and work units.[8]

The multiplicity of goals and objectives sought by agencies and subgroups within them need not necessarily be a problem for practitioners. However, there are at least two kinds of problems in relation to goals in social welfare organizations that may have a deleterious impact on the worker's morale and/or performance. The first of these is when practitioners perceive two or more goals as being incompatible so that the actions required to achieve both are difficult to reconcile. The dilemmas confronting workers in correctional and public assistance agencies, where the goals of social control and rehabilitation are simultaneously promoted, are perhaps best documented.[9] A variant of this conflict occurs when an agency's policies or procedures require workers to engage in activities that are antagonistic to their norms and ethics.[10] Under both these circumstances, practitioners often experience strain and confusion that, if unresolved, can give rise to low morale and withdrawal from clients.

A second type of problem situation occurs when agency goals are so vague and ill specified that the practitioner has no guidelines for determining what is purposeful or relevant activity, nor any criteria against which to judge his efficacy. In this poor-feedback context it is not uncommon for social workers to become preoccupied with techniques and procedures as ends in themselves rather than with the achievement of goals and outcomes.[11] Moreover, recent research indicates that there is a strong positive correlation between the satisfaction and performance of workers and specifically formulated, realistic, and easily understood agency goals.[12]

Agency goals, therefore, constitute an important element of the intra-organizational environment of the worker. To the extent that such goals and objectives convey clear and consistent messages to practitioners, the evidence would indicate that, other things being equal, workers are more likely to be satisfied and productive.

AUTHORITY RELATIONS

The distribution and exercise of authority is an issue that touches on the fundamental interests of both professional workers and the organizations that employ them. For the social worker, the locus and exercise of authority bears directly on the degree of freedom he can exercise in applying knowledge, skills, and values in work with clients. For the organization, authority is the instrument through which it obtains compliance from employees and coordinates their various activities toward a common end.

The authority structure of an agency may be defined in terms of centralization and formalization. Centralization refers to the locus of control and decision-making; the higher it is, the more centralized the organization. Formalization refers to the degree to which an agency prescribes and enforces rules and procedures to govern the employees' behavior; the more detailed the prescriptions, the more formalized the agency.[13]

Research indicates that a predominance of decision-making in upper echelons and a profusion of discretion-limiting policies, rules, and procedures tend to have a detrimental effect on social workers. One study of sixteen health and welfare agencies found, for example, that high centralization and formalization were both correlated with alienation from fellow employees and from work.[14] Other research has similarly shown that in agencies where workers were given little discretion to make practice-related decisions because of detailed rules, procedures, and instructions, job satisfaction was likely to decline.[15] Observational studies in public assistance agencies further confirm that a heavy overlay of inflexible administrative regulations not only impedes the worker's ability to respond to clients' needs, but generates serious problems of low morale, cynicism, and powerlessness.[16]

Any discussion of authority relations in social welfare organizations must address the central role of supervisor-supervisee relationships. Despite the criticism of supervisory practices in social welfare organizations[17] and efforts to experiment with alternative approaches,[18] close supervision is still ubiquitous in the field.[19] Indeed, evidence suggests that social workers are generally satisfied with the supervision they receive, especially when supervisors have expert knowledge relevant to the service to clients, play a supportive role with practitioners, and are prepared to grant the workers increasing autonomy.[20]

At the same time, significant minorities of respondents in several studies have expressed dissatisfaction with the supervision they receive.[21] In one recent national survey, for example, 15.4 percent of the supervisees sampled reported that they were fairly or extremely dissatisfied with their current supervision. Among the principal sources of dissatisfaction noted were supervisors' hesitancy to advocate the needs of supervisees and failure to provide specific criticism and instructive assistance to the workers in dealing with problems presented by clients.[22] Another study suggested that supervisors who are directive, paternalistic, and arbitrarily restrict the practitioner's autonomy are likely to create dissatisfaction and poor morale.[23]

In general, then, it would appear that social workers accept the oversight and direction that is implicit in supervision. However, when this relationship is based solely on the authority of position, with little attention given to solving the problems of cases or to professional development, it is likely to be negatively received and to have a deleterious effect on the practitioner's job satisfaction.

COMMUNICATION

Every organization has multiple networks of communication by which members relay and receive information. There are at least four main channels of communication along which messages are exchanged: the vertical, between supervisors and subordinates; the horizontal, between peers and colleagues; the diagonal, across units or departments, between people at different levels; and across agency boundaries, between organizational members and individuals and groups in the community.[24] This discussion will focus on the flow of information up and down the administrative hierarchy and its implications for the practitioner.

The quality and quantity of communication is probably one of the most important components of the practitioner's work environment. One recent study of workers in a variety of social welfare and rehabilitation agencies revealed, for example, a significant positive correlation between practitioners' job satisfaction and the degree to which they perceived organizational communication to be effective. A similar relationship was observed between the effectiveness of communication and the performance of workers.[25] It is important to note that in this study good communication showed a strong positive relationship to such other elements of agency climate as clear and realistic goals and effective supervision and a negative correlation with organizational control procedures that limited the workers' discretion and autonomy.[26] This would suggest that the quality of communications in an agency is closely related to other organizational variables that have been previously discussed.

A practitioner's access to superiors and the opportunity to participate in the development of agency policies and practices also appear to be an important aspect of the intraorganizational environment. Available evidence suggests that when workers have little opportunity to express ideas, needs, and experiences that relate to the work of the organization or find that such messages are blocked or distorted as they are conveyed up the line, problems of morale, cynicism, and alienation often occur.[27] It is interesting that studies of health and welfare organizations indicate that barriers to vertical communication between superior and subordinates are more likely to occur when decision-making is highly centralized among upper-echelon personnel and wide status differentials exist between administrative and nonadministrative staff.[28]

STRATEGIES FOR CHANGE

In the face of growing criticism in the 1960s from policy-makers, consumers, and numerous social movements, many of the policies and practices of social welfare agencies that had had the effect of denying or obstructing services to clients came under public scrutiny. Simultaneously, and perhaps partially as a result of this external criticism, practitioners and academicians in social welfare became increasingly aware of the constraints imposed on workers and clients alike by agency policies and procedures. This awareness helped lay bare the uncomfortable fact, long obscured by the close relationship between social work and social agencies, that it was often difficult to reconcile the social worker's role as a professional with his position as an employee. Some have asserted that this dual allegiance is irreconcilable and can only be resolved when social work services are provided outside the confines of the agency.[29] Others have argued the need for a fundamental, ideological realignment of the profession, to ensure that practitioners' values and commitments will be unequivocally oriented to the interests of clients.[30]

Short of these long-term solutions, consideration is being given to alternative actions that might feasibly be employed by practitioners who encounter agency conditions that, in their view, impede service delivery or create unwarranted hardships for clients.[31] Among the strategies that have been suggested to deal with such situations are participatory management,[32] case-by-case intervention,[33] unionization,[34] and internal advocacy.[35] Only the last will be dealt with here because of the limitations of space.

INTERNAL ADVOCACY

Internal advocacy may be defined as

> an activity engaged in by social work practitioners in their roles
> as professional employees, which is undertaken for the purpose of
> changing the formal policies, programs or procedures of the
> agencies that employ them in the interest of increasing the effectiveness of the services provided or removing organizational conditions
> or practices that are deleterious to the client population served.[36]

The advocacy system may be an individual practitioner, an ad hoc group of colleagues, or the formal subunit of an organization, such as a supervisory unit or department. Its purpose is to gain administrative approval for the proposal that seeks to benefit all or some portion of the organization's clientele. Specific advocacy efforts may include, for example, attempts to gain entitlements for individual clients who are denied benefits because of inflexible or arbitrary administrative procedures, to establish a mechanism to promote coordination of services between departments in an agency, to add clients to an agency board to achieve greater community representation in the policy-making process, or to create a new service or program to deal with a previously unmet need.

The intervention model for internal advocacy is not yet fully articulated, but it is thought to include at least the following interdependent components: identification of the organizational problem or dysfunction that gives rise to the need for change; clear specification of goals and concrete recommendations for altering the condition in question; analysis of sources of resistance to or support for the proposal for change; mobilization and maintenance of the advocacy system, including the recruitment and support of persons both within and outside the organization with the knowledge, skills, and power suited to overcoming anticipated resistance; formulation of a strategy of action that is based on a realistic assessment of the kinds of influence that will be required to obtain a favorable action from decision-makers; and implementation of tactics that are deliberately related to the strategy plan.

Strategic alternatives for internal advocacy may range from collaborative, in which both the advocacy system and the decision-makers agree on the need for change, to adversary, in which the two parties may disagree on the existence or nature of the problem or differ markedly on the best means for resolving the issue. In a collaborative strategy, the internal advocate is likely to utilize consensus-building tactics such as education, changes in attitudes, and mutual problem-solving. An adversary strategy, on the other hand, ordinarily involves more strident tactics such as confrontation, public exposure, mobilization of external pressures, negotiation, and bargaining.

There is little systematic evidence regarding the effectiveness of internal advocacy as an approach to changing agency policies, programs, or procedures. The limited data available suggest that efforts that seek to redistribute resources (such as power or money) or alter the goals of an agency are less likely to be successful than those aimed at modifying procedures or reorganizing existing programs.[37] However, much additional research is needed to establish a sound empirical basis for this mode of intervention and to determine the consequences of internal advocacy for agencies, practitioners, and clients.

Notes

1. Harold Wilensky and Charles N. Lebeaux, *Industrial Society and Social Welfare* (New York: Free Press, 1965), pp. 138–147; Harold W. Demone and Dwight Harshbarger, eds., *Handbook of Human Service Organizations* (New York: Behavioral Publications, 1974), pp. 22–31; and Robert Vinter, "Analysis of Treatment Organizations," *Social Work* 8 (July 1963): pp. 3–15.

2. Robert Vinter, "The Social Structure of Service," in *Issues in American Social Work,* ed. Alfred Kahn (New York: Columbia University Press, 1959), pp. 252–257; and Jack Rothman, *Planning and Organizing for Social Change* (New York: Columbia University Press, 1974), pp. 142–151.
3. Edwin Thomas, "Role Conceptions and Organizational Size," in *Social Welfare Institutions,* ed. Mayer Zald (New York: John Wiley, 1965), p. 499.
4. Ibid., p. 504.
5. Paul Weinberger, "Job Satisfaction and Staff Retention in Social Work," in *Perspectives on Social Welfare,* ed. Weinberger (New York: Macmillan, 1974), pp. 478–479.
6. Joseph Olmstead and Harold Christensen, *Effects of Agency Work Contexts: An Intensive Field Study* (National Study of Social Welfare and Rehabilitation Workers, Work and Organizational Contexts, vol. 1; Washington, D.C.: U.S. Department of Health, Education and Welfare, Social and Rehabilitation Service, 1973), pp. 107–125.
7. See, for example, Herman Stein, "Administrative Leadership in Complex Service Organizations," in *Social Work Administration,* ed. Harry Schatz (New York: Council on Social Work Education, 1970), pp. 288–292.
8. For an excellent discussion of goals, see Charles Perrow, *Organizational Analysis: A Sociological View* (Belmont, Calif.: Brooks-Cole, 1970), pp. 133–174.
9. Lloyd Ohlin, Herman Piven, and Donnel Pappenfort, "Major Dilemmas of the Social Worker in Probation and Parole," in *Social Welfare Institutions,* ed. Mayer Zald (New York: John Wiley, 1965), pp. 523–538; and Harry Wasserman, "The Professional Social Worker in a Bureaucracy," *Social Work* 16 (Jan. 1971): 89–95.
10. A. D. Green, "The Professional Worker in the Bureaucracy," *Social Service Review* 40 (March 1966): 74–83.
11. Alvin Gouldner, "The Secrets of Organization," in *Readings in Community Organization Practice,* ed. Ralph Kramer and Harry Specht (Englewood Cliffs, N.J.: Prentice-Hall, 1969), pp. 139–141.
12. Olmstead and Christensen, *Effects of Agency Work Contexts,* pp. 109–120.
13. Michael Aiken and Jerald Hage, "Organizational Alienation: A Comparative Analysis," in *The Sociology of Organizations: Basic Studies,* ed. Oscar Grusky and George Miller (New York: Free Press, 1970), pp. 518–519.
14. Ibid., pp. 522–525.
15. Olmstead and Christensen, *Effects of Agency Work Contexts,* pp. 107–110.
16. Wasserman, "Professional Social Worker," pp. 89–95; and Naomi Gottlieb, *The Welfare Bind* (New York: Columbia University Press, 1974), pp. 13–38.
17. See, for example, Nina Toren, "Semi-Professionalism and Social Work: A Theoretical Perspective," in *The Semi-Professions and Their Organization,* ed. Amitai Etzioni (New York: Free Press, 1969), pp. 169–184.
18. Joseph H. Kahle, "Structuring and Administering a Modern Voluntary Agency," *Social Work* 14 (Oct. 1969): 21–28.
19. Alfred Kadushin, "Supervisor-Supervisee: A Survey," *Social Work* 19 (May 1974): 288–297.
20. Ibid., pp. 291–292; and Olmstead and Christensen, *Effects of Agency Work Contexts,* p. 206.
21. See Alice Ullman, Mary Goss, Milton Davis, and Margaret Mushinski, "Activities, Satisfaction, and Problems of Social Workers in Hospital Settings:

A Comparative Study," *Social Service Review* 45 (March 1971): 22–26; Olmstead and Christensen, *Effects of Agency Work Contexts,* p. 206; and Kadushin, "Supervisor-Supervisee," pp. 291–292.

22. Kadushin, "Supervisor-Supervisee," pp. 291–292.

23. Ibid., pp. 291–295; and Olmstead and Christensen, *Effects of Agency Work Contexts,* pp. 197–204 and 109–115.

24. For a discussion of communication networks in organizations, see Daniel Katz and Robert L. Kahn, *The Social Psychology of Organizations* (New York: John Wiley, 1966), pp. 235–247.

25. Olmstead and Christensen, *Effects of Agency Work Contexts,* pp. 109–116.

26. Ibid., pp. 78–79.

27. Wasserman, "Professional Social Worker," p. 92; and Aiken and Hage, "Organizational Alienation," pp. 139–140.

28. Rothman, *Planning and Organizing,* pp. 463–464; and Jerald Hage, *Communication and Organizational Control* (New York: John Wiley, 1974), pp. 198–203.

29. Irving Piliavin, "Restructuring the Provision of Social Services," *Social Work* 13 (Jan. 1968): 34–41.

30. Willard Richan and Allan Mendelsohn, *Social Work: The Unloved Profession* (New York: Franklin Watts, 1973), pp. 44–50.

31. Under these circumstances it is the worker's responsibility to work with the agency to modify such practices or conditions. See Ad Hoc Committee on Advocacy, "The Social Worker as Advocate: Champion of Social Victims," *Social Work* 14 (April 1969): 16–22.

32. Harleigh Trecker, *Social Work Administration* (New York: Association Press, 1971), pp. 91–105.

33. See Gottlieb, *Welfare Bind,* pp. 123–144; and Archie Hanlan, "Counteracting Problems of Bureaucracy in Public Welfare," *Social Work* 12 (July 1967): 88–94.

34. Milton Tambor, "Unions and Voluntary Agencies," *Social Work* 18 (July 1973): 41–47.

35. The following discussion of internal advocacy draws heavily from the following sources: Hyman Weiner, "Toward Techniques for Social Change," *Social Work* 6 (April 1961): 26–35; George Brager, "Institutional Change: Perimeters of the Possible," *Social Work* 12 (Jan. 1967): 59–69; Rino Patti, "Limitations and Prospects of Internal Advocacy," *Social Casework* 59 (Nov. 1974): 537–545; and Robert Morris and Robert Binstock, *Feasible Planning for Social Change* (New York: Columbia University Press, 1966).

36. Patti, "Limitations and Prospects," p. 537.

37. See, for example, the following sources that present case studies of internal advocacy: Harold Weissman, *Overcoming Mismanagement in the Human Service Professions* (San Francisco: Jossey-Bass, 1973); and Martin Needleman and Carolyn Needleman, *Guerrillas in the Bureaucracy* (New York: John Wiley, 1974). For an empirical study of effects of internal advocacy in schools, involving the Teacher Corps, see Ronald Corwin, "Strategies for Organizational Innovation," in *Human Service Organizations,* ed. Yeheskel Hasenfeld and Richard A. English (Ann Arbor: University of Michigan Press, 1974), pp. 698–720.

Chapter 4   Organizational Characteristics of Agencies and the Distribution of Services to Applicants

James R. Greenley and Stuart A. Kirk

This chapter develops a theoretical framework for understanding how some organizational characteristics influence the way personal problems of applicants to health and welfare agencies come to be defined and serviced. It will argue that boundary control and domain are important concepts in understanding if and where an applicant's problem is serviced.

First, the topic will be located in the broader study of client careers. Second, key postulates of the framework to be developed will be introduced. Third, selected organizational variables will be defined and developed. Fourth, hypotheses will be derived from these postulates and concepts. Fifth, a reconceptualization of the health and welfare system in terms of the framework will be offered. Finally, several implications of this framework will be outlined.

CLIENT CAREERS

The notion of a "client career" refers in part to the sequence of relationships that a person may have with an agency. This aspect of a client career can be usefully divided into three phases. The first will be referred to as the pre-applicant help-seeking phase that encompasses the time a person first comes to define himself in need of help until he makes

Reprinted from the *Journal of Health and Social Behavior* 14 (March 1973): 70–79, with the permission of the publisher. The authors wish to thank C. David Hollister, Michael Aiken, and Jerald Hage for their helpful criticisms of an earlier draft of this paper.

contact with a help-giving agency. This phase has already received considerable attention.[1] The second phase may be called the applicant phase. It begins at the initial person-agency contact and terminates when the person is accepted at an agency for servicing or ceases to seek the services of help-giving agencies. The third phase, the client phase, refers to that period from his acceptance for service until the time he is no longer being helped by the agency. Although organizational characteristics influence all phases of client careers, this chapter focuses only on the applicant stage and examines conditions that influence whether agencies accept applicants as clients, whether they reject them without recommendation, or whether they attempt to refer them to another agency.

The conventional approach to the study of the applicant phase focuses on characteristics of the client and his problem and how these bear on diagnosis, acceptance, or referral,[2] the implicit assumption being that the client has an objective problem, that the evaluation, intake, or diagnostic process establishes the nature of that problem, and that recommendations for service—that is, acceptance, rejection, or referral—derive from the nature of the client's "real" problem uncovered by the evaluation. In short, the outcome of the applicant phase is viewed as determined primarily by characteristics of the client. This chapter begins with the notion that characteristics of the agency are also important. It will therefore attempt to develop some systematic hypotheses about the relationship between selected organizational characteristics and the applicant experience of acceptance, rejection, or referral.

POSTULATES

Once a help-seeker becomes an applicant by virtue of contacting an agency, his career is importantly shaped by the actions taken by its staff.

Postulate 1. When confronted with an applicant, staff members in many agencies have significant discretion in what definitions to apply to his problem and what service or agency to recommend to him.

The existence and extent of this discretion is not uniform across agencies, but is probably differentially distributed among agencies. This discretion is made possible by several factors. First, applicants are often not certain what the "problem" is or where to take it; they rely on staff to clarify the situation. Second, staff frequently find that personal problems are multi-faceted and ambiguous and do not always lend themselves to simple or standard categorization. Third, there are a variety of bases on which the staff can make the categorization—for instance, on the basis of presenting problem, observed symptoms, inferred or imputed underlying causes, or prognosis.[3] Finally, the ambiguity of the situation as well as the position of the staff vis-à-vis the applicant allows a staff member to impose his definition of the problem on the applicant.[4]

Postulate 2. Agencies in any given community tend to use different sets of problem definitions for defining their tasks.

Most agencies deal with a limited range of personal problems. That is, agencies view their tasks as dealing with problems that can be defined as falling within their chosen range of problem categories. So, we find agencies that service only people defined as alcoholic, unwed mothers, blind, delinquent, disabled, or even "multi-problemed." Admittedly, there are agencies that utilize a wide range of discrete categories for defining the problems of appropriate clients—for instance, a medical clinic or a mental health center. Yet, while some problem categories may be shared among several agencies, all agencies do not use all categories. And the historical trend is toward greater specialization of function[5] with consequent greater distinction among the problem categories used by agencies in a community. Thus, the agency where an applicant is accepted as a client limits the range of problem definitions that may come to be applied to him.

CENTRAL CONCEPTS

Exchange

Since applicants and clients can be seen as part of an organization's relevant environment,[6] and since an organization's essential relationship with that environment is one of exchange,[7] we may talk of exchange of service with applicants or exchange of applicants with other organizations. In one case, the applicant is the party with whom the exchange is made, and, in the other, he constitutes the item exchanged. An exchange of an applicant between organizations is commonly called a "referral." For our purposes, exchanges of applicants will be more broadly defined to include very formal and intentional transfers of applicants, transfers that result only from agency suggestions to the applicant that he seek help elsewhere, and transfers that agencies unintentionally set up by rejecting an applicant who subseqently receives help at another agency.

Boundary Control

Organizations have differential ability to control these exchanges with their environment or parts of it. We will refer to this ability to control exchanges as "boundary control." Although not employing this term, many authors have discussed the importance of an organization's ability to control its relationships with its environment.[8] Perrow, for instance, discusses a hospital's attempt to reduce its dependence on the environment and the consequences for its internal dynamics.[9] In a more general statement, Thompson refers to an organization's need to protect core technologies from fluctuations in the task environment through strategies that maximize the organization's power over its environment and thus minimize the relative power of that environment.[10] Although boundary control refers to the exchange of all elements, in this chapter we are primarily interested in the exchange of applicants. In regard to applicants, Thompson states that the degree of discretion the nonmember (e.g., applicant) can exercise and the organization's degree of control over its boundary personnel influence the outcome of their interaction.[11] Freidson, in his study of medical practice, found that the type of professional and lay referral system on which the medical practitioner is dependent affects the control he has over dealings with his patients.[12] Thus, a number of organizational processes have been related to an organization's ability to control its exchange with its environment and, even more specifically, its ability to control exchanges of and with applicants.

Since, as Thompson has indicated,[13] an organization's relationship to its task environment is multi-faceted, an agency's ability to exchange applicants varies depending on the particular applicant and the other agency involved in the exchange. Litwak suggests that each of these interorganizational linkages be examined separately.[14] However, for heuristic purposes, following Evans's admonitions,[15] we will characterize agencies by their general level of boundary control.

Domain

Boundary control implies the existence of a unit with a limited sphere of activity. The organization's sphere of activity has been called its "domain."[16] Levine and White define an organization's domain as "the specific goals it wishes to pursue and the functions it undertakes in order to implement its goals." Operationally for health agencies, it consists of the "claims that an organization stakes out for itself in terms of (1) disease covered, (2) population served, and (3) services rendered." The goals constitute the organization's claim to future "functions" and elements requisite to these functions, whereas the present or actual functions constitute the "de facto" claims to these elements. By "function" Levine and White mean "a set of interrelated services or activities that are instrumental, or believed to be instrumental, for the realization of an organization's objectives."[17]

There is one problem with this definition of domain. On the one hand, they define domain in terms of goals (*claims* to future services and resources) and functions (present or *actual* services). Operationally, however, they define domain in terms of only *claims*. For our purposes, we wish to recognize two domains that each organization has, a *claimed domain* and a *de facto domain*. An organization's claimed domain consists of its verbal and written pronouncements regarding the problems it deals with, the populations it serves, and the services it offers. Its de facto domain consists of the problems presently or actually dealt with, the populations served, and the services rendered.

Often the two domains are not congruent—they do not cover the same problems, populations, and services. Stanton, for instance, describes a clear example of this situation in a mental health association,[18] and Scott noted it with regard to blindness agencies.[19] This condition, in which claimed and de facto domains differ, will be called *domain discrepancy*.

Domain is relatively flexible, on both the claimed and de facto levels. Rather than constituting a fixed territory, it represents the outcome of the organization's continual negotiation with the relevant environment.[20] The claimed domain, on the one hand, is probably negotiated with a different segment of the environment than is the de facto domain; it is probably negotiated by a different level staff, for different purposes, and with potentially different organizational consequences. Typically, the claimed domain would be negotiated annually with funding or governing groups (e.g., community chests or councils, united funds, state legislatures, or agency boards), would be negotiated by the top administrative staff for the purpose of obtaining funds or raising prestige, and would have only limited impact on the routine operation of the agency. The de facto domain, on the other hand, is continually being negotiated with prospective applicants and referral agencies, is most commonly handled by line staff for the purpose of maximizing the utilization of limited resources, and has serious consequences for the daily life of the agency. In the absence of much research on the existence and character of these two levels of domain, the foregoing elaboration must remain suggestive.

Levine and White argue that exchange rests upon prior consensus regarding domain.[21] Their conclusion that "domain consensus is a prerequisite to exchange" follows from their conception of exchange as voluntary activity requiring some agreement. Yet, as Levine and White note,[22] parties to an exchange may not be interacting on equal terms and may employ sanctions or pressures. Thus, they seem to blur the meaning of "voluntary." Realizing that exchanges with or of applicants involve varying degrees of choice for the participants, we will not confine the concept of exchange to voluntary activity.

Therefore, domain consensus is not necessary for, although it may facilitate, interorganizational exchange. For example, the authors observed mental hospital staff members entirely misunderstanding the domain of a "homemakers" service, but nevertheless referring applicants there. And the staff of the homemakers service, after talking to the applicant, sometimes offered their help to the applicant for problems not even perceived by the personnel at the hospital. Hollister describes a different situation in which one agency dealing with juvenile delinquents disagreed with the domain of a second agency, even though they were familiar with it, but still found it necessary to exchange clients.[23] Exchanges may be facilitated by consensus about domains, but they do not require it.

BOUNDARY CONTROL AND CLIENT DISTRIBUTION

Boundary control is an organization's ability to influence the outcome of its exchange with its environment. One essential element that is exchanged among health and welfare agencies is applicants.[24] Since personal problems are subject to a variety of definitions (Postulate 1) and since these definitions are differentially employed by the various health and welfare agencies (Postulate 2), an agency's ability to control the exchange of applicants influences the range of possible definitions that may come to be applied to a given applicant.

Clients are sometimes seen as a resource without which a service agency cannot survive. However, clients may be a liability as well as a resource. As noted by several researchers,[25] few agency administrators emphasize a need for more clients. Although providing an agency with a raison d'être, clients can overburden an agency by demanding special attention or service, by requiring staff overtime, by consuming scarce resources (e.g., staff, equipment, or space) for long durations, or by failing to exhibit the proper improvement desired by the agency. Thus, the ability of an agency to dispose of an applicant, by rejection or referral, may be as important as the ability to obtain him. This is particularly true under conditions of a surplus or abundance of applicants.

Most communities have agencies with varying degrees of control over exchanges. Thus we might expect the following, assuming agencies act somewhat in their own self-interest:

Hypothesis 1. Agencies with high boundary control will, experiencing an applicant surplus, tend to accept fewer applicants as clients than low-boundary-control agencies. Conversely, agencies with high boundary control, experiencing a scarcity of applicants, may tend to accept more applicants as clients than low-boundary-control agencies.

Hypothesis 2. The applicants rejected by these high-boundary-control agencies will tend to flow, through referral or on their own initiative, toward agencies with lower boundary control where they will more likely be accepted for service.

Hypothesis 2 would follow from Hypothesis 1 if referrals and reapplications for service were only random in nature. Yet Hypothesis 2 is even more likely given that applicants are more likely to seek service where there are greater odds they will find it and agencies are more likely to refer applicants to agencies where the applicant is most likely to receive service.

Since agencies use different sets of problem definitions (Postulate 2), the above two hypotheses would suggest that an agency's boundary control influences how a person's problem may come to be defined or, on a community-wide level, how groups of applicants get sorted into problem categories.

This influence on problem rates will be exaggerated most in those communities in which high boundary control is associated with one particular type of agency. For example, if the agencies with domains dealing with mild psychiatric disorders all have relatively high boundary control, many people with problems that could have been defined as, say, "neurotic," will receive no treatment or will be distributed among other agencies—for instance, family service, child guidance, mental hospital, or medical clinic—and thus their problems will most likely be defined accordingly as marital problems, parent-child difficulties, serious psychiatric impairment, or possibly organic disease. Conversely, if those same psychiatric agencies have relatively low boundary control in that particular community, applicants to the other community agencies will tend to flow toward the psychiatric clinics. Thus, the rate of treated personal problems may be, in part, a function of the relative ability of agencies to influence applicant exchanges. Under conditions of applicant surplus, higher rates of rejection and deflated treated incidence rates should be associated with high-boundary-control agencies, and lower rejection rates and inflated incidence rates should be associated with low-boundary-control organizations.

By definition, agencies with high boundary control will be able to exercise more discretion in their selection of clients than will agencies with low boundary control. Assuming that agencies that are able to be more selective will choose those types of clients that they most want leads to the following hypothesis.

Hypothesis 3. Applicants accepted at high-boundary-control agencies will tend to be more homogeneous in regard to diagnostic, demographic, and other variables than those accepted at low-boundary-control agencies.

Furthermore, most agencies probably select clients from a relatively diverse applicant pool on the basis of characteristics the agency defines as desirable applicant traits—for instance, high social status or good prognosis.[26] Thus, in most cases the following should be true.

Hypothesis 4. Higher-boundary-control agencies, being better able to select, will have higher-status clients and those with a greater potential for improvement or rehabilitation than agencies with less boundary control. For example, compare the characteristics of mental patients at an exclusive, private psychiatric facility with those at a public state mental hospital.[27]

DOMAIN AND CLIENT DISTRIBUTION

Two types of agency domain are defined above: claimed domain, those verbal and written pronouncements regarding the problems an agency says it deals with, the populations it serves and services offered, and de facto domain, those problems actually dealt with, the populations actually served, and services rendered. Because agency personnel have discretion in how to deal with an applicant, both the patterning of claimed domains in a community and the relationship of the claimed to the de facto domain(s) may affect the relative distribution of applicants into problem categories.

Pre-applicant help-seekers and prospective referral sources base their decisions on whether to apply or refer to an agency largely on the basis of their perception of the agency. The more experience they have had with an agency, the more likely they will be familiar with what the agency actually does. To the extent that they do not know what an agency does, they will have to base their conceptions on what the organization claims about itself. Many referring agencies or applicants will probably not be in a position to assess an agency's de facto domain accurately; they will have to rely to some extent on the public information that the organization gives out to describe its services. Thus, most organizations and pre-applicant help-seekers probably orient themselves to some extent to other agencies in terms of those agencies' claimed domains.

Just as the claimed domain of one agency indicates the range of problems and services purportedly dealt with, the claimed domains of a community-wide network of agencies indicate the range of problems and services covered in that community.

Hypothesis 5. Health and welfare agencies in one community claiming to offer a more extensive set of services to a broader collection of people and problems than the agencies in another similar community will attract more applicants for service.

This may occur, not only because the public will initiate more applications for service, but also because any one agency in that community contemplating rejecting or referring an applicant will be more likely to make the referral if it perceives that another agency claims to deal with a problem that the applicant can be seen as having. Extensive claimed domains in a community may not only produce more numerous demands for service, but may actually result in more service given. For example, a community of agencies that claims that it deals with all the legal problems of the poor may find itself dealing with a good many more and varied situations than it anticipated or desired.

In most communities there are certain problem categories that are not within any agency's claimed domain. Since referral sources and applicants can utilize only existing services, they will be led to think and act in terms of existing agencies and their claimed domains.

Hypothesis 6. When some problem categories are not contained in a set of claimed domains there will tend to be an inflation of the number of applicants with problems defined in terms of those categories that are circumscribed by the existent claimed domains.

For instance, if an agency upon evaluating an applicant believes that his problem consists of the consumption of too much alcohol, but no agency in town claims to deal with alcoholic problems, it may refer the applicant to the family service agency, where his problem comes to be seen as a "marital problem" rather than an "alcoholic problem." In this way, both applicant and agency are encouraged to perceive and present the "problem" in terms of the categories contained in the available claimed domains, and thus the relative treated incidence rates in these categories tend to be inflated.

In most communities the degree of domain discrepancy will vary among the assorted agencies. To the extent that applicants orient themselves on the basis of claimed domains, the following hypothesis should be supported:

Hypothesis 7. Those agencies that have de facto domains that are smaller than their claimed domains will attract some applicants that they will not serve, and will tend to reject or refer more applicants than similar agencies without domain discrepancy.

Many health and welfare organizations both offer some services they do not give and give services they do not offer, producing overlapping domains rather than concentric ones. This possibly common type of domain discrepancy would produce a rather inefficient applicant distribution system where some applicants get serviced in unlikely settings and rejected at places where they were led to believe they rightfully belonged.

THE AMERICAN SYSTEM RECONCEPTUALIZED

The characteristics and problems of the American health and welfare system can be usefully explored by employing the concepts of boundary control and domain. In terms of boundary control and domain, the health and welfare system is quite diverse. Agencies' domains and degree of boundary control vary considerably for a host of historical reasons, not the least of which is the development of both public and private agencies, religious and secular ones, those funded and administered locally and those nationally, and those staffed by professionals and those by nonprofessionals.

In spite of the diversity, several persistent patterns or clusters can be discerned. Due to a number of historical developments and organizational strategies, an agency's boundary control and the size of its domain may often be related. Those agencies with the most control over the exchange of clients tend to be those agencies with rather specific and well-defined services. Conversely, those agencies with broad domains tend to have less control over the acceptance, rejection, or exchange of applicants.

The agency system, therefore, contains two major clusters of agencies. A first cluster of agencies, those with high boundary control and small domains, are often privately funded agencies which provide only one or several specific services to a select population who are thought to have good prognoses. Here are found many family casework agencies, private medical clinics, child guidance agencies, university-related psychiatric clinics, private mental hospitals, and other specialized agencies. A second cluster is composed of those agencies that have relatively low boundary control and broad domains. Here are found hospital emergency rooms, police departments, state mental hospitals, skid row missions, and public medical clinics. These two clusters, of course, are not inclusive of all health and welfare agencies; many agencies, admittedly, are not clearly in either cluster.

We suggest that within both of these groupings, and perhaps within the full range of agencies, there is widespread domain discrepancy. An agency may develop domain discrepancy for several reasons. First, relatively new agencies that are attempting to establish themselves in the existent agency network and in the community often claim to offer a wide variety of services covering a diverse population in order to attract funds and clients.[28] They are usually in a position of relatively little control over the selection of applicants (beggars can't be choosers) and are frequently unable to live up to their claims. Mental retardation facilities at the turn of the century, for example, made broad claims that they later could not and did not attempt to fulfill.[29] Second, as an agency is able to establish greater control over its exchanges, it is able to be more selective in its choice of clients, thereby narrowing its de facto domain and consequently increasing domain discrepancy. Third, an agency may choose to maintain a relatively larger claimed than de facto domain for public relations purposes.[30] For example, planned parenthood agencies often claim to offer fertility counseling in order to lower public controversy about birth control, although such services are rarely given.[31] The presence of this discrepancy, plus the existence of the two clusters described above, results in the familiar descriptions we hear of the American health and welfare system.

The American system is commonly characterized as a rather disjointed potpourri of agencies and services. Health and welfare services have been described as becoming more specialized and more embedded in bureaucratic structures.[32] Specialization, or narrowing of domains, has led to gaps in service, leaving some personal problems or combination of problems uncovered by the network of agencies.[33] Likewise, bureaucratic procedures, by functioning to buffer agencies against applicant demands for service and thereby providing the agencies with a mechanism of boundary control, may make service difficult to obtain. Similarly, the fragmentation of services (or domains) has made it more difficult for the help-seeker to know which agency is best suited to handle his particular problem.[34] Even if the applicant contacts what he thinks is an appropriate agency, the agency staff may feel that they do not want to deal with him or that his "real problem" is best serviced at another facility, thus necessitating an exchange. The continual exchange of applicants has been described by one observer of the American welfare scene as a "pinball" system,[35] wherein applicants are often expelled from the system or drop out without receiving help. The existence of agencies with high boundary control and small domains, then, results in applicants who are bounced among agencies until they are expelled from the system or are deposited in agencies that do not have the resources to reject them.

The sorting of applicants into agencies is made additionally difficult by the apparent lack of interagency coordination or integration.[36] In part this results from the existence of domain discrepancies that increase the probability that applicants will be rejected, thus increasing the need for coordination around referrals. The difficulty is further compounded by the ignorance agency personnel have regarding the claimed and de facto domains of other community agencies. Indeed, many agency personnel know little or nothing about 40 to 50 percent of other community agencies.[37] Most important in creating the problems of interagency coordination that have been observed is the differential ability of agencies to accept and reject applicants. Thus, it is boundary control that disrupts the smooth transition of applicants into clients.

In addition to the often-cited inadequacies of the health and welfare system is the problem of an abundance, or the appearance of an abundance, of prospective clients for most agencies. If agencies accepted and serviced all applicants, a surplus of them would not develop; applicanthood would be severely truncated. However, because most agencies have the ability to reject applicants, and their rejected applicants often remain in the applicant pool, there is a cumulative process that produces, in fact, too many applicants. The abundance, ironically, may be in part an artifact of agencies' boundary control, not necessarily a product of the rate of initial applications. Additionally, the existence of agencies with extensive claimed domains and relatively smaller de facto domains encourages many people to become applicants who otherwise would not, thus increasing the number of applicants, but not necessarily the number of clients.

The opportunity many agencies have to choose clients from among applicants allows these agencies to invest their efforts in helping only applicants who are most likely, or thought to be most likely, to benefit from their assistance. Consequently, those agencies with high boundary control often pick clients with the most remedial problems and reject those applicants who, though most in need of help, are thought least likely to show great improvement.[38] And thus the applicants with the most difficult problems often are serviced by the agencies with the fewest resources and least expertise to deal with the problems.[39]

Finally, when the American health and welfare system is conceptualized in terms of boundary control and domain, the rates of treated personal problems can be seen to be affected by the interplay of these two dimensions. When small domain and high boundary control occur together, as they often do, there is a tendency for them jointly to deflate the number of clients in their problem categories. Conversely, the problem categories used by the agencies with broad domains and lower boundary control will contain inflated rates of treated incidence.

IMPLICATIONS

The framework that has been developed has important implications for the study of client careers, for the social construction of public and personal identities, and for program planning.

There are numerous studies of client careers, but they often focus on either the pre-applicant help-seeking phase or on the experience of the individual once he has been accepted for service or treatment. We suggest that the applicant phase of a client's career is equally consequential and that the study of applicants should focus more on the organizational forces that operate to channel applicants toward and away from certain community agencies.

The individual applying for service personally enters into an organizational arena in which organizational factors affect the manner in which his problem, and indirectly his self, comes to be defined. Organizational factors, then, to some extent shape the process by which applicants are transformed into clients, and people with troubles are assigned new public identities. In the health and welfare field, for example, the troubled applicant who is passed from the medical clinic to the nursing home to the mental hospital is accompanied by a series of social definitions of the "problem" and indirectly definitions of himself as a social object.[40] These definitions that come to be assigned to the applicant may breed behavior conforming to the expectations generated by those definitions, expectations that encourage the very behavior social agencies are designed to change.[41]

Finally, health and welfare programs are often conceived and organized on the basis of perceived need for a given service. That need is often estimated on the basis of the size of current caseloads or the treated incidence rates in given problem categories. The framework outlined in this chapter would suggest that research based on the diagnosed problems of clients as well as programs based on such studies may overlook the extent to which the findings are shaped by the organizational characteristics of the agencies rather than by the problems of applicants.

CONCLUSION

To explore our hypotheses and their implications in future research would require data on both the help-seeking careers of applicants and on those organizations they contact. The help-seeking careers of a large contingent of applicants in a given community would have to be closely monitored in terms of the sequence of agencies contacted in person, by telephone, or by mail. When an applicant is accepted for service, one would have to note the problem category in which he was placed. Also, the health and welfare agencies in the community would have to be closely studied and carefully categorized in terms of the concepts developed in this chapter. Such a study would help ascertain the impact of boundary control, claimed and de facto domain, and domain discrepancy on the distribution patterns of applicants and their problems.

Notes

1. Cf. David Mechanic, *Medical Sociology* (New York: Free Press, 1968), pp. 130–131; Marian Radke Yarrow, Charlotte Green Schwartz, Harriet S. Murphy, and Leila Calhoun Deasy, "The Psychological Meaning of Mental Illness in the Family," *Journal of Social Issues* 11 (Oct. 1955): 12–24; Charles Kadushin, *Why People Go to Psychiatrists* (New York: Atherton, 1969); Harold Sampson, Sheldon L. Messinger, and Robert D. Towne, "Family Processes and Becoming a Mental Patient," *American Journal of Sociology* 68 (July 1962): 88–96; Eliot Freidson, *Patients' Views of Medical Practice* (New York: Russell Sage Foundation, 1961); and John E. Mayer and Noel Timms, *The Client Speaks* (New York: Atherton, 1970).
2. Freidson, *Patients' Views.*
3. Eliot Freidson, "Disability as Social Deviance," in *Sociology and Rehabilitation,* ed. Marvin B. Sussman (Washington, D.C.: American Sociological Association, 1966), pp. 71–99, and Robert A. Scott, *The Making of Blind Men* (New York: Russell Sage Foundation, 1969), pp. 71–89.
4. Freidson, "Disability," and Mayer and Timms, *The Client Speaks,* pp. 65–80.
5. Harold L. Wilensky and Charles N. Lebeaux, *Industrial Society and Social Welfare* (New York: Free Press, 1958), p. 247 ff.
6. James D. Thompson, *Organizations in Action* (New York: McGraw-Hill, 1967), pp. 27–28.
7. Ibid., p. 28.
8. Philip Selznick, *TVA and the Grass Roots* (Berkeley: University of California Press, 1949).
9. Charles Perrow, "Organizational Prestige: Some Functions and Dysfunctions," *American Journal of Sociology* 66 (Jan. 1961): 335–341.
10. Thompson, *Organizations in Action,* p. 19.
11. James D. Thompson, "Organizations and Output Transactions," *American Journal of Sociology* 68 (Nov. 1962): 309–324.

12. Eliot Freidson, "Client Control and Medical Practice," *American Journal of Sociology* 65 (Jan. 1960): 374–382.
13. Thompson, *Organizations in Action,* p. 29.
14. Eugene Litwak, *Towards the Multi-factor Theory and Practice of Linkages between Formal Organizations* (Washington, D.C.: U.S. Department of Health, Education and Welfare, 1970).
15. William M. Evans, "The Organization-Set: Toward a Theory of Inter-organizational Relations," in *Approaches to Organizational Design,* ed. James D. Thompson (Pittsburgh: University of Pittsburgh Press, 1966), pp. 173–191.
16. Sol Levine and Paul E. White, "Exchange as a Conceptual Framework for the Study of Interorganizational Relationships," *Administrative Science Quarterly* 5 (March 1961): 597.
17. Ibid., pp. 597–598.
18. Esther Stanton, *Clients Come Last* (Beverly Hills: Sage Publications, 1970).
19. Scott, *The Making of Blind Men,* pp. 90–104.
20. Anselm Strauss, Leonard Schatzman, Danuta Ehrlick, Rue Bucher, and Melvin Sabshin, "The Hospital and Its Negotiated Order," in *The Hospital in Modern Society,* ed. Eliot Freidson (New York: Free Press, 1963), p. 164 ff.
21. Levine and White, "Exchange," pp. 597–599.
22. Ibid., pp. 588–589.
23. C. David Hollister, "Interorganizational Conflict: The Case of Police Youth Bureaus and the Juvenile Court," paper presented to the annual meeting of the American Sociological Association, Washington, D.C., 1970.
24. Levine and White, "Exchange," p. 587.
25. Sol Levine, Paul E. White, and Benjamin D. Paul, "Community Inter-organizational Problems in Providing Medical Care and Social Services," *American Journal of Public Health* 53 (Aug. 1963): p. 1187.
26. Ibid., p. 1189; Scott, *The Making of Blind Men,* ch. 5; and Harry C. Brede-meier, "The Socially Handicapped and the Agencies: A Market Analysis," in *Mental Health of the Poor,* ed. Frank Fiessman, Jerome Cohen, and Arthur Pearl (New York: Free Press, 1964), p. 96.
27. August B. Hollingshead and Frederick C. Redlich, *Social Class and Mental Illness* (New York: John Wiley, 1958), ch. 9.
28. William R. Rosengren, "The Careers of Clients and Organizations," in *Organizations and Clients,* ed. Rosengren and Mark Lefton (Columbus: Charles E. Merrill, 1970), p. 121 ff.
29. Bernice M. Fisher, "Claims and Credibility," *Social Problems* 16 (Spring 1969): 423–432.
30. Cf. Stanton, *Clients Come Last.*
31. Elaine Cumming, *Systems of Social Regulation* (New York: Atherton, 1968), p. 51.
32. Wilensky and Lebeaux, *Industrial Society,* p. 233 ff.
33. Ibid., p. 250 ff., and Alfred J. Kahn, *Planning Community Services for Children in Trouble* (New York: Columbia University Press, 1963).
34. Kahn, *Planning Community Services,* p. 117 ff., and Gerald Gurin, Joseph Veroff, and Sheila Feld, *Americans View Their Mental Health* (New York: Basic Books, 1960), pp. 348–351.
35. Elaine Cumming, "Allocation of Care to the Mentally Ill," in *Organizing for Community Welfare,* ed. Mayer N. Zald (Chicago: Quadrangle, 1967), p. 130.

36. Ibid. and Kahn, *Planning Community Services.*
37. Levine et al., "Exchange," pp. 1190–1191.
38. Richard A. Cloward and Irwin Epstein, "Private Social Welfare's Disengagement from the Poor," in *Social Welfare Institutions,* ed. Mayer N. Zald (New York: John Wiley, 1965), p. 626 ff; Scott, *The Making of Blind Men,* pp. 69–70; and Bredemeier, "The Socially Handicapped," p. 96.
39. Cumming, "Allocation of Care," p. 145.
40. Cf. Erving Goffman, *Asylums* (Garden City, N.Y.: Doubleday, 1961), pp. 125–169.
41. Howard S. Becker, *Outsiders* (New York: Free Press, 1963); Edwin Lemert, *Social Pathology* (New York: McGraw-Hill, 1951); and Thomas Scheff, *Being Mentally Ill* (Chicago: Aldine, 1966).

Chapter 5   Social Workers versus Bureaucracy

Wilbur A. Finch, Jr.

Social work is often described as an organizational profession because most of its activities are carried out within formal agency settings. Thus, the vast majority of social workers carry at least three distinguishable roles: the role of practitioner or "helper," the role of professional working in a formal agency, and the role of bureaucrat who must negotiate the stresses and capitalize on the opportunities of organizational life.[1] Because most social workers cannot avoid contact with formal, bureaucratic organizations, one can assume that they have some perspective on the nature of such organizations and the ways in which workers may achieve personal and professional goals while working within their context. The success of professionals in organizations may ultimately depend on their acquiring a set of beliefs and values that helps them decide what is true, what questions need to be asked, and what is right or wrong in any given situation.[2]

The question of whether the pursuit of professionalism inevitably involves a conflict with bureaucracy has been of major interest to social work authors. While the demands of professionalism and the demands of work in a bureaucracy may be compatible in many ways, major sources of conflict exist that are usually related to the service ideal of professionals and their desire for autonomy in working with clients.[3] This chapter will review the potential sources of conflict for the social worker as these have been identified in the literature and will offer in light of recent changes in the field a redefinition of the problem of professionalism versus bureaucratization.

PRACTICE AND BUREAUCRACY

Basic to the argument that professionalism and bureaucratization are incompatible is the dilemma of professional autonomy versus bureau-

Reprinted from *Social Work* 21, no. 5 (Sept. 1976): 370–375, with the permission of the publisher.

cratic control. A number of social work authors believe a certain tension exists between the organization's need for the professional's expertise on the one hand and its requirement of employee loyalty that may, on the other hand, inhibit the worker's identification with the profession. Green argues that "when responsible to both a profession and a bureaucracy, the individual finds himself confronted by two sets of mutually incompatible demands."[4] For example, limits placed on professional activity by an organization may become viewed by the worker as impediments to the effective delivery of services. Similarly, the increased specialization of bureaucratic organizations may constrain the professional's ability to address client needs in their totality. Wasserman has posed a question that is therefore of basic concern to the social work practitioner: "How (and in what ways) does the bureaucratic structure support or constrain the worker's professional activities?"[5]

However, the controversy over professionalism versus bureaucratization has tended to obscure the accommodations that can be reached between professionals and the organizations in which they work. In order to effect accommodations, social workers may have to temper their feelings of professional and organizational identification, which can vary between the extremes of "high" and "low." By working from these two extremes, four possible categories can be examined.

Cell A, as indicated in Figure 5-1, represents the orientation of the worker whose professional as well as bureaucratic identification is high. One would expect compatibility to prevail between professionals having such an orientation and the organizations in which they work. Cell B represents an orientation in which identification with the organization is high but professional identification low. Workers having such an orientation might experience minimal conflict only with their agencies, although at the cost of isolation from their professional peers. When the worker's bureaucratic identification is low, as represented by Cells C and D, one

FIGURE 5-1
Cell Representation of Worker Identification
with Bureaucracy or Profession

Bureaucratic Identification	Professional Identification	
	High	Low
High	Cell A	Cell B
Low	Cell C	Cell D

would expect the development of intensified conflict between worker and organization.

Most studies of professionals in formal organizations emphasize that workers often go to polar extremes in their orientations. For example, professionals who adopt a bureaucratic identification give primacy to agency policies and procedures. This situation is represented by Cell B. Other workers who adopt a professional orientation give primacy to professional values, norms, and expectations. This orientation is represented by Cell C. However, the adoption of an orientation that is not extreme is an alternative available to the worker in an organization.

OTHER ORIENTATIONS

In studying patterns of orientation among professionally educated caseworkers in voluntary agencies, Billingsley has identified two subpatterns between the extremes of bureaucratic and professional orientations.[6] Because they conform to expectations that prevail both in their agencies and in the profession, he labels as "conformists" a group of social workers who evince a relatively high commitment to both agency policies and professional standards. Billingsley ranks this group highly in terms of their overall effectiveness within their agencies. The orientation of such a group is represented in Figure 5-1 by Cell A. Another group of workers termed "innovators" by Billingsley express a relatively low commitment to both agency policies and professional standards. Their feelings of commitment are represented by Cell D in Figure 5-1.

These findings raise an interesting question: Why are "conformists" significantly more prevalent on the staffs of family agencies and "innovators" more prevalent in protective service agencies? Billingsley believes this staffing pattern prevails because family agencies operate in terms of the professional education of their workers with more consistency than do protective service agencies.

As a means of coping with conflict between professional standards and organizational demands, Green believes that the individual consciously or unconsciously develops a pattern of accommodation.[7] His typology of accommodation therefore focuses on the internal dynamics of the individual rather than on the individual's behavior as a direct response to a bureaucratic environment. For example, the social worker who overidentifies with clients to the detriment of agency standards of performance and other organizational requirements is described as a "victim."

Although such an accommodation does not fit neatly into the cell analysis shown in Figure 5-1, because the "victim's" identification represents a distortion of professional norms and values, it may be included within Cell C for the purposes of this discussion.

Another pattern of accommodation is, according to Green, seen in the "immature professional," who has not successfully integrated professional principals into a coherent frame of reference. This individual accommodates by clinging to organizational procedures, thus fulfilling his need for structure and certainty. Such an accommodation may be considered an adaptation of that represented by Cell B. The orientation of Green's "social work reformer," who holds humanitarian sentiments above both organizational and professional requirements, may be included within Cell D.

Green's typology is useful in examining possible adjustments that can be made within the social worker who is practicing in an organizational setting. Nevertheless, attempts to categorize worker orientations leave important questions unanswered: Under what circumstances can an individual worker maintain a high identification with both his profession and his organization? For that matter, is high worker identification with both profession and organization desirable or even possible? Some social work authors are not certain that benefits are to be gained when the worker identifies highly with both his profession and the organization in which he is employed or that this kind of identification can in fact be sustained. They imply that such an orientation can be maintained only at the cost of a reduced commitment to professional values, norms, and expectations as feelings of employee loyalty dominate the worker's professional concerns.

Billingsley, for example, argues that "conformists," when forced "to choose . . . between professional standards and agency policies, . . . choose the latter more frequently."[8] As mentioned previously, however, he also rates such workers highly in terms of overall effectiveness, which leaves uncertain what conclusions might be drawn here about the relationship between effectiveness on the job and high professional identification. Pruger has also commented on the worker's identification with the organization: "A strong identification between helper and organization, however desirable, inevitably confuses the necessary distinction between them. When the environment is congenial, a special kind of commitment or strength is required to maintain an independence of mind."[9]

In contrast, Green has emphasized that the social worker's task is to function as best he can with a minimum of conflict within both the system of professional requirements and that of organizational demands. This requires the worker to integrate professional and organizational roles to some extent and to modify the demands of either or both.[10] The stance described by Green is not unlike what Schein has termed "creative individualism," meaning acceptance by the worker of only the organization's pivotal values and norms while mediating between professional and organizational standards.[11] Effecting such an accommodation enables the worker to avoid more extreme responses, such as rebellion or conformity. Because most social welfare organizations attach different importance to particular norms and values, one can hypothesize that potential conflict is reduced when "pivotal" norms and values are consistent with the professional beliefs of the individual.

Although many of those writing on the professionalism-versus-bureaucratization conflict have implicitly or explicitly taken sides—Wasserman, for example, has pointed his accusing finger at the organization, and Green has pointed his at the individual—their answers to the central question of the conflict remain incomplete. No one has clearly determined whether bureaucratic structures support or constrain the worker's professional activities nor have the ways in which they may do so been defined. Until this determination is made, potential conflict within different organizational structures cannot be predicted or anticipated. More important, conflict therefore cannot be reduced by changing the organizational structures in which it is commonly experienced by workers.

EXAMINING THE CONFLICT

The conflict between the professional and the organization has thus been a recurring theme in social work literature. Is there evidence that this conflict does in fact exist? Certainly, studies have documented the discontent of social welfare employees, but such conflict is often not limited to professional staff. A study conducted by the author found that social service employees interviewed were generally dissatisfied with their jobs. The study concluded that positions held within an organizational background were not factors determining how employees perceived their jobs and work environment.[12] The author of another study pursues this point:

> However, social workers who are not professionally trained, i.e., do not possess an MSW, also find themselves caught up in the same conflicting situations that face the MSW. They, too, often must choose between client need and agency policy and practice, between agency policy and community expectations, between agency policy and the standards of the social work profession; though they are not members of the profession, per se, many non-MSW

> social workers strongly identify with the profession and the
> values and norms therein.[13]

It becomes more difficult to define conflict between professional autonomy and bureaucratic control as a strictly professional problem if it is experienced by all social service employees in bureaucratic settings and not just by those who are professionally educated. A different question may be asked at this point: What are the organizational, personal, and professional characteristics associated with organization-worker conflict?

While studying workers in public welfare Blau focused on the orientation of caseworkers toward their clients and addressed the question of how the organization and social context of an agency influence worker orientation.[14] The attitudes of new workers toward clients is seen in his study as strongly positive, if somewhat sentimental and idealistic. These workers are highly vocal in their complaints about the organization, and compliance with rules and procedures is viewed by them as a hindrance to the delivery of services. The compliance of "old timers" is perceived by the new worker as rigidity. However, in the process of working with clients, situations that may cause them to change their idealistic orientation confront these new workers. For example, some clients lie to them, and others do not want their help. Blau observes that new workers actually provide clients with fewer services because they lack knowledge of agency procedures and rules and, therefore, focus more exclusively on determining whether clients have met eligibility requirements.

Paradoxically, then, Blau found that experience increases the worker's ability to serve clients but decreases his interest in doing so, at least during the initial three years of employment. In contrast, adjustment in older employees who continue beyond their initial three years of employment does not lead to greater rigidity or a lack of interest in helping clients but to a greater emphasis on providing services and a different, less emotional, client involvement.

If experience and length of service affect the way in which workers function in organizational settings, the source of conflict between the individual and the organization may not be solely professional in nature. Conflict experienced by a worker may be caused in part by personal concerns, stemming from the difficulty workers often have addressing client problems they have not solved for themselves.[15] If the source of dissonance between the individual and the organization is in part personal rather than professional, much of the conflict experienced by workers may result, for example, from their often having to use utilitarian, normative, and coercive measures while working with clients. Use of these measures may pose unique personal and moral problems for the practitioner.[16]

The professional has traditionally been viewed as flexible and creative, the bureaucracy as rigid, insensitive to the needs of clients, and unresponsive to their requests. However, one must remember that the behavior of professionals is largely determined by their expectations and perspectives, which in turn are derived from their education and work experience.[17] Social worker expectations, those beliefs about certain causes in the work environment bringing about certain effects, may grow increasingly incongruent as the nature, organization, and structure of professional practice change in social welfare agencies.[18] How does social work education currently influence the expectations of workers holding baccalaureate and master's degrees? Are expectations of worker autonomy being encouraged in social work students? Fostering belief in the possibility of autonomy within organizations may ultimately increase the dissonance between the worker and the organization. Similarly, students encouraged to perceive professional practice solely in terms of worker-client interactions may lack the organizational skills that they will increasingly need to support their helping activities.

PRESENT TRENDS

More and more often, organizational needs are being viewed as best served when workers of different education and training perform specialized functions.[19] In this situation different benefits are expected to accrue from the utilization of each kind of worker, and different criteria are used in measuring individual success. If technology is understood as the methods by which available resources are used to achieve a desired end, then selecting an individual worker to provide a particular service actually represents selecting a technology to address a particular area of client needs. A study conducted by the author concluded that this technology finds expression in certain critical interactions between worker and client and, depending on the individual worker involved, can determine (1) the particular client problem that will be addressed, (2) the way in which client problems may be defined, and (3) the particular problem-solving methods that will be used.[20] Workers of different education and training function differently, and the particular workers employed by an organization can determine the kinds of problems that it will be able to resolve.

When working within a system of specialization, the latitude allowed professionals in exercising discretionary judgment with clients will depend on whether their work can be completed alone: specialization means that workers with different skills perform complementary functions.[21] Segregating tasks and roles had traditionally permitted social welfare organizations to differentiate their control procedures among different kinds of personnel, thereby assuring that professionals and other employees were fulfilling their respective job functions.[22] Such differentiation can be sustained with relative ease among largely homogeneous groups of employees, but problems of unclear and debatable boundaries between job roles increase as the number of different kinds of workers grows. Boundaries may be further confused, as definitions of social work's special competencies, rather than remaining set and referential, continue to evolve.

Brown has argued that "effective organization is a function of the work to be done and the resources and techniques available for doing it."[23] Unless based on a clear understanding of the dynamic relationship between work performed within an organization and the organizational structure itself, managerial decisions can dramatically alter this relationship in totally unexpected ways. In many public agencies, a growing use of specialization has enabled new, frequently complex, and sometimes rapidly changing programs to be undertaken without a consequent disruption in overall organizational functioning. In such instances, only a relatively small group of employees learn and administer new programs. However, in spite of solving a number of problems effectively, specialization often represents what is in fact a short-term solution. Its introduction within an organization may cause long-term difficulties, especially when the increasing communication and coordination costs inevitably resulting from its use have not been anticipated. The author's findings elsewhere pursued this point in the following way:

> The specialization of social services in this organization means that organizational response to client needs increasingly occurs in terms of fixed roles and specified sets of behaviors. Although the relationships between these various roles permit some degree of interaction through formalized channels, such interaction appears to be increasingly controlled and limited. . . . Such practices appear to encourage a kind of parochialism of thought in the collection of information which relates only to the particular program and justifies its continuation, but offers little guidance for total agency response to the client. Frequent changes in worker assignments and the placing of specialized units in different physical locations further discourage interspecialization communication, except for the most persistent.[24]

As is evident, bureaucratic practices can encourage professionals to assume more limited and specialized responsibility for clients. If a social worker's assigned job activities do not involve the performance of complementary functions, the combined effect of services that might otherwise be achieved through the organization's helping processes are often lost to clients. The client is instead left with the impression of an ad hoc reactive approach to problem-solving, and experiences services as haphazard rather than as coherent attempts at help.[25] When bureaucratic specialization exists, furthermore, interaction between worker and client often rests on untested assumptions regarding activities performed by other workers who are seeing the client. In such a situation possible service gains may be lost in various ways. Perhaps a worker, unaware of what other workers are doing, may fail to support client efforts at problem-solving that are within the domain of another worker's specialization. It also becomes more likely that several workers will encourage the client in separate endeavors individually within his capability but cumulatively more than he can handle.

Hall has suggested that the number and quality of social services provided by an agency are not simply a function of the number of professionals employed there. The way in which the agency's work is organized and structured can be equally important in determining the services performed.[26] As specialization and the differential use of manpower increasingly appear within social work practice, many organizational and professional traditions may prove inadequate to the changing demands placed on service delivery by organizational complexity. Specialization requires that work be organized into categories, and this structuring of services predetermines how the organization and client are to interact. As social welfare organizations become more specialized, their inability to meet client needs falling outside of established work categories will be open to increasing criticism.

As specialization and the differential use of manpower increase, the structure and procedures needed to coordinate individual activities must be determined. Thompson suggests that in general organizations must face a new set of circumstances before adapting their structures to meet them, and social welfare agencies may well represent an example of this.[27] Hidden in present manpower patterns are both assumptions and costs that agencies eventually will have to weigh. For example, the greater the variety of workers and specializations involved with a particular client, the greater will become the need for a division of labor maximizing the use of individual worker skill. Similarly, the more workers are involved with a particular client, the more costly communication processes required for coordinated delivery of services will become.

Finally, as both the organization's workers and structure become more compartmentalized, the greater will become its need for coordination among operations and services.[28]

FURTHER DEVELOPMENTS

Growing trends toward differential use of manpower and increased specialization bring the importance of the organization, as opposed to the individual professional, into focus: only an organization will be able to undertake the varied forms of intervention increasingly needed to deal with client problems.[29] Trends such as these indicate that, except for a small number of social workers in private practice, the possibility of worker autonomy appears to be less a reality today than in the past. Continued concern with the issue of professional autonomy versus bureaucratic control may offer little help to future social workers who will perform professional functions primarily within a bureaucratic setting. Professional definitions of practice will increasingly preclude the possibility of autonomy; the organization and structure of social services will increasingly determine the number and quality of services provided to clients. Management functions such as control, coordination, direction, and planning will become predominant concerns for the profession in years ahead.

Several years ago, Meyer predicted that a new round of specialization would initiate a period of uncertainty in which the profession would have difficulty in clarifying job roles and functions.[30] This may be reflected in the recent decision of the Joint Board Committee of the Council on Social Work Education and the National Association of Social Workers to plan for a joint project to clarify the concepts of "core" and "specialization" in social work education.[31] Behind this action lies the belief that a core of social work education should be received at the BSW level and that specialization should begin with the MSW. It would not surprise the author if management eventually emerges as a major specialization at the MSW level.

If the social worker is to be subjected to bureaucratic controls, it is likely that the form and nature of these controls will be of growing concern to professionals. If anything, bureaucracy probably enfeebles the worker's service ideal more than it threatens his autonomy: organizational demands may increasingly preclude work routines such as prolonged intake procedures, which, although relatively time-consuming, are often viewed by workers as important in effectively meeting client needs.[32] Toren assumes that social workers will accept some degree of control exerted over their professional activities, and the same assumption can be made of the many different kinds of employees now comprising the social service manpower pool.[33] Professional concern may then focus on whether control is exercised by people who are knowledgeable and sympathetic. In the meantime, many social workers in organizational settings will remain discontented, clinging to their misconception of the organization as a thing of independent existence and will that interferes with their autonomy, rather than recognizing it as a group of interacting individuals who are similar to themselves.

The growing recognition within the field of the effects of organizational structure on service delivery has led to deliberate attempts at modifying organizational patterns and thereby eliminating the problems that clients encounter. Vinter has argued that the social worker "is a sophisticated and accomplished 'organization man'" and that his education, which combines both theory and actual practice, should do much to prepare him for his organizational roles.[34] However, the educational experiences currently available to students may not be accurate representations of the organizational world they will encounter as professionals. Gartner has commented on social work training in this way: "To the extent that the practice situation is juggled to meet training needs—by reducing the caseload or making it more selective—then practice loses some of the reality which is its uniqueness."[35]

Social workers surveyed by the author felt that their professional education had not adequately trained them to utilize their skills effectively within the organizational settings in which they now worked.[36] Subsequent observation of their work behavior revealed that these workers failed to perceive the influence of the work environment on worker behavior and to recognize its structure as potentially damaging rather than supportive in relation to service goals. This evidence suggests that many social workers are not ready to recognize the effects of organizational structure on service delivery or to search for alternative structures.

CONCLUSION

It is likely that the strains between social workers and organizations will increase as long as the beliefs that workers hold about cause and effect in their work environments do not fit changing realities in social welfare agencies. The success of social workers in organizational settings will increasingly hinge on their ability to recognize the ways in which organizational structure affects the delivery of services. The effective worker will be skillful at modifying the organization's patterns to remove impediments to practice.

Although adept in the role of practitioner or "helper," social workers too often lack skills needed to fill organizational roles in ways supportive of their service ideal, which allow them to pursue personal and professional goals within the organization. Filling an organizational role in a way that is personally satisfying may well require a more sophisticated and accomplished knowledge of organizational dynamics than many social workers presently possess.

Notes

1. Robert Pruger, "The Good Bureaucrat," *Social Work* 18 (July 1973): 26–27.
2. Carl F. Stover, "Changing Patterns in the Philosophy of Management," *Public Administration Review* 18 (Winter 1958): 22.
3. See, for example, Peter Blau and W. Richard Scott, *Formal Organizations* (San Francisco: Chandler Publishing, 1962), pp. 59–63.
4. A. D. Green, "The Professional Worker in the Bureaucracy," *Social Service Review* 40 (March 1966): 71.
5. Harry Wasserman, "The Professional Social Worker in a Bureaucracy," *Social Work* 16 (Jan. 1971): 89.
6. Andrew Billingsley, "Bureaucratic and Professional Orientation Patterns in Social Casework," *Social Service Review* 38 (Dec. 1964): 404–407.
7. Green, "The Professional Worker," pp. 74–76.
8. Billingsley, "Bureaucratic and Professional Orientation Patterns," p. 406.
9. Pruger, "The Good Bureaucrat," p. 31.
10. Green, "The Professional Worker," pp. 77 and 80.
11. Edgar H. Schein, "Organizational Socialization and the Profession of Management," *Industrial Management Review* 9 (1969): 6.
12. Wilbur A. Finch, Jr., "Education and Jobs: A Study of the Performance of Social Service Tasks in Public Welfare," unpub. DSW diss., School of Social Welfare, University of California at Berkeley, 1975, p. 83.
13. Neil A. Cohen, "The Public Welfare Department's Separation into Social Service and Income Maintenance Divisions: Its Impact on Role Conflict Perceptions and Job⋅ Orientations among Non-MSW Welfare Workers," unpub. Ph.D. diss., School of Applied Social Sciences, Case Western Reserve University, 1973, p. 32.
14. Peter M. Blau, "Orientation Toward Clients in a Public Welfare Agency," in *On the Nature of Organizations,* ed. Blau (New York: John Wiley & Sons, 1974), pp. 170–186.
15. Lydia Rapoport, "In Defense of Social Work: An Examination of Stress in the Profession," *Social Service Review* 34 (March 1960):62–74.
16. Nina Toren, "Semi-Professionalism and Social Work: A Theoretical Perspective," in *The Semi-Professions and Their Organizations: Teachers, Nurses, Social Workers,* ed. Amitai Etzioni (New York: Free Press, 1969), p. 166.
17. Eliot Freidson, "Dominant Professions, Bureaucracy, and Client Services," in *Organizations and Clients,* ed. William R. Rosengran and Mark Lefton (Columbus, Ohio: Charles E. Merrill, 1970), p. 74.

18. Lyman W. Porter, Edward E. Lawler III, and J. Richard Hackman, *Behavior in Organizations* (New York: McGraw-Hill, 1975), p. 52.
19. Sidney A. Fine and Wretha W. Wiley, *An Introduction to Functional Job Analysis* (Kalamazoo, Mich.: W. E. Upjohn Institute for Employment Research, 1971), p. 37.
20. Finch, "Education and Jobs," pp. 175–176.
21. Fred H. Goldner and R. R. Ritti, "Professionalization as Career Immobility," in *The Sociology of Organizations,* ed. Oscar Grusky and George A. Miller (New York: Free Press, 1970), p. 466.
22. Robert D. Vinter, "Analysis of Treatment Organizations," in *Human Service Organizations,* ed. Yeheskel Hasenfeld and Richard A. English (Ann Arbor: University of Michigan Press, 1974), p. 43.
23. Wilfred Brown, *Explorations in Management* (New York: John Wiley & Sons, 1960), p. 18.
24. Finch, "Education and Jobs," p. 145.
25. Ibid., p. 146.
26. Oswald Hall, "Organization of Manpower in Some Helping Professions," in *Manpower in Social Welfare: Research Perspectives,* ed. Edward E. Schwartz (New York: National Association of Social Workers, 1966), p. 59.
27. James D. Thompson, *Organizations in Action* (New York: McGraw-Hill, 1967), pp. 119–120.
28. Finch, "Education and Jobs," p. 181.
29. Henry J. Meyer, "Sociological Comments," in *Nonprofessionals in the Human Services,* ed. Charles Grosser, William E. Henry, and James G. Kelly (San Francisco: Jossey-Bass, 1969), p. 55.
30. Ibid., p. 56.
31. *NASW News* 20 (Sept. 1975): 10.
32. Harold Wilensky, "The Professionalization of Everyone?" in *The Sociology of Organizations,* (New York: Free Press, 1970), p. 491.
33. Toren, "Semi-Professionalism," p. 183.
34. Robert D. Vinter, "The Social Structure of Service," in *Issues in American Social Work,* ed. Alfred J. Kahn (New York: Columbia University Press, 1959), p. 242.
35. Alan Gartner, "Four Professions: How Different, How Alike," *Social Work* 20 (Sept. 1975): 357.
36. Finch, "Education and Jobs," p. 80.

Chapter 6   **The Professional Social Worker**

in a Bureaucracy

Harry Wasserman

The professional social worker in a public welfare bureaucracy serves two masters—his professional self, embodying intel-
lectual and moral criteria, and his employing organization, with its demands and constraints. In a previous article the author discussed the
general question of the comparative influence of social work education
and structural constraints on social work practice.[1] In this chapter he
discusses specifically the neophyte professional social worker's life in a
bureaucracy. Some of the areas that will be explored are the following:
How does the bureaucratic structure support or constrain the worker's
professional activities? What is the nature of the transactions and interactions he makes in order to perform his role as efficiently and effectively
as possible? How does he maneuver within the bureaucracy to gain what
he needs for his clients? In what ways does the bureaucratic structure
manipulate him?

POSITION OF RELATIVE POWERLESSNESS

The formal organization of the agency involved in this study places the
professional social worker at one of the lower levels of authority and
power. Administratively he is responsible to the following ascending
hierarchy: a supervisor who is his immediate superior, a deputy director
who fills the role of a chief of supervisors, a district director, and higher
administrators who are physically and operationally removed from the
worker's daily activities because they are located in the agency's central
office. Operationally, however, it is the supervisor to whom the worker
turns for expertise, guidance, and organizational support.

Reprinted from *Social Work* 16, no. 1 (Jan. 1971): 89–95, with the permission
of the publisher.

An analysis of supervisor-worker transactions reveals some aspects of the way the bureaucratic structure works. Each supervisor is administratively responsible for five workers and generally meets with each one on a regular basis (e.g., once a week or once every two weeks). The supervisor is also available as an emergency consultant at unscheduled times. During supervisory conferences, the worker explains what he has been doing, discusses problems in case management, negotiates for the fulfillment of clients' material needs, and seeks advice and guidance concerning the problems of specific clients. This practice is fairly typical of supervisor-worker transactions. It is quite striking, however, that the supervisor rarely meets with his five workers as a group except when new regulations, rules, and procedures must be explained. During the two-year span of the study there were no group meetings with a supervisor for the purpose of discussing case problems rather than administrative procedures. This fact raises the following questions: Why are so few group meetings of supervisors and workers initiated by the supervisor? Conversely, why is it that professional social workers never insist on having group meetings to discuss and grapple with the common recurrent problems and issues they face?

There are several factors that, when acting together, militate against group meetings. The administration can more effectively maintain control over the workers if workers must deal with their supervisor as individual entrepreneurs or contractors. For instance, a particularly resourceful and ingenious young worker, who is capable of providing special items for his clients, might inadvertently disclose in formal sessions the many ways to "work the system."[2]

By negotiating with the worker at the formal level of supervision as if he were a private entrepreneur, the administration avoids the introduction of resourcefulness and ingenuity into the formal system. On the other hand, by accomplishing things for his clients, the worker receives gratification that sustains him in his work. Paradoxically, however, it is clear that the individual worker's successes serve to gloss over or cover up the harsh inadequacies of the system. In struggling for successful outcomes within his own caseload, the worker tends to forget that the penurious institutional resources are abrasive and harmful to significant numbers of families and children whose social workers are less endowed with the qualities of resourcefulness and ingenuity.

The questionable legal maneuvers to protect clients from what, in the worker's opinion, are excessively harsh rules and regulations are justified by the worker as "situation ethics."[3] For example, the worker obtains an increase in a foster family's monthly grant because the foster child has a behavior disorder (the child actually does not, but the worker feels that because the foster parents are doing a good job they deserve a few extra dollars per month); an adolescent foster child earns enough money to necessitate recomputing his grant, but the worker "forgets" about it; or an AFDC mother has a friend who contributes financially, but the worker "forgets" about it. Although the worker may try to convince himself of the validity of his position, he does not quite succeed. He feels guilty, tense, and uneasy when he has acted in a questionable, unethical manner.

WORKERS' PERCEPTION OF SUPERVISION

Most of the workers in the study had more than one line supervisor during their period of employment with the agency; only three of the twelve judged their supervisors to be competent and therefore helpful. The majority of these young workers perceived the supervisory position to be primarily a bureaucratic control device; thus the way the supervisors functioned had little or nothing to do with social work values, knowledge, and skills.

The supervisor performs the function of organizational mediator; he makes judgments and decisions about workers' claims and demands on behalf of their clients on the basis of the agency's scarce resources. In other words, he negotiates on behalf of the organization with the worker who represents the clients.

The supervisor rarely sees the worker's clients except in emergencies. His role is to talk about clients, not to them. Thus he only knows the client through the worker and must make reasoned judgments and decisions based on a complex of variables that includes the client's actual situation, the worker's perception and definition of that situation, and the agency's capacity to provide an item or series of items. If the supervisor is responsible for five workers with a total of 175–200 cases or more, one questions whether he can make reasoned and balanced judgments about any problematic human situations, particularly when he must base his judgments on what the workers say about clients.

The majority of the new workers viewed their supervisors as insecure and frightened people who were unsure of their authority and power, conforming, lacking courage, unwilling to take a stand on critical issues involving either workers or clients, and more sensitized and attuned to organizational demands and needs than to those of the clients. They also believed that the system wanted passive, uninspired people in supervisory positions, that the need for supervisors with master's degrees was just another manifestation of our "credential society";[4] that credentials and conformity were more important for system maintenance than knowledge, competence, and skill; and that image and facade were valued more highly than reality and substance.

The agency's utilization, whenever possible, of graduate social work supervisory personnel and the lack of resistance of supervisory personnel to the impediments of the system probably accounted, in part, for the noticeable increase in cynicism among the new workers during the two-year period of study. This growing cynicism, plus the frustrations of working with difficult clients (many of whom were chronically in disastrous situations) and the cumulative reactions of physical and emotional fatigue, inevitably produced situations of great stress. The workers protected themselves in such situations, but the cost was the reinforcement of their natural defense mechanisms to the point of rigidity and brittleness.[5] Functionally this meant that they worked with many of their clients in a routine, uninspired way.

There are two solutions to such a dilemma. The worker can remain in the agency and eventually be promoted to a supervisory position, which will remove him from the clients, or he can leave the agency for another job (the solution chosen by six of the workers in the study).[6] If he remains and becomes a supervisor, he will adapt to the system. He may rationalize that he will do things differently and try to change the system, but he realizes that because bureaucracies do not change easily, structural change is a tremendously difficult, long-term undertaking. As Dahrendorf explains:

> Bureaucratic organizations typically display continuous gradations of competence and authority and are hierarchical. Within dichotomous organizations class conflict is possible; within hierarchical organizations it is not. This difference has an important consequence for the definition of bureaucratic roles. Insofar as bureaucratic roles are defined in the context of a career hierarchy, they do not generate a [class] conflict of interest with other bureaucratic roles.[7]

This means that all employees of a bureaucracy, regardless of their hierarchical status, are essentially "on the same side of the fence that divides the positions of dominance from those of subjection."[8] In the long run, it is extremely difficult for a professional social worker in a bureaucracy to be an impassioned advocate for his clients, because in so doing he must come into conflict with agency administrators as well as professional colleagues. If he cannot mobilize the support of both colleagues and welfare rights or other organizations that represent clients, he will be forced to leave the agency. If the new professional remains in the agency and eventually moves to the position of supervisor, he is constrained to "play the game," which includes accepting the meager systemic inputs and the dysfunctional aspects of the bureaucratic structure.[9]

WORKERS' VIEW OF THE ADMINISTRATION

Almost invariably the new professionals in this study looked on the higher administrators of the agency as "them." The administrators were not quite "the enemy," but they were viewed as being unconcerned about the worker's involvements with his clients, except when financial accountability was an issue. The most important indication of the administrators' lack of concern for clients, according to the observations of the workers, was the nature of the communication system, which was generally a one-way flow from top to bottom.

One of the assumptions of the "rational" system of organization is that knowledge, competence, authority, and important decision-making are at the top of the organizational pyramid and ignorance, passivity, and capacity for routine performance are on the bottom. As Blau and Scott point out, when the need for a highly coordinated organization is imperative, communication is of low organizational value.[10] This generalization also applies to the agency in which the flow of information from top to bottom is considered the normal pathway and direction of communication. It is true that workers can write memoranda to higher administrators through their supervisor, but these are rarely acted on. Therefore, the workers virtually have no way to voice their work needs, observations, good ideas, or creative innovations.

The social work education of these neophyte professionals apparently gave them no experience in working together as members of a professional collectivity, for example, in identifying their clients' needs or gaps in programs, social resources, and social utilities. As a professional group with a sense of collective responsibility, social workers do not pressure the system on behalf of clients—they accept the system. For example, the workers studied were prone to make such statements as the following: "You can't fight city hall," "The county supervisors [commissioners] are the real bosses," "What's the use of trying to change things when it's impossible to do so," and so forth. Such statements connote more than poor morale; they are part of a system of beliefs. Such defeatism and cynicism (as cognitive and emotional "sets") are psychological reflections of what Kenniston calls the "institutionalization of hypocrisy":

Of course, no society ever fully lives up to its own professed ideals. In every society there is a gap between creedal values and actual practices, and in every society, the recognition of this gap constitutes a powerful motor for social change. But in most societies, especially when change is slow and institutions are powerful and unchanging, there occurs what can be termed institutionalization of hypocrisy.[11]

The social welfare bureaucracy only expresses the profound hypocrisy of a larger society. The agency is neither the conspiracy of a small group nor the perpetual fiefdom of cruel men who have deliberately decided to harm or destroy families and children. The agency's cruelty reflects society's pejorative attitudes about broken, poor families who must rely on the public for special kinds of aid.

Dahrendorf explains the purposes and functions of bureaucracies and their power position in society as follows: "although . . . [bureaucracies] always belong to the ruling class, because bureaucratic roles are roles of dominance, bureaucracies as such never are the ruling class. Their latent interests aim at the maintenance of what exists; but what it is that exists is not decided by bureaucracies, but given to them."[12] Dahrendorf's conceptualization of the purposes and functions of bureaucracies is dramatically illustrated by the fact that financial accountability is the supreme value, and all other values are subordinate to it. For example, the social worker with a master's degree is not permitted to make a judgment or decision about a client's need for an extra grocery order; he must obtain authorization from two higher supervisor-administrators. If translated into whether the professional social worker is capable of making judgments and decisions about a client whose immediate future is hunger, the overriding organizational value of financial accountability means, in an objective sense, indignity and humiliation for the worker. Subjectively, some of the new workers felt this indignity and humiliation; others did not.

CLIENTS AS OBJECTS

Bureaucratic inefficiency is usually equated with an excessive amount of menial activities—red tape, paperwork, and the like. The new professionals in the study complained about the amount of paperwork, but, when emotionally unable to see clients, even the most committed workers found respite in paperwork and other office routines. Most professional social workers protest that such routine activities as maintaining files, keeping records, and collating statistics are beneath their professional competence; yet it is such menial work that allows them to objectify their clients—that is, to regard them as objects rather than people. To preserve his mental health, a worker must not be too sensitive about the clients' plight or become too involved with their "outcomes." Thus although bureaucratic procedures that cause dehumanization of clients are severely criticized, they are probably a psychic necessity for some workers.

What then is questionable and inevitably harmful in the process of client "objectification"? It is that the bureaucracy tends to dehumanize recipients by viewing them as cases and numbers or as objects related to financial accountability. If it is inevitable that workers will dehuman-their clients because psychologically they need to perceive them as abstractions, what does finally intervene on behalf of the client? It is simply the "sometimes" humanity of the worker. The word "sometimes" is critical, because it is psychologically impossible for a worker constantly to be a feeling, responsive human who is prepared at all times to cope with human disorder and disaster. However, the fact that the worker sometimes treats the client as a worthwhile human being keeps the system partially viable and, more important, the client feels that someone does care for him.

However, the cumulative effects of insufficient resources, bureaucratic structure, and personal fallibility finally can force the workers toward

> working on a different set of problems from those the . . . [organization] has set for them. . . . There is a sharp distinction that must be made between behavior that *copes* with the requirements of a problem and behavior that is designed to *defend* against entry into the problem. It is the distinction one might make between playing tennis on the one hand and fighting like fury to stay off the tennis court altogether on the other.[13]

The worker can defend himself by becoming overinvolved in paperwork, a specific case, informal meetings with colleagues, aimless driving, and so on. In other words, he can spend a large amount of time avoiding meaningful encounters with clients.

The bureaucratic system stimulates and reinforces defending rather than coping behavior by keeping the worker off balance. The constant changes in caseloads, rules, regulations, and procedures imposed from above produce a state of insecurity and instability in the worker. Thus the new professional's underinvolvement in initiating or participating in the creation of policies and procedures was undoubtedly another important cause of excessive defending behavior and low morale.

INFORMAL ORGANIZATIONS

According to Gouldner, informal organizations are "spontaneously emergent and normatively sanctioned structures in the organization."[14] Although one of the latent functions of the informal organization is to permit people to act as people rather than as occupants of specific positions or as incumbents of a structured role, organizational theorists generally assume that the informal organization in a bureaucracy tends to support the goals of the formal organization.

The informal organization—which must be understood specifically in this context as small groups of two or more people who are peers—primarily serves two functions: (1) it is the focal point for expressing complaints about the agency and (2) it is the most important social system for providing emotional support for workers and a sense of mutuality among them.[15] Workers let off steam in their informal meetings with colleagues while working at their desks, when they meet other workers accidentally in the halls, and during planned and unplanned coffee breaks. Their complaints cover a wide range of difficulties involving clients, other workers, supervisors, bureaucratic obstacles, and so on.

More important than the content of the complaints, however, are the latent functions of these informal gripe sessions: They provide emotional support for the worker in the sense that he can talk to a peer who understands, and they are a mechanism for draining off and deflecting the worker's need for a more formally organized, systematic approach to his problem as a worker in a bureaucracy. Thus although some of the verbal attacks against the agency are subversive in the sense that they frequently carry a high anti-authority component, the complaining done in the informal group is essentially functional to the maintenance of the formal system's equilibrium. As Coser has shown, much social conflict can be encapsulated within a social structure; in fact social conflict often supports it.[16]

In district offices where there were other professional workers, the new professionals were members of small informal groups. In those offices in which there were few, if any, professional social workers, the new professional was almost totally isolated. The workers who gave and received emotional support from informal relationships unquestionably had higher morale than those who were deprived of this experience. When the new worker was the only professional or one of few professionals, he tended to reject the camaraderie of the nonprofessionals because he saw himself as different from them. This was probably a defensive reaction against the nonprofessionals, who saw him as a threat because he was engaged in the same work but received greater financial rewards and a higher status.

CONCLUSION

The large public welfare agency—with its bureaucratic structure—is the embodiment of a profound moral ambivalence toward the people it serves. On the one hand, its manifest purpose is to help needy persons; on the other hand, its latent function is to "punish" those who are unable to maintain independent successful lives by failing to provide conditions by which they can help themselves or be helped. Its main aim is financial accountability—not accountability to the people it serves.

The social worker in such a bureaucracy is caught up in this brutal intersection of contradictory values. If he actually tries to help his clients and "buck" the organization, he often suffers from emotional and physical fatigue and becomes cynical and defeatist about the nature of social work. If he adapts to the bureaucracy, he at best experiences massive frustration; at worst he becomes a "mindless functionary."[17]

It is time for the social work profession, bureaucrats, and schools of social work to stop hiding their knowledge of bureaucracies. What we now need is new ideas, concepts, and models—in short, a new vision to reconstruct our working lives and new ways to relate to each other and to those we serve.

Notes

1. The study on which this chapter and the author's previous article were based involved observing twelve new professional social workers over a two-year period. For an overall discussion of the study and some general theoretical considerations, see Harry Wasserman, "Early Careers of Professional Social Workers in a Public Child Welfare Agency," *Social Work* 15, no. 3 (July 1970): 93–101.
2. In "working the system," some workers develop informal alliances with supervisors, cashiers, and clerks, who then serve as expediters. If the workers are relatively moderate in their demands, they can be quite successful in obtaining material goods for their clients, as well as jobs, housing, and medi-

cal care. Evidently, these alliances are known to those who must process special requests, and the worker may discuss some of his moves with others, but the extralegal moves are kept secret.

3. Joseph Fletcher, *Situation Ethics* (Philadelphia: Westminster, 1966).
4. See Edgar Z. Friedenberg, "Status and Role in Education," *Humanist* 28, no. 5 (Sept.–Oct. 1968): 13.
5. As reported in Wasserman, "Early Careers," three of the twelve new professionals in the study suffered from psychiatric difficulties that they believed were triggered by their work situations.
6. At the termination of the study, eight of the twelve new professionals had left the agency. Six of the resignations were voluntary and two were involuntary (one worker was drafted into the armed forces; the other moved to another city as a consequence of her husband's employment situation).
7. Ralf Dahrendorf, *Class and Class Conflict in Industrial Society* (Stanford, Calif.: Stanford University Press, 1959), p. 296.
8. Ibid.
9. In a bureaucracy a skeleton of "permanent cadre"—supervisors and administrators, professional and nonprofessional—maintain the system. Many of them have become thoroughly acclimated to the system. Little research has been done on either the self-concepts or the sociological functions of these long-term employes.
10. Peter M. Blau and W. Richard Scott, *Formal Organizations: A Comparative Approach* (San Francisco: Chandler Publishing, 1962), p. 242.
11. Kenneth Kenniston, "Youth, Change and Violence," *American Scholar* 37, no. 2 (Spring 1968): 239.
12. Dahrendorf, *Class and Class Conflict,* p. 300.
13. Jerome S. Bruner, *Toward a Theory of Instruction* (Cambridge, Mass.: Harvard University Press, 1966), pp. 3–4.
14. Alvin W. Gouldner, "Organizational Analysis," in *Sociology Today,* ed. Robert K. Merton et al. (New York: Basic Books, 1959), p. 406.
15. See Earl Bogdanoff and Arnold Glass, "The Sociology of the Public Assistance Caseworker in an Urban Area," unpub. master's thesis, University of Chicago, 1954.
16. Lewis A. Coser, *The Functions of Social Conflict* (London: Routledge & Kegan Paul, 1956).
17. Hannah Arendt, *Eichmann in Jerusalem: A Report on the Banality of Evil* (New York: Viking, 1964), p. 289.

Chapter 7 The Selection of Clients by Social Welfare Agencies: The Case of the Blind

Robert A. Scott

The purpose of social welfare is to promote the social betterment of a class or group of people who are defined as disadvantaged, handicapped, or deprived. A set of common problems is attributed to such persons based upon the nature of the trait or quality which sets them apart from the rest of society. Programs of social welfare are then planned to meet the needs which arise out of these problems.

It is believed that the form and content of such programs should be determined by the needs of the client. As his needs change, the programs themselves must change; conversely, the welfare of the client should be the primary factor to consider in making any policy decisions about changes in such programs.

In reality, other factors also exert a determining influence on social welfare programs. These factors are at least as important for setting policy as the clients' welfare and at times may even supersede it. Many such factors have been identified by other investigators.[1] Two are especially important. First, welfare services are characteristically distributed in our society through private philanthropy or government at its federal, state, and local levels. These programs are ordinarily incorporated in large-scale bureaucratic structures. As such, they are subject to the pressures and forces common to all complex bureaucracies. The preservation of the organization itself is a vital factor in setting program policy; and standardization based upon the criteria of efficiency, production, and costs is often applied to services which are intended to meet highly personal human needs.

Second, welfare programs must rely upon the public for their support, whether through legislative appropriation or private fund-raising efforts. The availability of services depends, at least in part, upon the kinds of support which the benefactors of welfare are willing to provide. When

Reprinted from *Social Problems* 14, no. 3. (Winter 1967): 248–257, with the permission of the journal, the author, and the Society for the Study of Social Problems.

the benefactors are the body politic, funds will ordinarily be made available for only those programs which the legislators believe are politically tenable to support. When the benefactors come from the private sector of society, the kinds of programs they are willing to support depend upon their personal conception of the nature of the problems of disadvantaged groups, and what they imagine constitutes a desirable and moral solution. In either case, such conceptions are generally responsive to broad cultural themes and values, especially those of youth, work, hope, contentment, and personal fulfillment.

At times, the personal welfare of the client, the needs of the bureaucratic structures through which services are supplied, and the benefactors' definition of the problems of the disadvantaged persons will coincide. Ordinarily these factors will coincide when the client possesses valued cultural attributes (e.g., youth, intelligence) and when valued cultural goals (e.g., employment, independence) are realistically attained for him. More often, however, these forces do not coincide; they may even conflict. Consequently, the public, whether through legislative bodies or private donations, may be unwilling to support programs for individuals with personal characteristics which are culturally devalued, although such individuals may be the majority of the disadvantaged group. From the point of view of organizational maintenance, it may be untenable to undertake extensive service programs for persons who, by virtue of their disability and other characteristics, may be unable to make a productive contribution to the society, even though they represent a majority of those who need service programs.

Social welfare programs are, therefore, set within and responsive to a variety of organizational and community pressures, which are highly determinative of program policy and implementation. By contrast, the problems of the recipient group ordinarily are caused by factors which are entirely unrelated to those which work upon the welfare agencies. The causes of the specific problems, and therefore the needs of a handicapped person, are not the same factors which determine what kinds of welfare services are offered to them. Clients' needs and the kinds of available welfare services run in two separate orbits, which may coincide only at certain points. It cannot be assumed, therefore that the services which are offered apply to all persons who belong to the disadvantaged group, nor can it be assumed that the persons who receive services are necessarily benefited by them.

These facts suggest a number of questions for research about the relationships between social welfare service programs, and the welfare problems of persons to whom the services are directed. First, it is necessary to determine the amount of congruence between services required by a disadvantaged group and those available to them. Second, it is necessary to determine the amount of congruence between persons who are in need of services and those who in fact receive them through existing structures. Finally, it is necessary to determine the consequences for a disadvantaged person of receiving services in existing welfare programs.

The purpose of this chapter is to provide data related to the latter two questions, by examining one type of social welfare program: services for the blind. I will compare existing services in this field to the population of blind persons, in order to identify what, if any, discrepancies exist in the present distribution of services. This will be done by describing the demographic properties of the blind population of the United States [in 1962]; and the corresponding distribution and properties of agencies which serve it. From these data, I will also examine some of the consequences for an individual, both for himself and in relation to the community, of receiving welfare services through existing agencies.

While the remainder of this discussion will specifically deal with agencies for the blind, my remarks apply with equal cogency to many types of welfare agencies, and especially to those which provide social services to persons possessing stigmatized and unimprovable deviant qualities.[2]

DEMOGRAPHIC CHARACTERISTICS OF THE BLIND

Approximately 955,000 persons in the civilian, noninstitutionalized population of the United States under the age of 80 are blind.[3] There are a number of significant facts about the blind population. First, a majority of them are elderly. Sixty-six percent are between the ages of 55 and 80; another 15 percent are in the age group of 45–54; 17 percent of all blind persons are in the age group of 18–44; and only about 2 percent are children under 18. According to these data, two thirds of all blind persons are in age groups where retirement is either pending or a reality, and only a small minority of blind persons are in age groups where either employment or education is realistic.

Second, blindness is much more common in women than in men.[4] Seven out of ten cases of blindness occur in women, and in all age groups there are more blind women than blind men, although the sex difference is greatest in the older age groups. Taking the factors of age and sex together, one half of all cases of blindness are among women 55 years of age and older; another 20 percent of the cases of blindness occur among women in the age group of 18–54. Elderly men account for 18 percent of all cases, and only 12 percent of the cases of blindness occur among men 18–54.[5]

Third, blindness is comparatively rare among children. There are estimated to be only about 27,000 blind children in the United States at the present time.[6] The blindness rate among children is only .35 per 1,000 of the population. In contrast, the rate for elderly persons is about 33 per 1,000 of the population.

Finally, the term "blindness" refers both to those who are completely without vision and to those who have severe visual impairments but who can see. Only a small number of blind persons are in fact totally blind; a majority of them have some measurable visual acuity. The available data suggest that there is a direct relationship between the amount of visual loss and age.[7] The older a blind person is, the more serious his visual loss is likely to be.

The adequacy and effectiveness of welfare programs can be judged in many ways. One such measure, which will be used in this chapter, concerns their completeness. By this I mean the degree to which welfare services are provided for all or most segments of the population in need. From this point of view, service programs for the blind may be regarded as adequate insofar as they reflect, in a general way, the composition of the blind population; correspondingly, they may be regarded as inadequate insofar as they apply only to special segments of the blind population.

It is recognized that this point of view is not commonly accepted among workers for the blind. They have argued that it is more worthwhile to supply services to those blind persons for whom there is the greatest expectation of success. Accordingly, it is held that resources are more wisely devoted to the education and training of blind children than to the care of elderly blind adults; and that it is more logical to aid the employable blind than those who are not employable. This argument is based on the assumption that resources for supporting service programs are limited, and that it is therefore necessary to establish these priorities. In reality, this assumption is generally incorrect in view of the fact that enormous sums of money are expended annually for services to the blind (for further information on this point, see footnote 16). The argument also contains an erroneous implication: that there is a correspondence between the way in which an individual experiences problems of blindness and the priority which his problems are assigned by the criteria of real or imagined economic and social factors. Because there are economic and social reasons why the problems of blind children might receive priority in service programs, we cannot assume that the older blind person experiences his problems as less serious.

If services for the blind roughly reflect the age and sex distribution of the blind population, then we can expect to find a major portion of the financial and manpower resources of this field invested in programs designed to meet the needs of those who are not expected to be self-supporting, and more particularly of the elderly. Conversely, we would expect that only a small portion of those resources would be invested in programs for educating and training children and employable adults. An analysis of services for the blind in this country reveals that the situation is exactly the opposite.

I made a study of the programs of all direct service agencies listed in a substantially complete directory of agencies for the blind in this country.[8] Seven hundred and ninety-eight separate agencies were identified, 274 of which are private and 520 governmental. Only 9 percent (71) of these agencies are concerned exclusively with elderly blind persons. By contrast, 67 percent (529) of the agencies have programs intended primarily for children and employable adults. The remaining 23 percent (187) are "mixed" agencies, which offer services to blind persons of all ages. The remaining one percent (1) do not offer direct services to the blind.

An analysis was made of programs in the 71 agencies and organizations which serve elderly blind persons exclusively. There are 21 domiciles which house and care for about 1,000 elderly blind persons. The remainder of these organizations are state offices responsible for administering the federal-state program of aid to the needy blind. In the mixed agencies, programs for the elderly are almost exclusively recreational, ranging from organized recreational programs to drop-in daytime clubs.

One hundred and thirty-four separate agencies serve blind children exclusively, and 395 agencies have programs primarily concerned with vocational rehabilitation and employment. Although mixed agencies do offer some recreational services to elderly blind persons, the primary emphasis of their programs is unmistakably on children and employable adults. Of the 187 mixed agencies, only a few have a separate division for the elderly blind; by contrast there are almost none which do not have a children's division or a division for employable adults.

These data show a clear bias in work for the blind in favor of children and employable adults and against elderly blind persons. About 90 percent of agencies in work for the blind place exclusive or primary emphasis upon serving less than one third of the blind population; and only 9 percent of the agencies are seriously concerning themselves with the bulk of blind persons.

Another important fact is not apparent from these data. Existing programs are not geared to serve all blind persons in a given age group.

Numerous services are available for the child who is educable, but there are almost no services for the multiply handicapped child. There are many services for the blind person who is thought to be employable, but few for the one who is thought to be untrainable or for whom employment is an unrealistic goal. Recreation programs for elderly blind persons are located in the agency itself, so that only those older blind persons who are mobile and independent enough to travel can take advantage of them. In effect, programs are geared to serve selected blind persons, and usually those who enjoy the highest probability for success; conversely, most service programs are ill-equipped to assist those for whom success is unlikely.

This systematic bias of work for the blind in favor of young blind children and employable blind adults, and the corresponding neglect of older blind persons, is reflected in another way—in the literature of work for the blind. An analysis was made of all articles which appeared in the *New Outlook for the Blind* (the principal professional journal of that field) from 1907 to 1963. This study showed that out of 1,069 articles, 36 percent dealt with children, 31 percent with rehabilitation, 15 percent with braille reading, 17 percent with specific services such as mobility, 21 percent with employment, and only 2 percent with geriatric problems. In short, 70 percent of the blind population (the elderly) received only 2 percent of the attention of writers in the major professional journal in work for the blind; whereas less than 30 percent of the population (children and employable adults) were discussed in 98 percent of the analyzed articles.

The reasons for the proliferation of services for a limited segment of the blind population are numerous and complex. I will try to discuss the most significant ones here. First, the same concepts which guided the pioneers of work for the blind 125 years ago make up a large part of contemporary theory. The demographic characteristics of the blind population then differed in several important ways from the present population. The number of persons in the general population who survived childhood and lived to old age was low, and the number of elderly blind persons was therefore correspondingly small.[9] A major cause of blindness in the adult population at that time was industrial accidents.[10] Ordinarily the eyes were the only organs involved, so that adult blind persons were healthy working people whose only handicap was blindness. Substantial numbers of children were blinded at birth because of diseases which specifically affected the eyes.[11]

Because a majority of the blind in the late nineteenth century were children and adults of working age, the concepts in this field stressed education and employment. Through the years, these concepts have not changed in response to changing social, economic, and public health conditions. In addition, workers for the blind have implicitly assumed that these problems of education and employment are inherent to the condition of blindness. They have mistaken these concepts for the problem of blindness itself. The blind to whom the concepts cannot be easily applied are viewed by workers as marginal to the "real work" in services for the blind. This work is believed to be educational and vocational; services for elderly, unemployable, or uneducable blind individuals are regarded as marginal activities. Education and employment are viewed as the only alternative solutions to the problems of the blind. If a person cannot benefit from either service, his problems are defined as unsolvable, and his case is closed. Consequently, elderly blind persons, the multiply handicapped, and the unemployable are considered apart from the "real problems" of blindness, because workers for the blind continue to employ archaic concepts in their service approach.

This tendency to employ archaic concepts can be viewed as a specific instance of a more general tendency by workers for the blind to resist any innovation or change in service programs. In the history of this field, there has been a characteristic and stubborn resistance to the adoption of any mechanical aids, educational devices, or concepts which in any way deviate from the status quo.[12] This tendency is itself a function of a complex set of factors, the nature of which can be only briefly delineated in this chapter. Essentially work for the blind is a low-prestige profession, one of that category of occupations called "dirty work."[13] Because the stigma associated with blindness may inadvertently rub off on workers for the blind,[14] this field is unable to attract the top persons in such fields as social work, psychiatry, psychology, education, ophthamology, and rehabilitation. In fact, in work for the blind, there is an unusual opportunity for individuals with very little formal training to attain positions of great power and responsibility.

This phenomenon has had many consequences for the field, one of which is a tendency to resist change. Many leaders in this field have power which derives from the agencies they control, and from their acquired expertise in certain specific service programs such as braille, mobility, rehabilitation, employment, or education. They lack generic professional training; consequently, it is difficult for them to move from one type of service program for the blind to another, or from services for the blind to services for other types of handicapped persons. Their expertise is highly specialized and is acquired by hard experience. Because of these limitations, little is transferable from traditional services to new ones which are proposed. Consequently, when changes are attempted in existing programs and agencies, such persons are faced with a major loss in power, status, and income. It would be impossible for them to secure comparable positions outside agencies for the blind because assignment to such positions would be based upon formal credentials such as education, rather than upon their specialized skills and acquired status in the field. The person with only a high school education who holds a powerful position in an agency for the blind stands to lose a great deal if that agency changes in any substantial way. Therefore, workers for the blind have traditionally had more intense commitment to the agencies they have built than to the persons whom they serve.[15] Concomitantly, they have tried to maintain the traditional base upon which their power rests and to rationalize these efforts by traditional concepts and theories of the field.

Another cause of client selectivity in service programs for the blind is the fact that agencies are dependent upon the public for financial support. All but a few private agencies rely upon fund-raising appeals to finance their programs, and public agencies are entirely dependent upon annual appropriations from state legislatures and from Congress. In either case, agencies for the blind are in stiff competition with one another, and with hundreds of other charities, for a share of the public's philanthropic dollars.

In this competitive situation, the success of fund-raising campaigns depends upon strong emotional appeals on behalf of the needy. In their fund-raising campaigns, agencies for the blind exploit a certain number of cultural stereotypes in our society. These stereotypes concern blindness, youth, work, and hope. The images of blind persons which are projected in these campaigns are either those of educable children, or of young, employable adults, who can be helped to overcome a serious handicap to become materially productive.[16] These appeals, therefore, leave the unmistakable but erroneous impression that blind people are young, intelligent persons who can be educated and employed. The public has come to expect results which are measurable in these terms. This consequence intensifies the agencies' search for the few blind people who in fact have these personal attributes.

At the same time, agencies are extremely reluctant to begin programs for other groups of blind persons unless there is good reason to believe that these programs will be supported by the public. It is assumed that appeals for funds to help persons from whom only modest gains can be expected, such as elderly blind persons and multiply handicapped children or adults, will not succeed in offsetting the costs of such programs. It has been argued by the agencies that funds obtained through appeals on behalf of blind children and employable adults can be partly diverted to support programs for other groups of blind persons. However, programs for children and employable adults involve enormous capital investments. These investments require increasing sums of money annually for maintenance and growth purposes. One consequence, therefore, of successful fund-raising has been that more and more money is needed simply to keep programs going.

I have compared the distribution of services for the blind in this country to the demographic characteristics of the blind population, and I have tried to indicate some of the reasons there is such a discrepancy between them. Now I want to consider another question—the avowed purpose of all programs for the blind to help the individual blind person to function as independently as he can. The question therefore arises, "What is the actual impact of agency programs upon those blind persons who do receive services?"

Since there are only about 950,000 blind persons in the entire country, the number of visually impaired individuals living in any particular geographical area is usually quite small. It is estimated that there are only about 40,000 to 50,000 blind persons in all of New York City, only about 10,000 in Philadelphia, and only about 14,000 blind persons in the Boston metropolitan area.[17] Yet, there are over 700 separate agencies and organizations for the blind in this country, a majority of which are situated in large urban areas. New York City has 50 separate organizations for the blind, 38 of which offer direct services; Philadelphia has 14 major direct agencies; and there are 13 major agencies in the greater metropolitan area of Boston.[18] Since a majority of these agencies offer services only to children and/or employable adults, there is obviously a very high ratio of agencies to clients. In New York City, for example, three major agencies and six smaller ones offer direct social and educational services to an estimated 1,000 blind children living in the area. Even if we assume that none of these children are multiply handicapped (which we cannot), the agency-client ratio is very large indeed. Twenty-two different organizations and agencies provide direct rehabilitation and vocational services to an estimated 13,000 blind persons who are of working age. This figure is inflated somewhat when we consider that between 50 and 60 percent of blind persons 18–54 years of age are women, for whom employment is not always a realistic or appropriate objective. Eleven other organizations specialize in the production and distribution of braille books and recordings for the blind. In addition, a number of state and federal services are available to the blind of New York City.

The disproportionately large number of agencies offering services has many consequences for blind persons, agencies for the blind, and for the community which supports them. One consequence is an intense and often highly spirited competition for clients among agencies for the blind. In some instances, this competition has become so keen that outside parties have had to intervene to protect the welfare of those involved. The pirating of clients is not unknown,[19] and great conflict between agencies ordinarily occurs in urban areas which have not been previously assigned to the competing agencies.

The intense and sometimes ruthless competition between these agencies for clients who fit their programs affects the agency's relationship to its clients. When an agency has the opportunity to provide services to a blind person who is suitable for its program, it is reluctant to let him go. The chances of finding a replacement for the client who leaves are not always good, and, without a substantial number of clients on hand, the agency may find it difficult to justify its expenditures to the supporting public. Clients are encouraged to organize their lives around the agency. Employment is secured for them in the agency's sheltered workshop, free recreational services are provided by the agency on a indefinite basis, and residential homes are maintained for them. Gradually a greater and greater portion of the client's contact with the larger community becomes mediated, and often determined by the agency, until the blind person is literally sequestered from the community.[20] At this point, the agency completely negates its original objective, which is to help the blind persons to become independent.

DISCUSSION

My analysis indicates that programs of services for the blind are often more responsive to the organizational needs of agencies through which services are offered than they are to the needs of blind persons. Moreover, by sequestering certain blind persons from the community, agencies for the blind are actually contributing to the very problems which they purport to be solving. The sociological concept which most appropriately applies to this phenomena is "displacement of organizational goals." This concept describes a situation in which an organization "substitutes for its legitimate goals some other goals for which it was not created, for which resources are not allocated, and for which it is not known to serve."[21]

This phenomenon, which has been observed in a variety of organizational settings, has been attributed to a number of factors, including the selection of organizational means and policies which preclude implementation of the goals,[22] the effects of bureaucracy on the personality and motivation of those who work in it,[23] elimination of the problems for which the organization was originally established,[24] and the requirement of the bureaucratic structure for resources and manpower.[25] The findings of a larger study of work for the blind, of which the data of this chapter are but one part, suggest that each of these factors plays a part in accounting for goal displacement in this field. In addition, another factor is suggested: the absence of any clear criteria by which to determine if the agency is or is not implementing its objectives.

It is generally agreed that the purpose of agencies for the blind is to help blind persons to maximize their ability to perform independently. Rehabilitation, which is a core service in any agency, seeks to restore the blind person "to the fullest physical, mental, social, vocational, and economic usefulness of which he is capable." The phrase "of which he is capable" is a crucial modifier, since there is no consensus among workers for the blind regarding what a blind person can or cannot do. In practice, this definition is often used tautologically, since any level of performance which a blind person happens to attain is regarded as the one "of which he is capable." It is difficult, and at times impossible, to know if an agency for the blind is actually attaining its goals.

Using the definitions often employed by workers for the blind, every client they serve is a successful case. By other criteria, such as amount of independent employment or degree of participation in the larger community, the conclusions with respect to the implementation of goals are more modest. In addition, when a blind person performs in a manner which everyone agrees is his maximum level of independence, it is difficult to demonstrate concretely that his independence is a result of the services which he has received. By the same token, when he is not functioning at a level believed to be his maximum, it is not known if this is because services have been inadequate, or because he is a victim of the erroneous beliefs of the larger society about blindness and its effects on human functioning. There is, therefore, a great amount of uncertainty concerning whether an agency is or is not attaining its goals. Criteria of measurement are nebulous, and so many factors might explain success or failure that it is impossible to demonstrate conclusively that a given agency has in fact implemented its goals.

A preoccupation with organizational means is one of the responses to the uncertainty which is generated by this situation. Over the years an intense interest has developed in the refinement of administrative procedures of service programs. This interest has been accompanied by a growing disinterest in the more fundamental questions concerning the necessity for a particular service, or its impact upon the client.[26] This preoccupation with administrative procedures provides workers with a feeling of certainty and accomplishment which would not otherwise exist. Since most workers for the blind are not professionally trained, and their competency to help the blind is therefore continually being challenged, we can see that this uncertainty regarding goal attainment is intensified. As a defense against this situation, workers bury themselves in the administrative details of their jobs. This preoccupation ultimately leads to the displacement of the organization's goals.

Ironically, the tendency toward the displacement of goals is not entirely dysfunctional when viewed from the perspective of the general public. There is a general resistance among most "normals" to become involved with stigmatized persons such as the blind, and avoidance is the characteristic initial response.[27] The blind have always complained that they are segregated from the rest of society, and that they are assigned a marginal and unsatisfying social role.[28] The tendency of agencies for the blind to sequester certain clients (i.e., those for whom there is the greatest probability of integration into the larger community) is consistent with the desire of the public to avoid blind persons. This response, of course, is not unique in welfare services for the blind; it applies with equal cogency to other groups of persons who are defined as disabled, handicapped, or otherwise socially undesirable.[29] The very fact that agencies for the blind exist creates a repository into which the blind may be placed by the larger community. Consequently, the fact that goals are displaced may have unfortunate consequences for particular blind persons, but not necessarily for society at large.

Notes

1. See, for example, Harold L. Wilensky and Charles N. Lebeaux, *Industrial Society and Social Welfare* (New York: Russell Sage Foundation, 1958), chs. 7 and 10.
2. Eliot Freidson, "Disability as Social Deviance," in *Sociological Theory, Research, and Rehabilitation,* ed. Marvin B. Sussman (Washington, D.C.: American Sociological Association, 1966).
3. This figure has been derived from data from two separate sources. For estimates of the prevalence of blindness in the noninstitutionalized civilian population of the U.S. between the ages of 18 and 79, see *Binocular Visual Acuity of Adults, United States, 1960–1962* (National Center for Health Statistics, ser. 11, no. 3). For estimates of the prevalence of blindness in children, see American Printing House for the Blind, *Annual Report* (Louisville, Ky., APHB, 1962).
4. *Binocular Visual Acuity,* table 3, p. 16.
5. Ibid.
6. This estimate is based upon the figures of the APHB for school-age children, and an educated guess by practitioners of works for the blind for preschool-age children.
7. *Binocular Visual Acuity,* table 3, p. 16.
8. *Directory of Agencies Serving Blind Persons in the United States* (14th ed.; New York: American Foundation for the Blind, 1965).
9. See Harry Best, *Blindness and the Blind in the United States* (New York: Macmillan, 1934), ch. 12.
10. Ibid., chs. 1 and 4.

11. Ibid., chs. 2 and 3.
12. For discussions of resistance to the adoption of the Hoover cane, see Thomas Carroll, *Blindness,* pp. 134–135; for discussions related to braille, see Robert Erwin, *As I Saw It* (New York: American Foundation for the Blind, 1966), pp. 1–56; for discussions related to seeing eye dogs, see W. M. Ebeling, "The Guide Dog Movement," in *Blindness: Modern Approaches to the Unseen Environment,* ed. Paul A. Zahl (New York and London: Hofner, 1962); also see Hector Chevigny and Sydell Braverman, *The Adjustment of the Blind* (New Haven: Yale University Press, 1959), ch. 9.
13. Marvin Sussman, "Sociology of Rehabilitation Occupations," in *Sociological Theory, Research, and Rehabilitation,* ed. Sussman, ch. 2.
14. Erving Goffman, *Stigma: Notes on the Management of Spoiled Identity* (Englewood Cliffs, N.J.: Prentice-Hall, 1963), ch. 1.
15. Chevigny and Braverman, *Adjustment,* ch. 9.
16. Such appeals have been enormously successful. I have estimated that in the state of New York alone, between $57,000,000 and $63,000,000 are annually expended by public and private organizations for services to the blind. This figure was compiled from data from a variety of sources, including the routine annual reports of governmental-sponsored service programs, the annual reports of private agencies which are routinely filed with the Charities Registration Bureau of the State of New York, and private correspondence with the numerous other organizations who do not ordinarily make financial reports public.
17. These estimates were derived by computing the blindness rate per 1,000 of the population and then multiplying them by the number of persons living in each city.
18. For a listing of most of these agencies, see *Director of Agencies Serving Blind Persons in the United States, 1965.*
19. Chevigny and Braverman, *Adjustment,* ch. 9.
20. This situation also applies to other types of welfare organizations. See, for example, Erving Goffman, *Asylums: Essays on the Social Situation of the Mental Patient, and Other Inmates* (Garden City, N.Y.: Anchor Books, 1961), and Harold Orlans, "An American Death Camp," *Politics,* Summer 1948, pp. 162–167.
21. Amitai Etzioni, *Modern Organization* (Englewood Cliffs, N.J.: Prentice-Hall, 1964), p. 10.
22. Robert Michels, *Political Parties* (Glencoe, Ill.: Free Press, 1949); Philip Selznick, *TVA and the Grass Roots* (Berkeley: University of California Press, 1949).
23. Robert K. Merton, *Social Theory and Social Structure,* (rev. ed.; Glencoe, Ill.: Free Press, 1957).
24. S. L. Messinger, "Organizational Transformation: A Case Study of a Declining Social Movement," *American Socological Review* 20 (Feb. 1955): 3–10.
25. B. R. Clark, "Organizational Adaption and Precarious Values," *American Sociological Review* 21 (1956): 327–336.
26. One manifestation of this trend is the shifting focus of papers and discussions at meetings of workers for the blind. At the beginning of organized programs of services for the blind, papers at such meetings were largely devoted to basic discussions of the appropriate goals of work for the blind; at the present time they are concerned almost exclusively with perfection of

the means. See *Annual Proceedings* of the American Association of Workers for the Blind.

27. Goffman, *Stigma,* ch. 1.
28. Alan Gowman, *The War Blind in American Social Structure* (New York: American Foundation for the Blind, 1957), pp. 5–9.
29. Goffman, *Stigma,* ch. 1.

Part II   Analyzing an Organization's Receptivity to Change

Practitioners who seek modifications in the policies, practices, or conditions of employing organizations must be centrally concerned with forces that may serve to facilitate, neutralize, or block the change proposed. This would seem too obvious to mention were it not for the fact that low-power practitioners frequently become so intensely committed to the substance of a proposal that they fail to give sufficient attention to factors that impede or support its acceptance and implementation. Yet experience suggests that the inherent value of an idea for change is only one of a number of variables that ultimately determines its destiny. This is sometimes difficult for subordinates to understand, especially when the proposal appears to be a reasonable answer to a documented problem or need with which they contend on a daily basis. The tendency, especially among neophytes, is to treat considerations not pertaining to the merits of the proposal itself as spurious or irrelevant to the change process. The concern expressed by superiors that the adoption of an idea may disrupt organizational routine, or give the appearance that one group of staff is favored over another, may, indeed, have little to do with the efficacy of the proposal. But the failure to recognize and strategically address these issues can frequently doom an otherwise promising innovation.

The chapters in Part II provide several analytic perspectives that may help human service practitioners to assess an organization's receptivity to changes initiated from below. Such an assessment is an essential component of the change process because it provides the basis for determining whether the change goal is feasible, what modifications and compromises may be necessary in order to minimize resistance and acquire support, what resources (for example, time, energy, people) will need to be enlisted in the change effort, and the type of strategy to be employed. (This latter point is dealt with more specifically in Part III.)

The chapter by Patti that begins this section provides a framework for assessing resistance to change in social welfare organizations. It is written from the perspective of the change agent who wishes to gain the approval of superiors for modifications in agency policies, programs, or procedures and directs his or her attention to four major potential sources of resistance: the nature of the proposal itself, the value orientation of the decision-maker, the organizational distance between the change agent and the decision-maker, and sunk costs in the arrangement to be altered. The variables addressed in this chapter do not exhaust those that may arise in any given change situation, but they do have the value of being readily observable and amenable to fairly systematic analysis.

Organizations of any complexity typically contain several factions with varying goals and interests. Though all these groups may have some commitment to the overriding purposes of the agency, each is also likely to have somewhat distinct interests and organizational perspectives that will condition how they perceive and evaluate the proposals for change. In Chapter 9, Binstock and Morris suggest one way of looking at factions in social agencies and the interests and values that each group is likely to consider as it entertains proposals for change. Although this selection examines resistance from the vantage point of the planner who is external to the system, the circumstances are similar to that of the internal change agent in the sense that both kinds of actors must ultimately rely on some authoritative body or set of persons in the organization to accept the innovation. This chapter also underlines the importance of identifying those groups that are likely to be the most influential in making the decision to adopt or reject a change. Too often change agents focus their efforts solely on persons who are officially responsible for such decisions, thereby failing to anticipate and address the resistance of groups that may actually be more influential in the decision-making process or in subsequent implementation. An analysis of the kind suggested by Binstock and Morris can assist change agents in avoiding this type of error. This analytic framework complements that in Chapter 8. Utilized in tandem, both chapters provide the low-power practitioner with a tool for estimating the sources and magnitude of resistance they may encounter in the change process.

It is not uncommon for change agents to be so enamoured of the righteousness of their proposal that they see resistance from any quarter as irrational or malevolent. In Chapter 10, Klein casts resistance to change in a somewhat different light, suggesting, among other things, that some forms of resistance are necessary to maintaining institutional integrity. Perhaps even more important is his argument that resistance can be a source of constructive information about the limitations and unforeseen negative consequences of a planned change. In this sense, opposition is not to be thought of as an undesirable impediment, but rather as an essential dynamic of the change process, which, if understood and addressed on its own terms, can strengthen the quality of the proposal.

The final chapter, by Hage and Aiken, focuses on structural attributes of health and welfare organizations that are associated with program change. Although the introduction of new programs is only one type of change with which professional change agents might be involved, the findings reported here may be applicable in other areas as well. Studies of this kind should be interpreted with caution by would-be change agents. Read literally, the findings might suggest that efforts to introduce change in organizations characterized by low complexity, high centralization, and high formalization are likely to fail and, therefore, should not be attempted. Such an interpretation would be unfortunate, since this research was not intended to generate prescriptions for practitioners in the field, but rather to produce knowledge and, it is hoped, explain why some organizations are more receptive to change than others. Rather, the utility of this study for practitioners is that it provides a conceptual framework for ordering observations about organizational variables that have some relationship to agency change and, therefore, for identifying conditions that may serve to facilitate or impede the acceptance of proposals. Armed with this assessment, the change agent is likely to be in a better position to assess the potential for support or resistance and to develop a strategy that takes these factors into account.

Supplementary References

Brager, George, and Stephen Holloway. *Changing Human Service Organizations*, pp. 30–128. New York: Free Press, 1978.

Johns, E. A. *The Sociology of Organizational Change*, pp. 33–62. Oxford: Pergamon, 1975.

Leeds, Ruth. "The Absorption of Protest: A Working Paper," in *The Planning of Change*, ed. W. G. Bennis, K. D. Benne, and Robert Chin, pp. 194–208. New York: Holt, Rinehart & Winston, 1967.

Monane, Joseph. *The Sociology of Human Systems*, pp. 113–162. New York: Appleton-Century-Crofts, 1967.

Weissman, Harold. *Overcoming Mismanagement in the Human Services*. San Francisco, Calif.: Jossey Bass, 1973.

Chapter 8   **Organizational Resistance and Change:**
The View from Below
Rino J. Patti

INTRODUCTION

Bureaucratic organizations have come to occupy a position of almost unique disfavor among human service professionals. Recognized by most as a necessary evil, such organizations tend in general to be characterized as sluggish, uncreative, and mired in rules and procedures which prevent the professional from offering the service he would otherwise be able to provide unfettered by these constraints. Bureaucracies are further criticized as being inherently preoccupied with maintenance and self-perpetuation, often to the extent that consumer welfare is sacrificed.[1] It is not my intent to elaborate on this critique except to point out that it has tended to obscure the necessity of analyzing each organization in terms of its receptivity or resistance to innovation. In too many instances, conventional wisdom about "the bureaucracy" has served as a substitute for careful differential assessments of organizations and their varying capacities for change.

In this chapter I direct attention to four variables which can provide the internal change agent[2] with a partial framework for analyzing the magnitude and nature of the resistance he will likely encounter in efforts to effect organizational change. The four variables to be discussed are (1) the nature of the change proposal; (2) the value orientation and decision-making style of the decision-maker; (3) the administrative distance between the practitioner and the decision-maker; and (4) "sunk costs," that is, the investment an organization, or some part thereof, has made in the arrangement the initiator of change intends to alter. In presenting this analytic framework my intent is to provide a practitioner with a tool that may enable him to make a differential assessment of resistance.

Reprinted from the *Social Service Review* 48, no. 3 (Sept. 1974): 367–383, by permission of The University of Chicago Press. © 1974 by The University of Chicago. All rights reserved.

Such an assessment, as I suggest later in the chapter, is crucial to making an informed choice of change objectives and interventional strategies.

In what follows, organizational resistance will be viewed from the perspective of the administrative subordinate who, in a given instance, must obtain the approval of his superior for changes he is proposing. Thus, in this context, the subordinate is any employee, be he administrator, supervisor, direct-service worker, researcher, or program analyst, who is actively attempting to influence decision-makers at some point further up in the administrative hierarchy to adopt his plan of action.

For the most part, discussions of organizational resistance tend to view the agency from the top down or, more specifically, from the vantage point of high-level administrators who generally have the authority to institute changes they consider desirable.[3] This is to be expected since these actors carry a major responsibility for initiating and managing change. At the same time this perspective has, at best, limited value for the low-power practitioner because his interest, his information, his experience, and, most certainly, his authority are likely to be distinctly different from those of his counterpart in higher administrative circles.

DEFINITIONS AND ASSUMPTIONS

Before proceeding with an analysis of those variables which have some bearing on resistance to change, it is first necessary to define some terms and state the major assumptions that will be central to the following discussion.

Change will refer to the formal acceptance of a proposed addition, modification, or deletion in administrative policy, program, or procedure by a person, or persons, with authorization to do so. I will not be concerned here with other kinds of changes, often just as important, that occur in the informal system (e.g., interpersonal relationships, communication, distribution of power) and for which no formal decision is required. Nor will I be concerned with modifications in policy, program, or procedure that fall within the authority domain of the practitioner himself. For example, if a caseworker decides to initiate group treatment for certain of his clients, or to modify his own record-keeping system, and has the authority to do so without gaining the formal approval of someone in the hierarchy, we will not consider this a change for our purposes.

Resistance refers to those forces or conditions within the organization that tend to decrease the likelihood that decision-makers will accept or act favorably upon a proposal for change initiated by an administrative subordinate. No effort will be made to address the resistance that may arise from a decision-maker's judgment that a proposed innovation is not sound or beneficial to the agency or the clientele it serves. Innovations are not inherently desirable, and in any given instance a supervisor may simply reject a new course of action out of a conviction that it will not add to, or may detract from, an agency's service capability. Resistance arising from this source will not be dealt with here.

In what follows, it will be assumed that the practitioner is attempting in good faith to effect change in the organization's policies, program, or procedures in order that it may be a more effective instrument for the delivery of social services. I will further assume that the change agent is competent and responsible in the performance of his professional role and that his involvement in the change effort is not intended to divert attention from or displace responsibility for his own personal or professional inadequacies. Finally, I will proceed on the assumption that he has conscientiously attempted to formulate his proposal on the basis of the best and most complete information available to him. It is necessary at this point to observe that unless these conditions have been met, the resistance the administrative subordinate encounters may be attributable more to him than to the organization he seeks to change.

THE CHANGE PROPOSAL

Since the range of change proposals made by practitioners may be as diverse as the activities that occur in the field of social welfare, I will attempt to focus this discussion by conceptualizing such efforts in terms of two dimensions: generality and depth. These dimensions are selected because on the face of it they seem to be critically related to organizational resistance.

Generality refers to the scope or pervasiveness of the proposal; in simple terms, the size of the organizational unit that will be affected by the changes sought. Three levels of generality are proposed here:

1. *Component*—those change efforts that seek modifications in organizational arrangements or operations which have relevance primarily for the change agent or for a small group with whom he interacts on a day-to-day basis (e.g., supervisory unit).

2. *Subsystem*—those change efforts that seek to alter the arrangements or operations of an entire unit or class of organizational participants (e.g., a department, district office, all caseworkers).

3. *System*—those efforts aimed at changing some aspect of the organization that will have operational implications for its entire membership.

In reality, changes at either of the first two levels of generality are likely to affect the third, but our concern here is not with the eventual ramifications of the change but with its intended, first-order consequences.

The second dimension concerns the *depth* of change that is sought.[4] Again, three levels are suggested:

1. *Procedural*—those proposed changes that seek to alter the rules and procedures guiding the day-to-day behavior of employees who are carrying out the policies or programs of the agency. The goal here is to facilitate the flow of work activities or to utilize resources more efficiently, not to alter the substance or purpose of the services provided. Examples might be improved methods of interdepartmental referral, the development of mechanisms for increased communication and coordination among staff (e.g., interdisciplinary team conferences), or the introduction of new statistical forms to enable an agency to monitor its work-load better.

2. *Programmatic*—those innovations aimed at modifying the operating policies or programs carried out by an organization in order to implement its basic purposes and objectives. The focal concern is to substantively alter the services that an agency provides so that it can more effectively accomplish its mission. Changes at this level may take the form of new treatment modalities (e.g., family therapy, behavior modification) or the addition of programs such as day care, job placement, or homemaker services.

3. *Basic*—those efforts that are aimed at changing the core objectives of an agency. The intent is to effect a fundamental shift in the organization's mission so that it will address itself to a different set of problems and outcomes. Examples here might be transforming a character-building agency into one that seeks to correct emotional disturbances in children, or changing a custodial institution into one that is committed to rehabilitation.

When these variables of generality and depth are related to one another, a ninefold classification of change proposals emerges. It is my premise that as either the generality or the depth of a proposal increases, the resistance to be expected from organizational decision-makers is, all other things being equal, also likely to increase. This is to be anticipated since the more fundamental and far-reaching the proposal, the greater the costs of innovation and the potential for instability are likely to be. Not only must the agency devote a greater than usual share of its resources to establishing new arrangements and behavior patterns, but the period of transition is almost certain to be accompanied by a lessening of the decision-maker's ability to predict and control employee behavior and the reactions of external support groups.

VALUE ORIENTATIONS OF DECISION-MAKERS

Practitioners in the lower reaches of social welfare bureaucracies may often assume that organizational decision-makers will be resistant to proposals emanating from below. Unfortunately, this assumption often serves to deter administrative subordinates who would otherwise promote their ideas for change. A more useful perspective would be to proceed on the premise that superiors vary considerably in their receptivity to innovation, and thus in how they react to proposals for change.[5]

One approach to making such a differential assessment involves an analysis of a decision-maker's value orientations. *Values* are defined here as the personal goals held by an official that serve to guide his organizational behavior, especially how he decides issues. They are a reflection of those conditions he believes will produce a sense of self-fulfillment, satisfaction, or accomplishment. The assumption here is that, notwithstanding limits to rationality,[6] a decision-maker consciously attempts to choose those courses of action for the organization which are most likely to maximize the prospect of attaining the goals he holds most important. Personal goals are not necessarily self-aggrandizing or selfish in the conventional sense. They may include values that the decision-maker perceives as altruistic or in the public good.

The following list of personal goals[7] indicates something of the range of values that may influence decision-making behavior. While all of these goals may be perceived as important, the decision-maker is likely to arrange them in a hierarchy so that some are more important in influencing his behavior than others. Thus the attention of the practitioner should be directed not toward the presence or absence of certain values but toward their relative position in the decision-maker's goal hierarchy. In other words, while all goals may be operative in some degree, it is likely that some are more consistently salient than others. The goals include:

1. *Power*—authority and control over organizational behavior.
2. *Money*—increases in income or income substitutes.
3. *Prestige*—respect and approval from those who are responsible for funding the agency, determining promotions, hiring and firing, and so forth.
4. *Convenience*—avoidance of conditions that will require additional personal efforts.

5. *Security*—protection against losses of personal power, prestige, or income.

6. *Professional competence*—respect from peers for knowledge, technical proficiency, or professionally ethical behavior.

7. *Client service*—achieving maximum program effectiveness and efficiency in the interest of better service to clientele.

8. *Ideological commitment*—maintenance of the agency as an instrument of an ideology or philosophical stance.[8]

This scheme does not exhaust the range of values that may motivate decision-making behavior, nor does it account for the fact that each proposed innovation may well call into play a somewhat different constellation of personal values from a superior. For example, under ordinary circumstances, if a decision-maker places high value on the retention of power but a particular proposal has no implications for his ability to achieve this goal, then another value (e.g., convenience) may become a dominant factor in his consideration. Nevertheless, despite its limitations, the scheme provides the change agent with a point of departure for assessing those goals that are likely to influence the superior's decision on his proposal at a given point in time.

An analysis of literature further suggests that these personal goals are not randomly distributed among decision-makers but rather tend to cluster characteristically in certain organizational role types. Brief profiles of each of three modal types—the conserver, the climber, and the professional advocate—are presented to illustrate the relationship between goals and decision-making behavior.[9]

The *conserver* is, as the name implies, largely concerned with maintaining his place and routine in the organization. His primary preoccupation is with security and convenience, that is, with maintaining whatever power, prestige, privilege, and income he now possesses. As one might expect, decision-makers who are conservers tend to consider any significant change in the status quo, especially if it affects their domain, an anathema. Such officials are often fearful, cautious, and lacking in self-confidence. They are likely to be alienated from the organization and its mission and secretly somewhat pessimistic about the effects of its programs. Cynicism about new efforts or ideas tends to be expressed in terms of failures associated with past similar ventures. Conservers frequently divorce job and social life, concentrating most of their creative energies in the latter arena. Although some administrators may be conservers by personality predisposition, such an orientation tends more often to be a product of longevity in the organization, advanced age, lack of promotional opportunities, and a declining sense of personal efficacy produced by years of frustration and disappointment while fighting the good fight.[10] This is not meant to imply that all officials approaching retirement are conservers but merely that there is a considerable tendency for those who have been in the bureaucracy a long time to develop this orientation.

The decision-making behavior of the conserver, as the preceding profile suggests, will tend to approximate what Gawthrop refers to as a "consolidative" orientation. He defines consolidation as "a deliberate and conscious effort to resolve demands for change regardless of source solely in the context of existing organizational structures, if at all possible."[11]

In contrast to consolidation, innovation (at the other end of the decision-making continuum) represents "a deliberate effort on the part of executive officials to search for improved performance programs, to diagnose organizational weaknesses in advance, and to predict as accurately as possible the consequences of innovative change."[12]

The consolidative bias of the conserver does not mean that such decision-makers indiscriminately reject all proposals for change, because to do so would obviously be to court disaster. Rather, consolidative behavior is more likely to be manifested by a failure to search for, or identify, emergent problems and issues. The conserver tends to be relatively impervious to informational inputs regarding program gaps or deficiencies until such information, through the sheer weight of repetition or wide popular acceptance, takes on the nature of conventional knowledge. Finally, when conditions requiring change are upon the organization and some response is imperative, the change implemented is likely to be incremental and modest.

The *climber,* the second modal type of decision-maker, is primarily concerned with acquiring power, position, and prestige.[13] He does this in a number of ways, including assiduously cultivating those in authority who have the power to affect his personal fortunes, taking on responsibilities or functions not previously associated with his job in order to increase the scope of his office, and moving opportunistically from one job to the next in search of more money and status. The climber's apparent commitment to the goals and programs of an organization is, in fact, likely to be an allegiance to the regime in power, whether this regime be the board, legislature, or chief executive. He thus systematically avoids dissenting from or criticizing organizational policies as well as interpersonal conflicts with superiors or important constituents. The climber is not excessively burdened with moral ambiguity or ethical conflicts and tends to resolve such matters as they arise, quickly and decisively. He values action, efficiency, and "getting things done." In short, his concern is with the "how" rather than the "why." It goes without saying that the climber is ambitious, but it is also true that he tends to be energetic and hardworking. The boundaries between work and personal life are extremely permeable, and frequently these dimensions become undifferentiated parts of his existence. The climber tends to become involved in a variety of community activities that bring him high visibility and contact with elites. It is these involvements that frequently provide opportunities for upward mobility.

It is probably most difficult to anticipate the decision-making style of the climber and thus his reaction to a specific proposal for change. In terms of Gawthrop's consolidative-innovative continuum, the climber's decision-making behavior would probably be characterized mainly by its inconsistency. That is, since he relates to his job opportunistically, one would expect him to act similarly regarding change. Accordingly, changes in public sentiment, funding patterns, or the views of important constituents are likely to be reflected in his decision-making behavior almost immediately. The climber's goal hierarchy makes him no more inherently disposed toward one style of decision-making than another. If stability and continuity are the currency of the time, then he is most likely to take a consolidative approach. If experimentation is fashionable, then he is likely to encourage and support proposals for change.

There are, however, two factors which over time would seem to constrain the climber's decision-making inconsistency. The first is that the climber, concerned as he is with upward mobility, must establish some kind of track record, a history of accomplishments. Since this is more likely to occur if he is doing rather than not doing something, we would expect him to be inclined to innovation. It is also probably true that the climber cannot afford an extreme image. He can afford to be tagged neither as timid or unimaginative on the one hand nor as brash and revolutionary on the other. This being the case, one might expect the climber to operate in the middle ranges of the consolidative-innovative continuum but seldom, if ever, and certainly not for long, at one end or the other.

The *professional advocate*[14] does not deny the goals that are characteristic of the climber, particularly with regard to power and prestige. The distinction lies in what each considers instrumental as apart from ultimate values. The climber considers the acquisition of power and prestige of paramount importance; the substance of what he is engaged in, the social goals of the enterprise, are his vehicle. The professional advocate, on the other hand, may acquire prestige, status, and power and may indeed actively seek such resources; their acquisition, however, is likely either to follow from or be used in the service of achieving some organizational objective.

The professional advocate is committed to his organization as an instrument of service. This commitment is more often to an image of what the organization can be and do rather than to what it is and is doing. He is likely to be identified with its goals and policies not because, as is true with conservers and climbers, this protects or advances some personal interest, but rather because it most closely approximates his professional ideals. The word "approximates" is crucial here because the advocate is seldom satisfied with what his organization is accomplishing and is likely to be its most severe critic. However, his displeasure does not ordinarily take the form of cynicism but is rather more likely to be expressed as a continual search for new approaches, personnel with fresh ideas, additional funds, enlarged jurisdiction, and the like. His dissatisfaction with what is leads him to experiment. Critical, ambitious, and sometimes even imperialistic, the advocate often finds himself in conflict not only with members of his own staff but with executives of other agencies and even, on occasion, his own board. His relations with those in authority stand in sharp contrast to the climber's. While the latter is likely to celebrate authority figures and defer to them on substantive issues, the advocate sees them as resources to be persuaded and enlisted in the cause of enhancing his organization's effectiveness.

Given this portrait of the professional advocate, one would expect his decision-making behavior to be strongly oriented toward innovation. This is likely to be reflected in a relatively high investment in searching the environment (both internal and external) for incipient or emerging trends, issues, and problems, feedback regarding current program operations, and proposals for change. Since the professional advocate places considerable emphasis on informational input, his capacity to receive unorthodox or unpopular recommendations will probably be somewhat greater than that of either the conserver or the climber, as will be his ability to tolerate the uncertainty and tension involved in receiving and processing such a wide range of stimuli. Concerned as he is with problem-solving and goal attainment, the advocate tends not to avoid rather considerable departures from existing policy and program directions, when such departures are in the interest of increased effectiveness. He is prepared, in short, to adopt fundamental and far-reaching changes and to bear the costs of instability and conflict that frequently accrue, if these changes promise an improved capacity for goal attainment.

While the professional advocate has a bias toward innovation, he can also be a staunch defender of the status quo if the changes suggested are contrary to the ideological or philosophical stance he espouses.

In summary, I have suggested in this section that administrative superiors, indeed all organizational actors, tend to behave in ways that will maximize certain personal goals that they consider most important. I have further suggested that a superior's goal hierarchy tends to be reflected in certain modal role orientations, most particularly in approaches to decision-making when change is called for. These modal types are seldom observed in their pure form, but my contention is that the practitioner who is attempting to promote an innovation can utilize this typology as a point of departure for analyzing the resistance that he is likely to encounter from decision-makers.

ORGANIZATIONAL DISTANCE

Another variable which appears to be crucial in assessing the potential resistance that may be encountered in efforts to change is what might be called *organizational distance*. In this context, organizational distance refers to the number of administrative levels between a subordinate who is making a proposal and the administrative superior who must ultimately decide upon it. All other things being equal, it is suggested that the greater the distance a proposal must traverse, the greater the likelihood that it will meet with resistance at the point of decision. Thus, if this premise is correct, one would expect to have greater success in gaining approval from an immediate superior than from, for instance, an agency executive who is three or four levels higher in the administrative hierarchy.

At the outset it is important to note that my concern is with those processes (forces and conditions) that are natural concomitants of organizational distance. These processes can be augmented or neutralized by the actors in a change scenario, that is, they can be consciously manipulated by subordinates and decision-makers to affect the outcome of the change proposal. In the discussion that follows, however, I will focus only on ways in which distance itself can generate resistance to changes initiated by subordinates. Two major aspects are considered here: the processes that affect the substance and relevance of a proposal as it is communicated through one or more intermediaries; and the conditions under which the proposal is considered and decided upon.

The greater the number of intermediaries through which a proposal for change must be communicated, the more vulnerable it becomes to information loss, distortion, and delay.[15] One or more of these may have the effect of altering a proposal's substance or diminishing its timeliness.

First, it is in the nature of multilevel organizations that every subordinate must condense the information he conveys to his superior. Were this not the case, the sheer bulk of information emanating from below would soon grow to unmanageable proportions. The caseworker communicates only a portion (indeed a small portion) of what he considers relevant information to his superior, who in turn further collapses the information for presentation to his superior. This "winnowing process"[16] occurs at each level and inevitably entails a certain amount of information loss. While proposals (suggestions, recommendations) are less subject to condensation than information bits, here too the pressures of time frequently require that they be simplified or abbreviated in the course of passing through the communication network. As a consequence, it is not at all unusual for a proposal initiated several levels down to be only a skeleton of itself when presented to the decision-maker. That this occurs is evidenced by the frequency with which change agents can be heard to complain that their proposal was oversimplified or inadequately represented in the decision-making forum.

In addition to information loss, a proposal for change often becomes distorted as each intermediary inevitably filters it through his own perceptual screen. Values, vested interests, past experiences, feelings toward the practitioner—all these influence the intermediary's perception of what will be favorably or unfavorably received in the upper echelon. A proposal that may incur disfavor from superiors, for example, is often presented with somewhat less enthusiasm and vigor.

There is finally the matter of time. Since the timeliness of the proposal is often as crucial as its substance, delays that occur in the process of communicating across several administrative levels can have a determinate influence on the outcome. Such delays need not be motivated by opposition, although the popularity of phrases like "pigeonholing" and "sitting on" is testimony to the fact that they often are. More pertinent here is that intermediaries often delay transmitting a proposal because their superiors are preoccupied with other matters or overloaded.

Singly or in combination, these processes can have the effect of making a proposal for change less acceptable to decision-makers. This need not occur inevitably, but it seems fair to conclude that the greater the number of intermediaries, the greater the likelihood that information loss, distortion, or delay will take its toll on a proposal for change.

Organizational distance would also seem to be important to an assessment of potential resistance insofar as it is related to the conditions under which change proposals are considered and decided upon. First, the further removed a practitioner is from the ultimate decision-maker, the more likely it is that their respective organizational perspectives and criteria for decision will differ. The needs, interests, and priorities of incumbents in various echelons do differ, and these differences tend to become more sharply delineated as organizational distance grows. While these varying perspectives need not be in conflict, it frequently happens that they are.

Second, and not unrelated to the point just made, the more distance there is between the change agent and the decision-maker, the less opportunity there will be for sustained face-to-face interaction between them. In very practical terms this means less opportunity for the change agent to elaborate, argue, persuade, and compromise. This is perhaps best illustrated by the not unusual experience of being given fifteen minutes on the crowded agenda of an executive staff or board meeting to present a proposal. The constraints of time, unfamiliarity, and differences in language become formidable barriers to a persuasive presentation. Under these circumstances, it is not unusual for the subordinate to feel that he has not adequately represented his recommendations. Contrast this with a proposal made to an immediate supervisor with whom the practitioner has day-to-day interaction: this context permits the actors to explore their respective points of view, probe motivations, develop common referents, and negotiate differences. The obvious point is that the context in which a proposal is made and a decision arrived at is itself an important determinant of the outcome.

Finally, the higher a change agent must go in the administrative hierarchy for decision, the more likely his proposal is to come into competition with the interests of other groups. At each successive level in the administrative hierarchy, the decision-maker is confronted with an increasingly complex array of contending interests that must somehow be mediated. For the practitioner, this fact has important ramifications because it means, in effect, that as the array of competing interests becomes more varied and complex, his proposal will be weighed against a set of criteria that go beyond the merits of his proposal. The further removed the initiator of change is from the decision-maker, the less likely he is to have the information needed to anticipate or counteract these competing interests.

In summary, then, I am suggesting that the distance between the initiator of change and the decision-maker can itself be a crucial determinant of the amount of resistance that a proposal will encounter. There are, of course, ways to counteract or neutralize the consequences of distance, but before these can be developed, the change agent must be aware of their potential for generating resistance.

SUNK COSTS

The variable of *sunk costs*[17] may also constitute a source of resistance to change efforts initiated by administrative subordinates. Sunk costs refer to the investments that have been made by an organization (or its members) to develop and sustain any institutional arrangement or pattern of behavior that is currently in force. Investments are here defined broadly as inputs of money, time, energy, or personal commitment. They might include, for example, the staff time and energy that have been devoted to recruiting, developing, and maintaining foster homes over a period of time, or the funds that have been expended to train workers in a new mode of treatment (e.g., behavior modification). More specifically, sunk costs might be represented in the money that has been spent to remodel and furnish a building so that it can accommodate program activity. An equally important, if more subjective, element of sunk costs is the personal commitments made by members of an organization to an existing arrangement. It might be difficult, for instance, to attach a dollar figure to a social worker's effort to establish interdisciplinary team conferences on a surgical ward, but the worker will surely be able to attest to the energy costs that have been incurred in the process.

This latter aspect of sunk costs is frequently associated with length of employment in an organization.[18] That is, the longer a person has worked in an agency, the more likely he is to have a personal stake in its existent programs, procedures, and objectives. Since this dimension of sunk costs is subjective and often difficult to elicit (who would admit that he is opposed to change?), length of employment can sometimes be used to make an assessment of potential resistance. One way to gain an indication of resistance to innovation in a bureaucracy might be to sum the total number of years of employment for all persons in the department or unit that will be affected by the proposed change, and divide it by the number of employees. The dividend, when compared to those of other departments, may provide one measure of the relative opposition to be expected.[19]

Generally, it would appear that the greater the magnitude of an organization's investment in some arrangement or pattern of behavior, the more likely it is that a change in that arrangement will be resisted. Sunk costs, in other words, generate an organizational bias toward continuity. There are, of course, conditions that serve to counterbalance this bias. If, for example, the benefits gained from an investment have been less than anticipated, or existing arrangements have produced dysfunctional consequences (e.g., unfavorable community reaction, client dissatisfaction, loss of funding), an organization may be willing to write these costs off as a bad investment and strike out on a new course of action. External inducements that promise rewards greater than those currently received can also make it worthwhile for an agency to sacrifice its investments. Nevertheless, where sunk costs are large, organizations are not likely to make such judgments quickly. They are rather more likely to opt for continuity than for change.

IMPLICATIONS FOR CHANGE AGENTS

Assessing potential resistance to a proposal for change does not of necessity predict the fate of that proposal. Indeed, the purpose of being able to anticipate resistance is precisely that the change agent can mobilize resources and conduct interventions in a way that will decrease or neutralize opposition. Thus, it is my position that this kind of analysis is crucial preparation for a low-power subordinate who, with limited resources, wishes to maximize the effect of his efforts.

The action implications which flow from an analysis of resistance are manifold and cannot be fully explored here.[20] For illustrative purposes, however, I will suggest several ways in which the kind of analysis previously developed can inform a practitioner's interventions.

Feasibility. A change agent's ability to achieve a goal is very likely to depend upon whether he chooses a feasible goal in the first place. But how is feasibility assessed? Following Morris and Binstock, we would contend that "if the proposed innovations are resisted by the target organization, the *feasibility* [emphasis added] of the planner's goals is determined by his capacity for overcoming that resistance."[21] An analysis of organizational resistance can be useful in determining feasibility by putting into sharper perspective the resources the change agent will need to achieve approval and implementation of his goals. If the practitioner finds that one or more of the sources of resistance are likely to be operative in the change situation, he is then in a position to appraise whether it is possible to mobilize the resources that will be needed to overcome that opposition. Is it likely, for example, that he will be able to generate sufficient pressure to convince a "conserver" decision-maker to adopt a change that requires a major redirection of organizational focus? Can he reasonably expect to convince such a decision-maker that his interests (goals) are better served by anticipating change than by waiting until it is foisted upon the agency? If the conserver approves a proposal, can a staff that is heavily committed to the status quo be expected to implement it?

Answers to questions like these, even when one allows for the vagaries of prediction, can assist the change agent in deciding whether the resources he has, or can likely mobilize, are sufficient to the task at hand. If they are not, he may find it preferable to redefine his goals in terms that are more consistent with the resources he can muster.

Focus of intervention. An assessment of resistance can also aid the practitioner in determining where to focus his interventions. If he finds, for instance, that the decision-maker with a professional-advocate orientation is favorably disposed to a proposed change but declines to give approval because of anticipated adverse effects on the morale or efficiency of staff, then it may be a better use of the subordinate's time and energy to focus his attention on the staff. Efforts to persuade or influence them to accept a proposal may not only free the decision-maker to give his approval but ensure that the change, once authorized, will be effectively implemented.

In another situation, the change agent may find that the major obstacle to gaining approval for his recommendations is simply his failure to represent his ideas adequately to the decision-maker. Here again, he may decide that it is not pressure upon the superior which is indicated so much as efforts to increase the likelihood that his proposal will be given a full hearing. This might be accomplished by cultivating the support of intermediaries in the communication network, dramatizing the proposal to draw the attention of the decision-maker, going around the administrative hierarchy directly to the superior, and the like. Finally, in those cases where the administrative superior's role orientation and decision-making style resemble those of the "climber," the practitioner may find that a most effective point of leverage is to achieve the support of some community influential who has access to the superior.

Type of intervention. An assessment of resistance may also enable the practitioner to make a more informed choice of strategy. Let us assume for the moment that an administrative subordinate is proposing a change that is both high in generality and basic in character. Let us further assume that the worst possible combination of resistive forces is at work, that is, a conserver decision-maker at some distant point high up in the hierarchy and a staff that has for many years worked at developing and maintaining the agency's programs. Under these circumstances, the change agent who would pursue a consensually oriented strategy, based solely on information-giving and rational persuasion, is very probably doomed to fail. A more suitable strategy in this scenario is likely to be one that makes it costly for the organization to pursue its present course, one that assumes fundamental differences between the subordinate and the decision-maker, in short, a strategy characterized by aggressiveness, stridency, and coercion. The practitioner may not be inclined to pay or impose the costs that are associated with this approach, but he should not assume that the kind of change he is seeking can be accomplished without this magnitude of commitment.

On the other hand, one who is seeking approval for a modest program or procedural change in a relatively new agency with a professional-advocate executive and a shallow hierarchy is equally misled if he adopts a conflictually oriented strategy. To do so under such circumstances may not only elicit spurious resistance to his proposal but use up personal credit the change agent might wish to call on in future endeavors.

CONCLUSION

This chapter has been an effort to translate selected aspects of organizational theory into analytic concepts that can have some practical utility for administrative subordinates who are attempting to promote change in their agencies. The four variables discussed—the nature of the change proposal, the decision-maker, organizational distance, and sunk costs— are suggested as analytic focal points for the practitioner who wishes to assess the resistance he is likely to encounter in seeking change. While a certain degree of resistance is to be expected in virtually any proposal for change, the contention of this chapter is that it will vary significantly from one situation to another depending upon the particular configuration of variables that obtains. It is further argued that an assessment of the quality and quantity of resistance is crucial if the change agent is to make an informed choice of intervention strategy.

It is important to note that the four variables discussed in this chapter are only some of those that will determine an organization's resistance to change. Others that could not be dealt with here, but which require attention, are the nature of an organization's external environment (including its sources of legitimation and funding), its stage of development, and its technology. All of these appear to have some bearing on resistance and should eventually be part of an analytic scheme employed by change agents.

It is my hope that this paper serves simultaneously to provide low-power change agents with a beginning framework for organizational analysis and to stimulate further inquiry into this crucial aspect of change methodology.

Notes

1. See, for example, Robert Presthus, *The Organizational Society* (New York: Random House, Vintage Books, 1962): and Warren G. Bennis, "Beyond Bureaucracy," in *American Bureaucracy,* ed. Warren G. Bennis (Chicago: Aldine, 1970), pp. 3–16. Critiques more specific to social welfare can be found in Irving Piliaven, "Restructuring the Provision of Social Services," *Social Work* 13 (1968): 34–41; and Robert Pruger, "The Good Bureaucrat," *Social Work* 18 (1973): 26–32.

2. Hereafter the terms "practitioner" and "administrative subordinate" are used interchangeably with "change agent."

3. See, for example, Alvin Zander, "Resistance to Change: Its Analysis and Prevention," in *Social Work Administration*, ed. Harry Schatz (New York: Council on Social Work Education, 1970), pp. 253–257; and Paul Lawrence, "How to Deal with Resistance to Change," *Harvard Business Review* 47 (1969): 4–13, 166–76.

4. This scheme for classifying depth of change is adopted from Anthony Downs, *Inside Bureaucracy* (Boston: Little Brown, 1967), pp. 167–168.

5. The empirical evidence on this point is scanty and somewhat inconsistent. Weinberger's analysis of agency executive behavior led him to the conclusion that administrators tend to resist making decisions that involve the reordering of goals or the reallocation of resources (Paul E. Weinberger, "Executive Inertia and the Absence of Program Modification," in *Perspectives on Social Welfare*, ed. Weinberger [New York: Macmillan, 1969], pp. 387–394). Tangential but apparently supportive evidence is reported by both Epstein and Heffernan, who found agency executives to be conservative in their attitudes toward social change strategies that are likely to have a disequilibrating effect on agency behavior (Irwin Epstein, "Organizational Careers, Professionalization and Social Worker Radicalism," *Social Service Review* 44 [1970]: 123–131; Joseph Heffernan, "Political Activity and Social Work Executives," *Social Work* 9 [1964]: 18–23). A somewhat different profile of executives' reactions to change emerges from Hanlan's partial replication of Epstein's study. He concludes, for example, "On the basis of these limited findings, these executives cannot be characterized as a group within the profession who are most resistant to social action strategies," and later, "The study findings reported here, while limited to a small selected sample, provide some challenge to the assumption that these social work executives are co-opted into conservative and non-social action directions by nature of their occupancy of hierarchical positions" (Archie Hanlan, "Social Work Executives, Recent Graduates, and Social Action Strategies," unpub. paper [n.d.], pp. 11, 13). One source of the inconsistency reported in these studies may be the fact that executives, as I suggest here, fall into sub-groupings with distinctly different value orientations.

6. In the context of a single decision-making episode, insufficient information, emotional stress, inability to foresee consequences, and the like may prevent the decision-maker from rationally choosing, from among the available courses of action, those that will maximize the potential for goal attainment.

7. This is a modification of a list suggested by Downs, *Inside Bureaucracy*, pp. 84–85. Goals 6, 7, and 8 are different from those suggested by Downs. The modification is necessary to reflect some of the distinct features of the culture of social work.

8. This goal category refers to those decision-makers whose primary goal is to preserve or maintain an agency because of their commitment to some broad principle like the maintenance of ethnic identity or the value of private or volunteer philanthropy. The preservation of the agency becomes a vehicle for promulgating a particular ideology which, in the administrator's view, serves the public interest.

9. This typology was constructed from an analysis of several classification schemes that attempt to relate goals and role orientation to the behavior of

organizational officials. While these schemes conceptualize organizational behavior in rather different ways, there are notable areas of agreement and overlap among them (Downs, *Inside Bureaucracy,* pp. 88–111; Presthus, *Organizational Society,* pp. 164–268; Alvin Gouldner, "Cosmopolitans and Locals: Toward an Analysis of Latent Social Roles," *Administrative Science Quarterly* 2 [1957]: 281–306, 444–480; and Leonard Reissman, "A Study of Role Conceptions in Bureaucracy," *Social Forces* 27 [1949]: 305–310). The designations "conserver" and "climber" are borrowed from Downs.

10. See Downs, *Inside Bureaucracy,* pp. 96–99.

11. Louis C. Gawthrop, *Bureaucratic Behavior in the Executive Branch: An Analysis of Organizational Change* (New York: Free Press, 1969), p. 181.

12. Ibid., p. 182.

13. Presthus (*Organizational Society,* pp. 164–204) refers to these officials as upward mobiles.

14. The professional advocate shows characteristics of Presthus's "ambivalent" and Gouldner's "cosmopolitan," but differs from both because of his high commitment to the agency.

15. An elaboration of impediments to upward communication in bureaucracies can be found in Daniel Katz and Robert L. Kahn, *The Social Psychology of Organizations* (New York: John Wiley & Sons, 1966), pp. 245–247; and Gordon Tullock, *The Politics of Bureaucracy* (Washington, D.C.: Public Affairs Press, 1965), pp. 137–141.

16. Downs, *Inside Bureaucracy,* p. 117.

17. See James G. March and Herbert A. Simon, *Organizations* (New York: John Wiley & Sons, 1966), p. 173; and Downs, *Inside Bureaucracy,* pp. 195–196.

18. Jerald Hage and Michael Aiken, *Social Change in Complex Organizations* (New York: Random House, 1970), p. 97. Some functional aspects of personal commitment to organizational arrangements are discussed in Donald Klein, "Some Notes on the Dynamics of Resistance to Change: The Defender Role," in *Concepts for Social Change,* ed. Goodwin Watson (Washington, D.C.: National Training Laboratories, 1967), pp. 26–36.

19. Victor Thompson, *Bureaucracy and Innovation* (University: University of Alabama Press, 1969), pp. 61–88. See this source for suggested approaches to measuring resistance to innovation in complex organizations.

20. A further discussion of factors that should be considered in choosing and planning change strategies can be found in Rino Patti and Herman Resnick, "Changing the Agency from Within," *Social Work* 17 (1972): 48–57.

21. Robert Morris and Robert H. Binstock, *Feasible Planning for Social Change* (New York: Columbia University Press, 1966), p. 94.

Chapter 9   **Organizational Resistance to**

Planning Goals

Robert Morris and Robert H. Binstock

In attempting to achieve a preference goal the planner is immediately confronted by questions of feasibility. When his goal embodies a proposal for a change in the policy of an organization, his success, most simply expressed, lies in his ability to get the "target" organization to accept that proposal. A "policy change" is an innovation in the organization's allocation of its resources. This may include changes in the amount allocated, the combinations allocated, the purposes for which they are allocated, the timetables for allocation, the procedures of allocation, and the criteria for allocation. These changes may affect programs, procedures, activities, and behavior patterns—all the expressions of an organization's purposes as well as the ways in which they are carried out. If the proposed innovations are resisted by the target organization, the feasibility of the planner's goal is determined by his capacity for overcoming that resistance.

For a number of reasons, organizations are predisposed to resist changes embodied in social planning goals. One of the primary reasons is that the "organization does not search for or consider alternatives to the present course of action unless that present course is in some sense 'unsatisfactory.' "[1] The "existing pattern of behavior has qualities of persistence; it is valuable in some way or it would not be maintained."[2]

Social planning goals are not formulated primarily in an attempt to solve unsatisfactory conditions within a target organization.[3] Rather, major attention is directed toward finding a solution to an unsatisfactory condition of social welfare. Moreover, target organizations are not often selected with attention to the current states of satisfactoriness in their internal affairs. And even if the organization's present course is in some sense unsatisfactory, it is unlikely that the allocative innovation presented by a social planning goal will be perceived by the organization as

Reprinted from *Feasible Planning for Social Change* (New York: Columbia University Press, 1966), pp. 94–112, with the permission of the publisher.

a solution to its problems. It should not be surprising, then, that preference goals are frequently resisted by target organizations.[4]

Resistance to planning goals has many bases and is expressed in a variety of ways. If an organization is functioning satisfactorily, innovative proposals threaten attachments to old ways, introduce the uncertainties of new practices, and may disrupt the comfortable balance. A change may violate the culture or ethos that provides the foundation for organizational cohesion and financial support. Suggested innovations may appear senseless, insignificant, or without worthwhile purpose. Some alterations may be resisted primarily because they seem to require subordination of the organization to the will of outsiders. Others, of course, are rejected because, in the view of the target organization, the cost of adopting them apparently outweighs the benefits. While any one of these factors may be the most important in a given situation, usually several are operative to some degree when organizations resist planning goals,[5] as was evident in the Ford projects.

CASE STUDIES

San Francisco

One of the early undertakings of the San Francisco project director was an attempt to develop a health screening program for the elderly. The proposal called for the establishment of program units in five municipal health clinics, each to be staffed by a physician, a nurse, a social worker, and a health educator. The clinics were to provide case-finding, diagnostic, and educational services; staff members were expected to see to it that patients who needed medical care obtained it from appropriate community facilities.

In developing this proposal, the planner recognized a strong tradition in which voluntary and public health services of San Francisco are compartmentalized. For example, all general medical clinics are administered by voluntary hospitals and supported exclusively by fees and philanthropic contributions. Yet these private clinics are the sole source of out-patient medical care available to persons with limited incomes who cannot afford private fees. While the city health department administers a public hospital for in-patient care, it is not integrated with any of the private out-patient services. The success of the planner's attempt to establish the health screening program depended upon good working relationships between the private and the public health systems, which in turn required the cooperation of both the San Francisco medical society and the health department.

Both organizations approved the screening plan in principle although the health department indicated that it would make only one, possibly two, of its centers available. While the medical society registered no objections at the outset, it soon became clear that the society would reject any arrangement which implied that existing patterns of private medical practice were in any way inadequate. Proposals for case-finding, diagnosis, and health education services were resisted. ("We're not going to beat the bushes for patients." "There'll be no laying on of hands." "No patients will be disrobed for examinations.") Although the medical society eventually agreed to administer a watered-down version of the program, it refused to apply for funds when it learned that a grant from the federal government would probably have to be obtained. ("That's tainted money.")

Another problem tackled by the San Francisco project was the uneven distribution of recreational services for the elderly, provided at the time by some forty social agencies. Despite a plethora of agencies and a variety of auspices, less than 3 percent of the aged population participated in programs with any regularity. Some neighborhoods had no recreational programs at all; where programs existed, participation was often limited to persons of certain ethnic or religious backgrounds. The need for programs serving socially isolated older persons in the downtown rooming-house district was dramatized by a series of well-publicized incidents in which the public library barred them from its reading room and lavatory facilities.

To meet these deficiencies, the planner attempted to persuade various agencies to extend their programs into additional neighborhoods and to acquire more diversified clientele. Both types of proposals were resisted. Some agencies pleaded a lack of funds for program expansion and indicated no willingness actively to seek additional support from any source. Sectarian agencies generally resisted the suggestion that their service responsibility could or should extend beyond their own group.

Contra Costa County

Prior to the inception of the Ford project, the West Contra Costa Council had decided that additional visiting nurse services were needed, and in September 1961 the project director (planner) was asked to act on this matter. She found that the local Visiting Nurse Association was interested in expanding the range of its program and that other health and welfare agencies had recently called attention to the need for non-medical home services. A discussion with the county health officer convinced the planner that new nursing and homemaking services should be combined within a single agency, and that such a program would have to be county-wide in order to secure requisite resources. With these premises it became clear to her that cooperation from the county public welfare department was essential for success, and that the participation of certain other organizations would be valuable—the county health department, the county hospital, the heart and cancer associations, and the county medical society. The only likely source for initial funding of the program seemed to be the U.S. Public Health Service.

Several of these organizations expressed immediate reservations, however, when the planner presented her proposal. The county welfare director was reluctant to endorse the program, stating that administrative and legal restrictions prevented him from accepting the proposal that he arrange for the purchase of services from the new voluntary agency, for the benefit of welfare clients. (No doubt the increase in the department's budget which this would entail was a factor, as well as a preference that such services, if introduced, be directly controlled by his department rather than by a new agency.) Other potential participating agencies were inclined to support development of separate nursing and homemaker services. The regional office of the Public Health Service felt that the program as first proposed lacked sufficient innovative character and experimental promise to qualify for a demonstration grant.

Opposition was also encountered within the planner's own organization, the newly established Contra Costa Council of Community Services. The faction from the older, relatively well-developed western region was inclined to oppose the notion of a combined program because it posed a competitive threat to the financial support of the separate nursing and homemaking services already established in that sector of the county. Moreover, the proposal that the new program be county-wide reactivated latent regional antagonisms that had recently been exacerbated when a prominent and aspiring member of the western faction failed to become the executive director of the new county organization.

Another objective of the Contra Costa project director was the construction of low-rent housing for the elderly. When the planner approached the municipal housing authorities in Richmond and San Pablo, cities containing two thirds of the total population of the western region, she found them generally receptive to her aims. However, according to state law, local housing authorities must submit their plans for housing construction to public referenda in their communities. Since the West Contra Costa Board of Realtors had taken a vigorous public stand that no new housing for the elderly was needed, the housing authorities were reluctant to move ahead and thereby expose themselves to the risk of defeat in referenda campaigns.

Other efforts to develop housing for the elderly in unincorporated areas falling within the jurisdiction of the county housing authority found even less responsiveness. After much discussion, the director of the authority agreed to undertake a preliminary survey of need, but he was unimpressed with the urgency of the situation because the proportion of elderly residents was small, their average income was relatively high, and a great deal of middle-income housing had been recently constructed in the county.

Denver

One of the goals of the Denver project was to expand and improve recreational programs for the elderly by bringing about the federation of some thirty-five clubs of older persons. The programs of these clubs were meagre and sporadic. By consolidating the memberships of many small groups the planner expected to find a fresh demand for a rich and varied program, important enough to require full-time staff supervision and coordination. With this expectation, he sought a commitment of staff from the municipal department of parks and recreation. The department, already operating a day center for the aged, rejected the planner's proposal: any expansion of its program for older citizens would have required diversion of its limited resources from programs for other age groups. The planner also encountered resistance in his attempt to federate the clubs. It soon became evident that club members were relatively satisfied with the pattern of their activities. Perhaps an even more important factor in their reluctance to band together was their obvious fear of losing autonomy.

The Denver project also attempted to develop a program for improving the medical services to chronically ill older persons. His approach was to bring together forty-five health and welfare agencies from the metropolitan area, to get them to agree on the need for better coordination, and to develop for themselves new patterns of procedure for interagency relations. While these agencies did participate in a series of meetings and generally agreed that there was some need for coordination, they did not seriously attempt to undertake innovations. They were confounded by a dilemma well stated by the planner as he presented them with two precepts to guide them in their deliberations:

A program on chronic disease is inherently an all-or-nothing program. . . . It cannot be segmented but must reflect integration of services.

Chronic disease is too big a problem to solve in one fell swoop, and it would be best to start realistically with one aspect of the program and build gradually.

Given this contradiction and the initial participation of forty-five (later sixty) organizations, it is not surprising that this conference group was not able to agree upon a single proposal in the course of three years.

Worcester

The aim of the Worcester project was to establish a center for the elderly which would provide an extensive battery of health and social services. The planner chose two basic approaches as he tried to achieve this goal. One was to seek funds with which to rent facilities and to hire staff; the other was to solicit contributions of staff and space from various organizations in the community.

The primary targets of the planner's search for funds for the multi-service center were the Priorities Committee and the board of directors of the Worcester Planning Council. From the outset there were strong indications that both targets were opposed to the creation of this new agency for the elderly. The Priorities Committee gave the proposed center such a low rating in its periodic evaluation of worthy community causes that the Golden Rule (United) Fund never gave serious consideration to proposals for financial support. Low rating also hampered efforts to secure funds from other likely sources because the decisions of the Priorities Committee as to worthy and unworthy causes are generally respected in Worcester's tightly knit welfare system. After an extended period of frustration for the planner, the Planning Council seemed to relent in its opposition when it granted permission for the project for the aging to undertake independent, local fund-raising. But this seeming change of attitude was illusory. Leading figures in the Fund and Council took pains to let important potential contributors know that the multi-service center was not important, and this message was also subtly delivered to a fund-raising specialist who had been ready to manage a campaign for the center on a contingency basis.

Organizations from which the planner was seeking contributions of facilities and staff also resisted his efforts. Several organizations seemed to be promising targets for the contribution of facilities. The YWCA was currently constructing a large modern building in the downtown area, and several of its board members had hinted that the Y might be persuaded to let the age center use some available space on the ground floor. But other members of the organization resisted the suggestion on the grounds that "dirty old men hanging around the lobby" might corrupt the morals of the Y's young women. The decision of the Priorities Committee reinforced the hesitancy of those who had reservations. Ground-floor space in Worcester's public housing projects also seemed suitable locations for the multi-service center, but the director of the housing authority took the position that housing projects were not appropriate sites for social service programs. For a while it seemed that the Junior League of Worcester would provide volunteer staff for the proposed center program, but effective communications from Fund and Council members led to withdrawal of the offer.

The Worcester project director also tried to alleviate the plight of older persons living in substandard housing in the center of the city. The established practice of the city housing authority was to build "garden" projects in outlying residential areas. The planner proposed the construction of high-rise apartments in the downtown section, suggesting that most older persons already living in that area seemed to prefer the location and benefited from their ready access to nearby health and social service agencies. While the director of the authority had no general objection to housing for the aged, he gave a number of reasons for rejecting the proposals: neither downtown business interests nor the redevelopment authority would allow such potentially valuable sites to be used for tax-exempt purposes; older persons preferred to live in quiet and restful residential areas; automatic high-speed elevators required for high-rise apartment projects would befuddle and frighten aged residents.

DOMINANT FACTIONS IN ORGANIZATIONS

The propensity of organizations to resist innovative proposals embodied in social planning goals poses important practical questions for the planner. Is it possible to predict or anticipate which target organizations are especially likely to resist? How extensively? No classification has yet been developed which provides systematic guidance for predictions as to which organizations, under what circumstances, will resist certain types of planning goals. Further research into organizational behavior may eventually produce refined predictive criteria, but, for the present, social planners must rely upon a sensitive reading of each new situation against an extensive backdrop of relatively intimate knowledge of the pertinent organizations.

While the history of each organization's previous response to various proposals for policy change is helpful, it is at best a very rough guide, since from the viewpoint of the organization the current proposal for change may differ importantly from past ones in ways not readily apparent to the planner, an outsider. Similarly, decision criteria within the organization may alter over time, often in ways so subtle that even key individuals in organizational operations may not have recognized the change. The planner may also be able to read day-to-day clues indicating that an organization considers its situation unsatisfactory in some sense and, consequently, may be predisposed to accept innovations.[6] But the planner cannot really come to grips with the phenomena of organizational resistance by viewing an organization as if it were a single entrepreneur calculating the value of various courses of action. As March and Simon suggest:

> Although tangible . . . costs often can be and sometimes are evaluated in monetary terms, it is seldom possible to make accurate estimates of the costs of innovation, and even in situations where it is possible, such estimates are seldom made. Individuals and organizations give preferred treatment to alternatives that represent continuation of present programs over those that represent change. But this preference is not derived by calculating explicitly the costs of innovation or weighing these costs.[7]

The innovative proposal presented by the planner's preference goal is not evaluated by a monolithic organization with a single goal. In complex organizations, many types of roles are performed, each role defined by a different set of constraints, each set of constraints having some effect upon organizational policy. It is safe to say, however, that most innovative proposals presented to an organization are tested against a set of constraints which is widely shared within the organization; moreover, this set has its strongest roots in the major concerns of those persons who are in dominant organizational roles.[8] It is by directing his efforts at the persons who play the dominant roles (not officially, but actually) within the organization that the planner can be most effective in his efforts to overcome resistance. The critical considerations for the planner are who plays the dominant roles in the organization's decision-making, and, in their organizational roles, what are their primary concerns?[9]

Many individuals and groups within an organization may formally participate in decisions or informally affect them, but in any organization certain factions tend to dominate.[10] A single faction may be in control, or decision-making may be shared among several—a coalition. By and large, four types of factions tend to assume dominant roles within organizations at one time or another: boards of directors; executives; employees; and general membership. While dominant factions differ from one organization to another, it is possible to distinguish the type that dominates in a given organization and to isolate those matters to which it is sensitive. The planner needs information of this kind in selecting his tools for overcoming resistance and deciding how to employ them because the dominant faction is the most promising target for effecting a policy change.

The Board of Directors

Whenever there is a board of directors, it is officially expected to dominate policy in the interests of the organization's constituency. In the case of profit-making concerns, the pertinent interests are those of the owners of the corporation. For voluntary welfare organizations, private universities, hospitals, churches, and other nonprofit, quasi-public organizations, the board performs the functions of guarding and providing for the interests of consumers or clients; consequently, board members are often termed "trustees" or "overseers." The board of a public corporation or agency is expected to make policy "in the public interest." Since the relevant public is the electorate of a given jurisdiction, public directors, frequently designated "commissioners," attain their positions through election, appointment by elected officials, or appointment by administrative officials, such as city managers.[11] In contrast, the incumbent boards of business concerns and quasi-public institutions often play guiding roles in the selection of their succesors.

Official distinctions between the major policy matters to be determined by the board and the minor policies that are the responsibility of executives and administrators are frequently quite vague. Directors are expected to control decisions as to the purpose, scope, and character of the organization's activities; administrators are expected to carry out these decisions as efficiently and effectively as possible. In their very nature, of course, decisions as to the purpose, scope, and character of an organization's activities can define the nature of routine operations quite explicitly, especially if the board meets frequently to review administrative activities in the light of broader policy. By the same token, everyday operations can have a significant impact upon over-all policy, particularly if the board seldom meets and does not take an aggressive interest in the affairs of the organization.

Often the board abdicates, or is precluded from performing its expected function. It "rubberstamps" decisions already made, while continuing to perform ceremonial functions. On the other hand, groups much like boards—advisory committees, for example—may not be expected to make policy but often do so in the absence of a strong board or executive.

In a great many organizations, however, the board of directors plays its official, dominant role in policy determination. This is not to suggest that other factions in the organization contribute nothing to policy formation, but merely that, in the last analysis, the board is decisive. Often, a very few members of the board may become the key figures in organizational determinations. The larger the board, the more likely it is that this will happen. On occasion, even a single individual will dominate the board of directors because of his official position (perhaps as chairman), or his personal influence, or the apathy and indifference of the others.

Persons who serve on boards frequently do so for the probable rewards of prestige and sociability:

> Among the trustees and directors of universities, hospitals, and welfare organizations . . . the personal prestige which membership provides is often a strong incentive. Board members not only contribute prestige to such boards, but their own prestige is enhanced through association with other high-status community figures and with the institutions themselves.[12]

Board members are thus responsive to activities which enhance the organization's prestige and stature and thereby enhance their own opportunities for recognition.[13] Not all boards, of course, are dominated by such concerns; the boards of some organizations are primarily interested in achieving some ethical or moral goal. Still other boards are comprised of persons who feel obligated to carry on an established pattern of family or group responsibility; these tend to be occupied with the perpetuation of traditions.

It is, of course, important to distinguish between the personal concerns of a board member and those that guide him in his organizational role. While the board member's view of organizational interests is almost always influenced by his own interests, the latter do not fully determine his decisions in an organizational role; nevertheless, organizational considerations rarely conflict with personal ones.[14] It is safe to say that a proposal which violates the personal concerns of board members will be resisted by the organization. By the same token, the planner's efforts to overcome organizational resistance will have to be tailored with an eye to these interests.

The Executive

In some organizations, particularly governmental agencies, there is no board of directors. While general policy may be set by legislation or by higher administrative directives, most policy decisions are in the hands of the agency's managing executive. As in the case of board domination, other internal elements may contribute to policy formation, but decisions are dominated by the executive.

In the presence of a board of directors, control may pass to an executive by default. But even if a board is actively exercising its prerogatives, some of the executive's routine functions may enable him to dominate policy. Through the cumulative impact of routine decisions, through the preparation of budgets and agendas, through control of information flow, through his personnel policies, and through his position at the heart of organizational communications he can play a decisive role in policy development.[15]

The primary concerns of the executive differ from those of a board of directors. He is especially interested in the maintenance and enhancement of the organization, in a smooth and efficient performance. Resources must be managed so as to keep his directors, staff, contributors, and consumers relatively satisfied. Since these elements may require different and sometimes conflicting incentives to satisfy them, the executive must see to it that each receives a sufficient supply to hold the organization together.[16] The executive is also desirous of gaining recognition from members of his own organization and from others in his field. The planner's tools for influencing an executive must be selected for their relevance to such matters.

The Staff

Official responsibility for policy decisions is rarely lodged with employees, but they sometimes have an active voice in determining policy. On rare occasions when customary decision-making patterns break down because employee satisfaction has not been sufficiently taken into account, employees may be able to assume a dominant though temporary, role.[17] Issues of salary, benefits, working conditions, and professional opportunities and ethics may enable a staff to dictate policy in a period of crisis. Such crises are infrequent in social agencies, where professional employees are loath to challenge established procedures and regulations, even when they conflict with their assessment of sound professional practice and clients' interests.[18]

While the staff rarely dominates the entire policy range of an organization, professionals in social agencies do tend to have a decisive voice in policy matters directly concerned with client selection.[19] Regardless of official agency policy, their acceptance and rejection of applicants for service inevitably shape the program.

Members and Consumers

While the general membership of an organization may periodically select directors or officers to serve as its representatives for determining policy, the candidates are usually part of a predetermined slate composed by incumbent directors. Occasionally, the policies of public agencies are settled by a referendum on a specific question. A few private organizations with a relatively small membership submit issues directly to their constituents.[20] But for the most part the general membership of an organization rarely plays a dominant or even an active role in a policy decision.

Members and consumers (who are in some sense "members" of an organization) may dominate briefly when they are both greatly dissatisfied and sufficiently organized to pose a threat to organizational survival. This usually occurs when their primary interests, the quantity and quality of the organization's product and the ease of their access to it,[21] are grossly neglected. For any given member the criteria for satisfaction may be any among a wide variety of immediate material necessities and states of social and psychic well-being. The subjective character of these criteria[22] makes it difficult for the planner to be guided by an understanding of these concerns in his attempts to overcome organizational resistance.

Opportunities for members and consumers to determine policy are severely limited because they are not usually organized for this purpose. If they are organized, and if the central issue which brings them together is sufficiently strong, they are likely to withdraw to form a separate organization. If the issue is weak, the opportunity to control policy is short-lived because the coalition will fall apart, lacking sufficient incentive to bind together the otherwise constituent elements.

TARGETS FOR OVERCOMING RESISTANCE

The relatively distinctive concerns of these various groups that can dominate organizational policy are of critical importance to the planner as he attempts to overcome resistance to the innovation presented by his preference goal. When one faction dominates, it, in effect, is the channel through which the planner must direct his efforts to change policy. The special lenses through which the faction views innovative proposals are the planner's guide to the feasibility of his undertaking.

Whether or not the planner's goal violates the fundamental viability of organizational life, as it is interpreted by board, executive, staff, or membership, determines whether there is a channel open to the planner for overcoming resistance. If the goal is within the range of organizational purpose as interpreted by the dominant group, then that group's special interests are also a guide to the tools which will be needed for overcoming resistance and to where and how they must be employed. Tools which will influence an executive (in line with his preoccupation with organizational maintenance and enhancement and his desire for career recognition) may be quite different from those needed to influence a board of directors (in accordance with its interests in prestige, sociability, and the discharge of traditional obligations). For a planner's goal to be feasible, he must have access to the dominant group and the appropriate means of influencing it. In the rare instances when several factions dominate as a coalition, sharing equally in the power to determine policy, the planner's job is more difficult. Each of the several targets must be attacked if the planner is to overcome resistance. He must possess a wide variety of tools in order to have the necessary chance of success in each channel. And they must be especially powerful because the diversity of primary concerns operative in the policy considerations of such organizations leads to considerable internal conflict in response to innovative proposals. Consequently, it is difficult for coalition-dominated organizations to make any change at all. It is far easier for a planner to overcome the resistance of an organization that is dominated by a single faction.

In some situations it is relatively easy for a planner to know which faction is dominant and to be confident in his assessment of its primary concerns. In San Francisco, for example, the planner knew from his own direct contact with the local medical society that its policy was determined by a board composed of physicians in private practice. While it is not always safe to assume that such a group is primarily interested in maintaining the traditional patterns of medical care in a community, specific evidence was available to buttress this assumption. At that time the medical society was deeply embroiled in a public campaign of opposition to medicare, arguing that the existent system of medical care for the aged was more than adequate. In this light it should have been quite clear from the outset that the Ford project's plan for a health screening program for the elderly, as proposed, would be vigorously opposed by the medical society. The proposal, in itself, clearly implied that the existing system of private medical care in San Francisco was inadequate for meeting the health needs of many older persons. Indeed, it was developed by the planner and his committee because they thought that system to be inadequate.

In this instance, of course, it would have been easy enough to predict the intransigent resistance of the medical society to the planning goal. The organization was not particularly large and complex; it was not difficult to identify the dominant faction. Moreover, its interest in preserving traditional patterns of medical care was well known. However, a planner cannot be expected to be attuned to the factional situation within each complex organization from which he is seeking a policy change; nor can he always be aware of the overriding interests of dominant factions. Considerable stu•ly and analysis of factions and interests dominant in various types of organizations will be needed before planners will have sufficient guidance for making reliable predictions as to resistance likely in a variety of situations.

But in the absence of reliable instruments for prediction, attention to factions and their interests is more likely to provide an understanding of a planning situation than an analysis that is built upon an identification of an organization's "functions" and "responsibilities in the community." It is easy enough, of course, to second guess. But it would seem that the extensive waste of time and energy spent by the San Francisco project, in a fruitless attempt to use logic in overcoming the medical society's resistance, could have been predicted. Attention to the dominant interests of the medical society, rather than to the logic of its role as "community representative of private physicians," might have suggested more feasible approaches for achieving many if not all of the aims embodied in the health screening program proposal.

Numerous examples can be found in the records of the Ford projects in which attention to similar matters might have led to more feasible and effective planning.

Notes

1. James March and Herbert Simon, *Organizations* (New York: John Wiley, 1966), current scholarship on theories of organization and decision-making, 1966) p. 173. For a brief, cogent evaluation of current scholarship on theories

of organization and decision-making, and for a bibliography of major pertinent works, see Karl Deutsch and Leroy Rieselbach, "Recent Trends in Political Theory and Political Philosophy," *Annals* 360 (1965): 154–155.

2. Herbert Simon, Donald Smithburg, and Victor Thompson, *Public Administration* (New York: Knopf, 1961), p. 453.

3. For an explication of the determinants of the criteria of satisfaction, see March and Simon, *Organizations*, pp. 182–183.

4. To suggest that an organization resists a planning goal is not also to suggest that it is generally resistant to change. As will be suggested further on, an organization may often resist a specific innovative proposal even though it is generally disposed to make a change (ibid., p. 174).

5. See Simon, Smithburg, and Thompson, *Public Administration*, pp. 439–441.

6. As March and Simon have expressed it: "To explain the occasions of innovation is to explain why a program of action that has been regarded as satisfying certain criteria no longer does so (*Organizations*, p. 182). March and Simon present a systematic treatment of "the occasions of innovation" (pp. 182–186).

7. Ibid., p. 173.

8. Simon, "On the Concept of Organizational Goal," *Administrative Science Quarterly* 9 (1964): 21. It would be fair, of course, to refer to this set of constraints (as Simon does) as organizational goals.

9. Ibid.

10. Regardless of rules for the acquisition of official power in organizations, designed to achieve and preserve widespread participation in making decisions, the power to make decisions tends to be accumulated in the hands of a few. This is especially true of those organizations committed to mass participation. It was the observation of this tendency in political parties that led Robert Michels to formulate his "iron law of oligarchy." See his *Political Parties* (New York: Dover, 1959).

11. In the broadest sense, state legislatures and city councils also function, in effect, as boards of directors. Indeed, in the theory of the council-manager form of city government, the city council is regarded as the board of directors of the municipal corporation. See Don K. Price, "The Promotion of the City Manager Plan," *Public Opinion Quarterly* 5 (1941): 563–578.

12. Peter Clark and James Q. Wilson, "Incentive Systems: a Theory of Organizations," *Administrative Science Quarterly* 6 (1961): 141.

13. Murray Ross and Charles Hendry, *New Understandings of Leadership*, New York Association Press, 1957.

14. As Simon has observed: "If we examine the constraint set of an organizational decision-making system, we will generally find that it contains constraints that reflect virtually all the inducements and contributions important to various classes of participants. These constraints tend to remove from consideration possible courses of action that are inimical to survival. They do not, of course, by themselves, often fully determine the course of action" ("On the Concept of Organizational Goal," p. 21). Also see Clark and Wilson, "Incentive Systems," and Chester Barnard *The Functions of the Executive* (Cambridge, Mass.: Harvard University Press, 1938).

15. See C. A. Harrell and D. G. Weiford, "The City Manager and the Policy Process," *Public Administration Review* 19 (1959): 103.

16. See Clark and Wilson, "Incentive Systems," where an analysis of incentives that explains organizational behavior from the viewpoint of the executive is presented.

17. See, for example, the report of an experience in Philadelphia by Hyman Weiner, "Towards Techniques for Social Change," *Social Work* 6, no. 2 (1961): 26–35.

18. See Andrew Billingsley, *The Role of the Social Worker in a Child Protective Agency,* (Boston: Society for the Prevention of Cruelty to Children, 1964).

19. "The social services, which have helped to nourish them, depend to an increasing extent on the valuable skills and specialized knowledge of these occupational groups [the professions]. Because of the contribution they can make, there is a tendency to give these groups more representation upon policy-making and advisory bodies . . . A possible consequence is that, collectively, more power may come to reside in the hands of these interests" (Richard Titmuss, "Social Administration in a Changing Society," in *Essays on the Welfare State* [New Haven: Yale University Press, 1959]).

20. For example, the Family Service Association of America and local units of the YWCA follow this practice.

21. See, for example, Herman Somers and Anne Somers, *Doctors, Patients and Health Insurance,* (Garden City, N.Y.: Doubleday, Anchor, 1961), pp. 194–203.

22. See Edward Banfield, "Does Consumers' Freedom Need Redefining?" paper delivered at Florence Heiler Graduate School for Advanced Studies in Social Welfare, March 1965.

Chapter 10 **Some Notes on the Dynamics of Resistance to Change: The Defender Role**

Donald Klein

The literature on change recognizes the tendencies of individuals, groups, organizations, and entire societies to act so as to ward off change. Though it is generally acknowledged that human beings have a predilection both to seek change and to reject it, much of the literature has isolated the latter tendency for special emphasis. In fact, studies of change appear to be taken from the perspective or bias of those who are the change agents seeking to bring about change rather than of the clients they are seeking to influence. It seems likely, therefore, that our notions of change dynamics are only partially descriptive. It is interesting that Freud used the term "resistance" to identify a phenomenon which, from his viewpoint, had the effect of blocking the attainment of his therapeutic objectives. One wonders whether patients would use just this term to refer to the same sets of interactions between themselves and their therapists.

Freud, of course, emphasized that resistances were a necessary and even desirable aspect of the therapy. He pointed out that without resistance patients might be overwhelmed by the interventions of the therapist, with the result that inadequate defenses against catastrophe would be overthrown before more adaptive ways of coping with inner and outer stimuli had been erected.

DESIRABILITY OF OPPOSITION

The objective of this chapter is to suggest that, as in patient-therapist dyads, opposition to change is also desirable in more complex social

Reprinted from Goodwin Watson, ed., *Concepts for Social Change* (Washington, D.C.: National Training Laboratories, for the Cooperative Project for Educational Development, 1967), pp. 26–36, with the permission of the publisher.

systems. It further suggests that what is often considered irrational resistance to change is, in most instances, either an attempt to maintain the integrity of the target system in the face of real threat or opposition to the agents of change themselves.

Opposition to Real Threat

Change of the kind we are considering consists not of one event but of a process or series of events occurring over a period of time, usually involving a more or less orderly and somewhat predictable sequence of interactions. Though it involves the reactions of individuals, it also entails reorganization of group, organizational, or even community behavior patterns and requires some alteration of social values—be they explicit or only implicitly held.

Few social changes of any magnitude can be accomplished without impairing the life situations of some individuals or groups. There is no doubt that some resistance to change will occur when an individual's livelihood is adversely affected or his social standing threatened. Elderly homeowners gain little from and sometimes must spend more than they can afford for new public school buildings or for the adoption of kindergartens by their communities. Some administrators may lose their chances for advancement when school districts are consolidated to achieve more efficient use of materials and resources. Other examples of real threat could be cited from public health, urban renewal, and other fields.

However, there are more fundamental threats posed by major innovations. Sometimes the threat is to the welfare of whole social systems. Often the threat is not clearly recognized by anybody at the time the change occurs; it emerges only as the future that the change itself helped shape is finally attained.

For example, the community which taxes property heavily in order to support kindergartens or costly educational facilities may very well be committing itself to further homogenization of its population as it attracts young families wealthy enough to afford the best in education and drives out working-class groups, elderly people, and those whose cultural values do not place so high a priority on education. The community which loses a small, poorly financed local school in order to gain a better equipped and perhaps more competently staffed district facility may also be committed to a future of declining vigor as its most able young people are more readily and systematically siphoned off into geographically distant professional, industrial, and other work settings.

It is probably inevitable that any major change will be a mixed blessing to those undergoing it in those instances when the status quo or very gradual change has been acceptable to many or most people. The dynamic interplay of forces in social systems is such that any stable equilibrium must represent at least a partial accommodation to the varying needs and demands of those involved. Under such circumstances the major change must be desired by those affected if it is to be accepted.

Maintenance of Integrity

"Integrity" is being used here to encompass the sense of self-esteem, competence, and autonomy enjoyed by those individuals, groups, or communities who feel that their power and resources are adequate to meet the usual challenges of living. Unfortunately, integrity sometimes is based on a view of reality that is no longer tenable. When changes occur under these circumstances, they force us to confront the fact that our old preconceptions do not fit present reality—at least not completely. Dissonance exists between the truths from the past and current observations. In some cases relinquishing eternal verities would resolve dissonance but would also entail a reduction of integrity. However irrational, the resistance to change may have as its fundamental objective the defense of self-esteem, competence, and autonomy.

In our complex, changing world the assaults on individual, group, and community integrity are frequent and often severe. The field of public education is especially vulnerable to such assaults, so much so, in fact, that one sometimes wonders whether there are any truly respected educational spokesmen left who can maintain the self-esteem, sense of competence, and necessary autonomy of the schools against all the various changes which are being proposed and funded before they have been adequately tested.

Resistance to Agents of Change

The problem is further complicated, first, by our society's growing capacity, indeed necessity, to engage in massive programs of planned change and, second, by the development of ever-growing cadres of expert planners who are capable of collecting and processing vast bodies of information, of organizing that information into designs for the future apparently grounded on the best available expertise, and of marshalling arguments capable of persuading great numbers of political, business, and other civic leaders that action should be taken. The difficulties which arise stem from the very magnitude of the changes being projected, from the rapidity with which changes can occur, and from the troubling realization that changes often are irreversible as well as far-reaching, ensuring the prolongation of error as well as accuracy.

However, the most important generator of defense would appear to be the frequent alienation of the planners of change from the world of those for whom they are planning. The alienation is one of values as much as of simple information. Alienation is perhaps most apparent in the field of urban renewal, where planners have yet to devise mechanisms for adequately involving their clients in the planning processes. But other examples can be cited: Health professionals feel that matters of the public health should be left in the hands of the experts most qualified to assess the facts and to take the necessary action. They often decry the involvement of the public in decisions about such matters as fluoridation through referenda or other means. Educators are often loath to encourage the development of vigorous parent groups capable of moving into the arena of curriculum planning, building design, or other areas of decision-making.

Few expert planners in any field are prepared to believe that their clients can be equipped to collaborate with them as equals. What can the lay person add to the knowledge and rationality of the technical expert? And is it not true that the process of involving the client would only serve to slow down if not derail the entire undertaking? If decisions can be made and implementation secured without involving his public, the planner's job is greatly simplified. The result is that each planning project proceeds without taking the time to involve those who will be affected by the planning until it is necessary to gain the client's consent.

It is little wonder that planners typically do not engage in collaborative planning with clients on specific projects: It is costly, time-consuming, irritating, frustrating, and even risky. However, failure to work collaboratively contributes to the well-known American mistrust of the highly trained, academically grounded expert. Under the most benign circumstances, the client may be skeptical of the planner's recommendations. Given any real threat to livelihood or position, or given any feared reduction in integrity, a client's skepticism may be replaced by mistrust of the planner's motives and open hostility towards him.

The motives of innovators are especially apt to be suspect when the planning process has been kept secret up until the time of unveiling the conclusions and action recommendations. By this time, the innovators have usually developed a considerable investment in their plans and are often far more committed to defending them than to attempting to understand objections to them. They are not prepared to repeat with newcomers the long process of planning which finally led them to their conclusions. And they are hardly in the most favorable position to entertain consideration of new social data or of alternative actions which might be recommended on the basis of new information. The result often is that opposition to the recommended change hardens and even grows as the ultimate clients sense that their reactions will not materially influence the outcome in any way short of defeating the plan in open conflict.

DEFENSE AS PART OF THE PROCESS OF INNOVATION

Studies in such fields as agriculture and medicine have helped clarify the sequence of processes involved in successful introduction of new practices. Even in fields where results can be more or less objectively judged in terms of profit, recovery rates, and the like, successful innovation occurs only after initial resistances have been worked through.

Innovation in any area begins when one or more people perceive that a problem exists, that change is desirable, and that it is possible. These people then must decide how best to go about enlisting others to get the information needed to assess the problem and to develop a strategy leading to implementation of a plan of action. However, we know that those people who are prepared to initiate change within their own groups, organizations, or communities are often in a very unfavorable position from which to do so. In stable groups especially, it is the marginal or atypical person who is apt to be receptive to new ideas and practices or who can economically or socially afford to run the risk of failure. Thus it has been found necessary to carry out sustained efforts at innovation in which experimentation with new ideas can be followed by efforts at adapting or modifying them to fit more smoothly into existing patterns until finally what was once an innovation is itself incorporated within an altered status quo.

The Importance of Defense in Social Change

Up to this point, this chapter has touched on some of the factors contributing to the inevitability of resistance to change and has presented but not developed the major thesis that a necessary prerequisite of successful change may be the mobilization of forces against it. It has suggested that just as individuals have their defenses to ward off threat, maintain integrity, and protect themselves against the unwarranted intrusions of others' demands, so do social systems seek ways in which to defend themselves against ill-considered and overly precipitous innovations. The

existence of political opposition within local, state, and national government virtually ensures such defense to the extent that the party out of
power is sufficiently vigorous. The British system of the loyal opposition
probably epitomizes the application of the concept of necessary defense
in the area of political life.

In more implicit ways, nongovernmental aspects of community life
have their defenders, individuals and groups who constitute the spokesmen for the inner core of tradition and values. They uphold established
procedures and are quick to doubt the value of new ideas. Their importance stems from several considerations:

First, they are most likely to perceive and point out any real threats
to the well-being of the system which may be unanticipated consequences
of projected changes.

Second, they are especially likely to react against any change that
might reduce the integrity of the system.

Third, they are sensitive to any indication that those seeking to produce change fail to understand or identify with the core values of the
system they seek to influence.

The Defender Role

The defender role is played out in a variety of ways depending on such
factors as the nature of the setting itself, the kind of change contemplated, the characteristics of the group or individual seeking to institute
change, and the change strategy employed. In a process of orderly and
gradual change, the defender role may be taken by a well-established,
respected member of the system whose at least tacit sanction must be
gained for a new undertaking to succeed. In a situation of open conflict,
where mistrust runs high, the defender role may be assumed by those
able to become more openly and perhaps irrationally vitriolic in their
opposition. They are often viewed by the proponents of change as im-
possibly intractable and dismissed as "rabble-rousers" or "crackpots."
This was frequently the attitude of profluoridationists toward the anti's.

Though crackpots may emerge as defenders under certain circumstances, so long as they are given support by a substantial segment of
the population, even though it may be a minority, they are expressing a
reaction of all or part of the target system against real threat of some
kind. In one community, I observed a well-educated group of residents
vote overwhelmingly against fluoridation at a town meeting, even though,
as I viewed it, the small body of antifluoridationists expressed themselves
in a highly emotional, irrational way. In later conversations it appeared
that many who voted against fluoridation actually favored it. They were
influenced not by the logic of the defenders but by other dynamics in the

situation, which presumably the defenders also were reflecting. Some of those who voted "no" were unprepared to force fluorides on a minority; others pointed out that those presenting the case for fluorides had neglected to involve the voters in considering the true nature and extent of the problem of tooth decay; and a third group wondered why the health officer and others fighting for the change were so insistent on pushing their plan through immediately rather than asking the town to consider the problem at a more leisurely pace through the more usual committee procedure. The profluoridationists, on the other hand, were discouraged by the vote, felt rejected by fellow townspeople, and had grave doubts about bringing the issue up again in view of the fact that "they don't want to protect their children's teeth."

In the instance of fluoridation, the defenders usually have been drawn from the ranks of those who do not hold public office and who do not consider themselves to be members of the "establishment." This is not always the case, however. In civil rights controversies the change agents typically are the disenfranchised; the defenders occupy public office or appear to be close to the sources of existing power. But no matter whether the innovation comes from top down or bottom up, in each situation the defenders are representing value positions which have been important not only to themselves but to larger groups of constituents, and presumably to the maintenance of the culture itself.

In the Boston controversy over de facto school segregation, the school committee chairman was elected by an overwhelming vote of those who, however bigoted many of them may be, believe they are defending their property values, the integrity of neighborhood schools, and their right to stand up against those who are trying to push them around. If any of us were faced in our neighborhoods with the prospect of a state toll road sweeping away our homes, we, too, might convince ourselves that we could properly rise up in defense of the same values. The point is not whether the schools should remain segregated; they should not. Rather, as change agents we must be concerned with the opposition's values and recognize that, to a great extent, their values are ours as well. Moreover, it would help if we could grant that, in upholding these values, the defenders—however wrong we believe they are in the stands they take and the votes they cast—are raising questions which are important in our society and which we must answer with them. It is far too easy to dismiss neighborhood schools as a reactionary myth or to hold that they are unimportant in face of the larger objective of reducing intergroup barriers. The issues become far more complex when we grant that neighborhood schools were established because, in the judgment of many educators and citizens, they had merits apart from the current controversy over segregation. Once having granted this, the problem becomes one of seeking solutions which can minimize the losses in respect to such merits and maximize the gains in respect to integration. I would predict that if change agents were to consider seriously the defenders' concerns in the case of school integration, many of them would no longer feel so embattled and would no longer require the kind of school committee leadership which was recently overwhelmingly renominated in Boston.

But what about the motives of those who lead the opposition to good causes? Are they not likely to seize on virtuous issues simply as ways to manipulate opinion and to rally more support? No doubt they are. Nonetheless, I think the point still holds that the virtues are there to be manipulated. They can be used as a smoke screen by demagogues only so long as those who follow them are convinced that the agents of change are themselves unscrupulous, unprincipled, or unfeeling. Therefore, we add to the anxieties and opposition of those who are being rallied by the demagogues if we dismiss the demagogues and fail to come to grips with the concerns of those who uphold them.

Of course, demagogues and rabble-rousers do more than articulate the *values* of their followers. They also dare to give voice to the frustration and sense of helpless rage which the followers feel but usually cannot express. Those who are the targets of change usually do not feel it safe to give vent to their true feelings. The man who is a demagogue in the eyes of his opponent is usually a courageous spokesman to the follower whom he is serving as a defender.

How the Change Agent Views the Defender

Thus, an important implication for the change agent is that the defender, whoever he may be and however unscrupulously or irrationally he may appear to present himself and his concerns, usually has something of great value to communicate about the nature of the system which the change agent is seeking to influence. If the change agent views the situation with a sympathetic understanding of what the defenders are seeking to protect, either a modification of the change itself or of the strategy being used to achieve it may prove desirable. In certain situations the participation of defenders in the change process may even lead to the development of more adequate plans and to the avoidance of some hitherto unforeseen consequences of the projected change.

It is important, therefore, for those seeking change to consider the costs of ignoring, overriding, or dismissing as irrational those who emerge as their opponents. To ignore that which is being defended may mean to ignore flaws in the planned change; it may also mean that the process of change becomes transformed into a conflict situation in which energies become increasingly devoted to winning rather than to solving the original problem.

Outcome of the Defender Role

What happens to the defender role during a period of change is no doubt a function of many factors: the nature of the issue, previous relationships between opposing sides, the various constraints of time, urgency of the problem, and so on. We are all familiar with situations in which defenders and protagonists of change have become locked in fierce conflict until finally the defenders have either won out or been shattered and forced to succumb. Frequent examples can be found in the early history of urban renewal, when entire urban neighborhoods were destroyed and their defenders swept away as a consequence. (The West End of Boston is one example.) It is also possible for conflict to continue indefinitely with neither side able to gain the advantage, with the result that both sides contribute to the ultimate loss of whatever values each was seeking to uphold. Labor-management disputes which shatter entire communities are instances where the interplay between innovative and defensive forces ceases to be constructive.

Often in communities the defenders of values no longer widely held become boxed in and remain in positions of repeated but usually futile opposition to a series of new influences. The consensus of the community has shifted in such a way as to exclude those who may once have been influential. In their encapsulation these individuals and groups are no longer defenders in the sense the term is being used here; for they no longer participate meaningfully in the changes going on around them.

Finally, as has already been suggested, the defenders may in a sense be co-opted by the change agents in such a way as to contribute to an orderly change process.

School Administrator: Defender or Change Agent?

Within school systems the balance between innovation and defense must always be delicate, often precarious. The history of education in this country is full of examples of major innovations, accomplished by an outstanding superintendent, which, no matter what their success, were immediately eliminated by his successor. Sometimes disgruntled citizens who have been unsuccessful in opposing innovations are better able to mobilize their opposition when no longer faced with powerful professional leadership. Sometimes teachers and staff members who have conformed to, but not accepted, the changes feel more secure to express their opposition to a new superintendent.

It has been pointed out by Neal Gross and others[1] that the superintendent of a public school system faces the almost impossible task of mediating between the conflicting demands of staff, community, and other groups. He is almost continuously confronted with the opposing influences of innovators and defenders, not to mention the many bystanders within the system who simply wish to be left alone when differences arise. Under the circumstances it may well be that one of the most important skills a superintendent can develop is his ability to create conditions in which the interplay between change agents and defenders can occur with a minimum of rancor and a maximum of mutual respect. As we have seen in New York City and elsewhere, however, controversies do arise—such as in civil rights—in which the superintendent seems unable to play a facilitating role.

In situations that are less dramatic and conflict-laden, the superintendent and other school administrators are usually in a position where they can, and indeed must, be both change agents and defenders. In the face of rapid social change they face the challenge of learning how to foster innovation while, at the same time, finding the most constructive ways in which to act in defense of the integrity of their systems. It is also important that they learn how to differentiate between change which may pose real threat and change which is resisted simply because it is new and feels alien. Perhaps most important of all, they have the opportunity of educating the change agents with whom they work, either those inside their systems or those from the outside, to the point where the change agents perceive, understand, and value the basic functions and purposes of the schools.

The Force Field of the Defender

In human relations training we have frequently used Lewin's force field model[2] as a way to introduce learners to the objective analysis of the forces driving towards and restraining against a desired change. Here, too, we have tended to view the change field through the eyes of the protagonists. I think it would be illuminating, for example, in any study of educational innovation, to attempt to secure an analysis of the force field from defenders as well as change agents at several stages of the innovative process. Comparative analysis of the views of protagonists and defenders might help illuminate the biases of the change agents and clarify more adequately the underlying origins of the opposition within the target system. It also should provide us with a better understanding of the dynamics of the defender role and how it can be more adequately taken into account in programs of social innovation.

Notes

1. Neal Gross, A. W. McEachern, and W. S. Mason, *Explorations in Role Analysis: Studies of the School Superintendency Role* (New York: John Wiley & Sons, 1958).
2. Kurt Lewin, *Field Theory in Social Science* (New York: Harper & Brothers, 1951).

Chapter 11 **Program Change and Organizational Properties**

Jerald Hage and Michael Aiken

A major problem in the study of organizations is the analysis of organizational change. One of the difficulties in studying change is the determination of an adequate definition of organizational change.[1] Etzioni has suggested that most organizational studies implicitly, if not explicitly, involve the study of change of some variable or property.[2] This difficulty has been labeled by Parsons as the problem of change within a system as opposed to change of the system.[3] The difficulty lies in determining which kind of change results in a change of the organizational system. New techniques may be adopted, new models may be tried, and new rules and policies may be formulated; yet these are changes that do not necessarily imply fundamental changes in the organizational system. We shall offer a tentative solution to this problem by limiting our analysis to one kind of change within the system—the adoption of new programs or services. This kind of change appears to be an important one albeit not the only kind because it can imply changes in techniques, rules, or even goals. We are interested in studying the relationship between different organizational properties and the rate of program change, and we assume that the rate of program change, as well as other organizational properties, can be conceived most advantageously as variables in a system. We assume that a change in one variable leads to a change in other variables. If different rates of program change are related to different configurations on other organizational properties, then we can speak of different systems. This is our approach to the problem of studying organizational change.

In our study, we have measured the rate of program change in sixteen organizations over a five-year period.[4] This rate is then related to other organizational properties, for example, job satisfaction, codification of rules, decision-making, which are measured cross-sectionally, not longitudinally. While this prevents our making any statements about cause and effect, it does allow us to examine how different rates of program change are associated with various organizational properties.

To this end, we studied sixteen social welfare organizations staffed largely by professionally trained personnel. These organizations provide a particularly interesting testing ground for hypotheses relating rate of program change to other organizational properties, since the organizations provide services for the physically handicapped, emotionally disturbed, or mentally retarded. It might be assumed that each agency would attempt to add as many new programs as resources allow, but this was not the case. Some welfare organizations were primarily concerned with the quantity of client service. Given additional financial resources, these organizations would probably either reduce the caseload of staff members or increase the number of clients serviced. For example, a county children's welfare department had added only one new program in the previous five years and had no plans for future changes. This agency was primarily concerned with reducing the caseloads of its social workers. The rationale was not to improve the quality of service but, rather, to reduce turnover among its social workers, since the caseload was usually high in this agency, well beyond typical limits. Similarly, the head of a private home for emotionally disturbed children reported that no new programs had been added in his agency in the previous five years. In contrast, some welfare organizations were primarily concerned with the quality of client service. These organizations would probably use additional financial resources to add new programs or techniques. A county mental hospital, the organization in our study with the highest rate of program change, had added eight new programs in the past five years, including a sheltered workshop, a training program in group therapy for the attendants, and a placement service. In addition, there were already plans afoot for future changes. Similarly, a private home for emotionally disturbed boys had added six new programs in the last five years and had plans for still more. One of the greatest concerns in this organization was that the caseload might increase, since the agency head felt that the major emphasis should be placed on improving the quality rather than the quantity of client service. The contrasting policies of these organizations cut across the different kinds of goals and are reflected in the varying rates of program change among the sixteen organizations. The rate of program change by type of organization is shown in Table 11-1. While rehabilitation centers have the greatest incidence of program change, and social casework agencies the least, there are still considerable variations among these categories of organizations that ostensibly have similar goals. Furthermore, the crucial question is whether a re-

TABLE 11-1

Average Number of Program Changes by Type of Organization

Type of Organization	Number of Organizations	Average Number of Program Changes	Range
Rehabilitation centers	3	4.67	3–6
Hospitals	3	4.67	3–8
Special education departments—public schools	1	4.00	4
Homes for emotionally disturbed	3	2.67	0–6
Social casework agencies	6	1.33	0–3

habilitation center with a low rate of program change has organizational characteristics that are similar to a social casework agency with a low rate of program change.

The assumption of an organization as a system implies that certain organizational configurations are most likely to be associated with a high rate of program change. This also implies that if a high rate of program change occurs in an organization, it is likely to bring about changes in the working conditions of the organization.[5] Our data are not longitudinal, and thus it becomes impossible to stipulate any cause or effect relationships.[6] That is, we are unable to stipulate if program change brings about alternatives in other organizational properties or if new programs are introduced because of the presence of some other organizational characteristics. While our study is framed in the latter sense, this is simply for the convenience of the presentation of our findings. We would like to know organizational scores at both the beginning and end of the five-year period to unravel this problem, but unfortunately we only know organizational characteristics at the end of the five-year period.

Our purpose in this chapter, then, is to relate the organizational characteristics of complexity, centralization, formalization, and job satisfaction to the rate of program change. We hypothesize that the rate of program change is positively related to the degree of complexity and job satisfaction, and negatively related to the degree of centralization and formalization.[7] The rationale for each hypothesis is discussed below as the data are examined.

STUDY DESIGN AND METHODOLOGY

The data upon which this study is based were gathered in sixteen social welfare agencies located in a large midwest metropolis in 1964. Ten agencies were private; six were either public or branches of public agencies. These agencies were all the larger welfare organizations that provide rehabilitation, psychiatric services, and services for the mentally retarded as defined by the directory of the Community Chest. The agencies vary in size from twelve to several hundred. Interviews were conducted with 314 staff members of these sixteen organizations. Respondents within each organization were selected by the following criteria: (*a*) all executive directors and department heads; (*b*) in departments of less than ten members, one half of the staff was selected randomly; (*c*) in departments of more than ten members, one third of the staff was selected randomly. Nonsupervisory administrative and maintenance personnel were not interviewed.

This sampling procedure divides the organization into levels and departments. Job occupants in the upper levels were selected because they are most likely to be key decision-makers and to determine organizational policy, whereas job occupants in the lower levels were selected randomly. The different ratios within departments ensured that smaller departments were adequately represented. Professionals, such as psychiatrists, social workers, rehabilitation counselors, and the like, are included because they are intimately involved in the achievement of organizational goals and are likely to have organizational power. Nonprofessionals, such as attendants, janitors, and secretaries are excluded because they are less directly involved in the achievement of organizational goals and have little or no power. The number of interviews varied from seven in the smallest to forty-one in one of the largest agencies.

It should be stressed that in this study the units of analysis are organizations, not individuals in the organizations. Information obtained from respondents was pooled to reflect properties of the sixteen organizations, and these properties are then related to one another.[8] Aggregating individual data in this way presents methodological problems for which there are yet no satisfactory solutions. For example, if all respondents are equally weighted, undue weight is given to respondents lower in the hierarchy. Yet those higher in the chain of command, not those lower in the chain of command, are most likely to make the decisions which give an agency its ethos.[9]

We attempt to compensate for this by computing an organizational score from the means of social position within the agency. A social position is defined by the level or stratum in the organization and the department or type of professional activity. For example, if an agency's professional staff consists of psychiatrists and social workers, each divided into two hierarchical levels, the agency has four social positions: supervisory psychiatrists, psychiatrists, supervisory social workers, and social workers. A mean was then computed for each social position in the agency. The organizational score for a given variable was determined by computing the average of all social position means in the agency.[10]

The procedure for computing organizational scores parallels the method utilized in selecting respondents. It attempts to represent organizational life more accurately by not giving disproportionate weight to those social positions that have little power and that are little involved in the achievement of organizational goals.

Computation of means for each social position has the advantage of avoiding the potential problem created by the use of different sampling ratios. In effect, responses are standardized by organizational location— level and department—and then combined into an organizational score. Computation of means of social position also has a major theoretical advantage in that it focuses on the sociological perspective of organizational reality. We consider an organization to be a collection of social positions which we call jobs, not simply an aggregate of individuals. Ideally, sociological properties are more than a summation of psychological properties. We feel that our computation procedures are, hopefully, more consistent with a "sociological imagination."

ORGANIZATIONAL PROPERTIES AND RATE OF PROGRAM CHANGE

Following the work of Pugh et al., we find it useful to make a distinction between structural variables and performance variables as two special kinds of organizational properties.[11] The former refer to the arrangements of positions or jobs within the organization, for example, the utilization of different professional specialties or the degree of complexity, the distribution of power or the degree of centralization, the utilization of rules or the degree of formalization. The latter refer to the outcomes of the arrangements of positions, for example, the rate of program change, the degree of job satisfaction, the volume of production. In addition we examine a personality characteristic of the individuals who work in the organization, namely, their attitudes toward change. Since we are interested in rates of program change, it is entirely possible that this is affected not only by the structural and performance characteristics of the organization but also by the general orientations of the individual members. Admittedly these are not the only distinctions that can be made, but they provide a useful framework for distinguishing among major kinds of variables, helping to isolate the characteristics that are part of the system.

STRUCTURAL VARIABLES:
THE DEGREE OF COMPLEXITY

Since the publication of the English translation of Durkheim's *The Division of Labor,* the degree of complexity, or specialization, has been a key concept in the organizational literature.[12] Yet this variable has seldom been systematically related to other organizational properties. For our purposes, we define organizational complexity with three alternative empirical indicators: occupational specialties, the length of training required by each occupation, and the degree of professional activity associated with each occupation. The greater the number of specialties, the greater the length of training required by each occupation; and the greater the degree of professional activity, the more complex the organizational structure. The term "specialization" has frequently been used to describe both this phenomenon and the minute parceling of work such as that of an assembly line, where training of job occupants is minimized. From our perspective, the latter is the opposite of complexity. In order to avoid terminological confusion, we prefer to use the word "complexity" to refer to the former phenomenon, since we feel that this is more consistent with Durkheim's usage of the term.[13]

A recently published axiomatic theory hypothesizes a direct relationship between complexity and the rate of program change.[14] There are several reasons why these two properties should be related in this way. The addition of new programs frequently necessitates the addition of new occupations. Job occupants of such occupational specialties often have a particular organizational perspective which leads to the introduction of still other new programs. Further, the professional activities of job staff members function as communications links between the organization and its competitors, providing a source of information about new ideas and techniques. In addition, conflicts among the different occupational specialties in an organization act as a further dynamic force for the creation of new programs. The more professionalized the occupations, the greater the struggle to prove the need for expansion.[15]

In our interviews with staff members of organizations, each respondent was asked to describe the nature of his duties, the extent of his training, and the amount of his professional activity. Just as the number of jobs reflects the complexity of the organization, it was our belief that the more the training required, the more the probable complexity of the job itself, so that this needed to be considered as well. Furthermore, the more the professional activity of the job occupants, the more likely there would be continued increases in the complexity of the job. On the basis of the respondents' answers to our questions, three indicators of organizational complexity were computed. The first indicator is the number of occupational specialties, which was measured by counting the numbers of different kinds of work that exist in an agency. There is a correlation of .48 between the number of occupational specialties and the rate of program change. A variety of occupational perspectives is associated with a higher rate of change.

We have already stated that we are unable to determine causation because our data are taken at one point of time. Since occupational specialties more than any of our other variables can be closely linked to the programs that are added, we reconstructed the number of occupational specialties that existed in each organization prior to 1959, the beginning of the five-year period we used for measuring the rate of program change. While the number of occupational specialties was altered in several organizations, the correlation between these two properties remained virtually unchanged $(r = .45)$.[16]

The amount of professional training is another indicator of the complexity of organizations. This was measured by computing an index reflecting the degree of formal training and other professional training for each social position in the organization.[17] As can be seen from Table 11-2, there is a weak but positive correlation between the organization score of professional training and the rate of program change $(r = .14)$. Thus the amount of professional training in an organization is positively associated with the rate of program change.

To measure the extent of the extra-organizational professional activity of members of each organization, the respondents were asked to report the number of professional associations to which they belonged, the proportion of meetings attended, the number of papers given, and offices held, all of which represent professional involvement.[18] The higher this score, that is, the greater the extra-organizational professional activities of members of the organization, the more likely it was to have a high rate of program change, as shown in Table 11-2 $(r = .37)$. It should be noted that the amount of professional involvement is more highly related to program change than the amount of professional training.

TABLE 11-2
Rate of Program Change and Other Organizational Properties

Organizational Properties	Pearson Product-Moment Correlation Coefficients of Each Organizational Characteristic with Rate of Program Change*
Structural variables:	
Degree of complexity:	
Measure of the number of occupational specialties	.48
Measure of the amount of extra-organizational professional activity	.37
Measure of the amount of professional training	.14
Degree of centralization:	
Measure of the degree of participation in organizational decision-making	.49
Measure of hierarchy of authority	—.09
Degree of formalization:	
Measure of the degree of job codification	—.47
Measure of the degree of rule observation	.13
Performance variables:	
Degree of satisfaction:	
Measure of job satisfaction	.38
Measure of expressive satisfaction	—.17
Personality variables:	
Motive of self-interest and negative attitudes toward change	—.04
Motive of values and positive attitudes toward change	—.15

*The measures of association reported here are Pearson product-moment correlation coefficients. The units of analysis in this report are the sixteen organizations in our study, not our 314 individual respondents. Product-moment correlation coefficients are highly sensitive to even slight modifications of numerical scores with so few cases. We rejected the use of nonparametric measures of association because our scales are lineal and not ordinal; nonparametric statistics necessitate our "throwing away" some of the magnitude of variations in our data. Since these sixteen organizations represent a universe of organization, tests of statistical significance are inappropriate.

Involvement in extra-organizational professional activities evidently heightens awareness of programmatic and technological developments within a profession.[19] Professionally active job occupants introduce new ideas into the organization, and the outcome is a high rate of program change. Similarly, new programs require the addition of new job occupants who are highly trained. A plausible line of reasoning is that greater extra-organizational professional activity implies a greater emphasis on the improvement of the quality of client service, whether the clients are emotionally disturbed or mentally retarded. Such an emphasis requires a continual application of new knowledge, whether reflected in new programs or in new techniques. The number of occupational specialties and the amount of extra-organizational professional activity were themselves related; the correlation coefficient was .29. The sheer presence of different occupational perspectives, implying the idea of occupational conflict, appears to heighten professional involvement, as was suggested by Durkheim.[20]

STRUCTURAL VARIABLES: THE DEGREE OF CENTRALIZATION

There are many debates in the organizational literature about the relative merits of centralization as opposed to decentralization of decision-making. On the one hand, Weber argued that strict hierarchy of authority increased both the volume of production and the efficiency of an organization.[21] On the other hand, the human relations specialists have argued that decentralization increases job satisfaction and reduces resistance to change.[22] Both arguments are probably correct.

In our study the staff members were asked how often they participated in organizational decisions regarding the hiring of personnel, the promotions of personnel, the adoption of new organizational policies, and the adoption of new programs or services.[23] The organizational score was based on the average degree of participation in these four areas of decision-making. As can be seen from Table 11-2, the greater the participation in agency-wide decisions, the greater the rate of program change in the organization ($r = .49$). Decentralization allows for the interplay of a variety of occupational perspectives. As Thompson has suggested, a centralized organization is one in which change can be, and frequently is, easily vetoed.[24]

Agency-wide decisions are not the only kind that are made. Other decisions are those concerning the performance of a specific job. Agency-wide decisions are basically decisions about the control of resources, while job decisions are basically decisions about the control of work. It is at least logically possible that the centralization of the former kind of decision-making can be associated with the decentralization of the latter kind of decision-making. We measure the degree of decision-making about work with a scale called the "hierarchy of authority."[25] This scale was found to have little relationship with the rate of program change, although it was in the predicted direction ($r = -.09$). It is the centralization of decisions about organizational resources, not the centralization of work control, that is highly related to low rates of this kind of organizational change.

STRUCTURAL VARIABLES: THE DEGREE OF FORMALIZATION

Rules or regulations are important organizational mechanisms that may be used to ensure the predictability of performance. There are two aspects of the use of rules as a mechanism of social control; one is the number of regulations specifying who is to do what, where, and when; we call this the degree of job codification. Another is the diligency in enforcing those rules that specify who is doing what, where, and when; this we call rule observation. The latter is important because many organizations may not enforce all regulations. The degree of formalization is defined as both the degree of job codification as well as the degree of rule observation.

While it has been commonplace to argue that bureaucracies retard change, there have been few studies that have examined this proposition in a comparative framework. One of the essential elements of bureaucracy is its emphasis on formalization. Our hypothesis is that the two aspects of formalization outlined above retard the adoption of new programs because they discourage individual initiative.[26] Clearly codified jobs that are closely supervised to ensure conformity also reduce the search for better ways of doing work. Such a use of rules encourages ritualistic and unimaginative behavior.

The two indexes of formalization were constructed on the basis of a factor analysis of scales developed by Hall.[27] At best these scales are only rough indicators of the degree of formalization in an organization. As indicated by Table 11-2, job codification is inversely related to the rate of organizational change ($r = -.47$). The relationship between the degree of rule observation and the rate of program change is much weaker and is in a direction opposite from our prediction ($r = .13$).

In order to determine whether each of the observed relationships between each of our indicators of various structural properties and the rate of program change is spurious, multiple and partial correlation analyses are introduced.

As shown in Table 11-3, only two of these variables have strong and independent relationships with the rate of program change: the degree of job codification ($rp = -.47$) and the degree of participation in decision-making ($rp = .39$). It should be noted that the β weights for participation in decision-making are greater (.555), however, than the β weights for job codification ($-.379$).

The number of occupational specialties and the degree of hierarchy have moderate but independent relationships with the number of program innovations, although the latter variable is related in the opposite

TABLE 11-3
Multiple and Partial Correlation Analysis of the Number of Program Changes and Other Organizational Properties

Organizational Properties	Partial Correlation Coefficient*	β Coefficients in Standard Form†
Degree of complexity:		
Measure of the number of occupational specialties‡	+.24	+.202
Measure of the amount of extra-organizational professional activity	+.08	+.104
Measure of professional training	−.10	−.137
Degree of centralization:		
Measure of the degree of participation in organizational decision-making	+.39	+.555
Measure of hierarchy of authority	+.23	+.231
Degree of formalization:		
Measure of the degree of job codification	−.47	−.379
Measure of the degree of rule observation	+.15	+.134
Coefficient of determination		.558
Multiple correlation coefficient		.75

*These are the partial correlation coefficients between each variable and the rate of program change, controlling for the other six structural variables. Thus, each is a sixth-order partial correlation coefficient.
†These are β coefficients in standard form, i.e., β weights.
‡This is the number of occupational specialties as of 1959, before the program changes discussed in this chapter were introduced.

direction when the other six variables are controlled. The degree of extra-organizational activity, the degree of professional training, and the degree of rule observation have little relationship with the number of program innovations after controlling for the other factors, although rule observation remains virtually unchanged.

PERFORMANCE VARIABLES:
THE DEGREE OF SATISFACTION

Since the famous French and Coch experiment, the advocates of the human relations approach to organizational analysis have emphasized the importance of morale as a factor in understanding differential acceptance of change and, therefore, implicitly differential rates of program change.[28] We developed two different measures of morale—an index of job satisfaction and an index of satisfaction with expressive relations.[29] There is a correlation of .38 between job satisfaction and rate of program change. On the other hand, satisfaction with expressive relations is negatively correlated, albeit the size of the correlation is small ($r = -.17$). This suggests a plausible explanation for several contradictory viewpoints in the literature concerning morale and organizational change. The work of Coch and French suggests a positive relationship between morale and change, but a series of studies by Mann, Hoffman, and others at the University of Michigan have noted that change creates social strain in the organization.[30] One may infer, not necessarily from our data, that job satisfaction may be a necessary precondition for the introduction of changes, but after this change has been introduced it may have disruptive and negative effects on social relationships among members in an organization. It is also plausible to argue that the organizational conditions that facilitate the introduction of change, namely, occupational diversity and decentralization, reduce satisfaction with expressive relationships because of the conflicts they engender.

PERSONALITY VARIABLES:
GENERAL ORIENTATION TO CHANGE

It is argued by some social psychologists and psychologists that all collective properties of organization, such as the degree of centralization, the degree of formalization, or the degree of complexity, are ultimately reducible to psychological factors. Since this is a common argument, we attempted to measure several personality variables that might account for differences in organizational rates of program change. It could be argued that change occurs in organizations because the organization has a high proportion of individuals who are favorably oriented to social change. Selznik has suggested the idea of selective recruitment of certain personality types; that is, when an organization needs new job occupants, the attempt is made to recruit individuals who have personality attributes consistent with organizational needs.[31] Mann and Hoffman have hypothesized the obverse of this process, namely, that individuals who cannot tolerate change will leave changing organizations and seek work in more stable ones.[32] Finally, Homans and others have argued that sociological variables are fundamentally reducible to psychological variables.[33] While we do not accept this argument, we included measures of individual orientations toward change developed by Sister Marie Augusta Neal in an attempt to test the validity of such assertions.[34]

The Neal batteries of self-interest motives, value motives, pro-change motives, and anti-change motives were factor analyzed and yielded two clear factors; one factor contains items representing attitudes of self-interest and a negative attitude toward change, while the second factor contains items representing attitudes of ideals and a positive orientation toward change. We would expect the former to be *negatively* associated with rate of program change and the latter to be *positively* associated with program change. We found only a modest relationship between these measures of attitudes toward change and the amount of organizational program change.

The measure of self-interest and anti-change was virtually unrelated to program change ($r = -.04$), while the measure of ideals and pro-change was related to program change opposite from the expected direction ($r = -.15$).

An organization can have a high proportion of job occupants who are favorably disposed toward change in their personal orientations, and yet the organization does not necessarily adopt new programs. The reverse pattern is equally true.

What this suggests is that the personality attributes included in our study add little to our understanding of organizational change as we have measured it. On the other hand, there is the possibility that there are other personality variables that are appropriate for the understanding of organizational change.

It would be desirable to know the relative importance of performance variables, such as job satisfaction and the structural properties, but the limited size of our universe of organizations ($n = 16$) makes a multiple correlational and partial correlational analysis (reported in Table 11-3) for all the variables that we have measured inappropriate. It should be understood that there is a very strong relationship between the degree of centralization and job satisfaction in particular.[35] At the same time, the concept of a system assumes that there is this high degree of interdependence. The precise importance of each of these variables must be determined with a much larger number of organizations and preferably with longitudinal measurements.

CONTEXTUAL VARIABLES, ORGANIZATIONAL PROPERTIES, AND RATE OF PROGRAM CHANGE

The fact that there are varying rates of program change for our different kinds of agencies, as indicated in Table 11-1, suggests that there may be disparate situations faced by each of our organizations. The rate of technological change may be faster in rehabilitation than in social casework agencies.

In particular, the organizations in our study vary considerably in their ease of access to resources, whether personnel or finances. They differ considerably in their age and autonomy. These and other indicators of their environmental situation can have an impact on the organization and its ability to adopt new programs. By studying the impact of such variables as auspices, size, and function, it becomes possible to view the process by which organizations are likely to develop one or another system. It also allows us some insight into the generalizability of our findings. If one of these variables accounts for most of the observed relationship between the rate of program change and the organizational properties, then we are aware of a significant limitation on our findings.

In a recent review of the organizational literature, Pugh and his associates suggest a number of contextual variables that can be used either as controls or as independent variables when examining the relationships among organizational properties. The variables that they discuss are: origin and history, ownership and control, size, charter technology, location, resources, and interdependence.[36] Presumably, each of these factors could have an impact on the characteristics of the organization, including the rate of program change. In particular, there is always the possibility that any of the relationships reported in Table 11-2 are simply a function of some of these contextual variables. For example, there is a standard organizational hypothesis that increasing size means more centralization and formalization, and, therefore, one might expect large organizations to have low rates of program change as a consequence. Another standard hypothesis is that older organizations are likely to be more bureaucratic and therefore to have lower rates of change.

To explore the relative importance of these environmental factors for the relationships discussed above, we employed partial correlations. A fourth-order partial correlation was computed between each of the organizational properties and rate of program change, controlling for size, auspices, age of organization, and major function.

Size represents the rank order of organizations by number of employees in the organization; it is the same as the contextual concept discussed by Pugh et al.

Auspices, that is, whether the organization is public or private, is similar to their concept of ownership and control. Since none of our organizations is a business, most of the analytical distinctions that they discussed do not apply. It should be noted that "auspices" not only includes the idea of the nature of the accountability of the chief executive, but it suggests the sources of revenue, an idea contained in the concept of resources. The public agencies are largely tax-supported, while the private agencies rely upon donations, grants, and fees. In other words, the distinction between public and private carries many implications; therefore, the word "auspices" appears to be a more appropriate one than either ownership or resources.

The age of the organization is only one aspect of the organization's origin and history, but it is an attempt to measure some of the ideas discussed by Pugh et al.

Finally, function is our attempt to divide a relatively homogeneous universe of organizations into at least two kinds of goals and technologies. We separated our organizations into those that deal with their clients for a relatively short period of time, the typical casework situation found in the social welfare agencies, and those that deal with their clients for a relatively long period of time, the sheltered workshop, the school, and hospital situations. The one-hour interview and the total institution reflect different kinds of technology, at least in terms of their intensiveness, even though all of our agencies are concerned with providing rehabilitative and psychiatric services.[37]

Location and interdependence are two contextual variables discussed by Pugh et al. that are not included in our analysis. Location is impossible to include because all of our agencies are in the same metropolitan area. We feel that interdependence is an exceedingly important contextual variable, but we are still in the process of collecting data on it. A separate analysis of this contextual variable and its impact will be made at a later date.

Not all of the four contextual variables are related to the rate of program change. Both age ($r = -.03$) and auspices ($r = -.06$) were unrelated to this kind of organizational change as we have measured it. But size ($r = -.61$) and function ($r = .58$) were highly related to the rate of program change. The larger the size of the organization and the more time the client spends in the organization, the higher the rate of program change. Since these contextual factors are themselves interrelated (larger organizations were much more likely to be total institutions) and since these factors do have an impact on rate of program change, the question remains whether the relationships between our dependent variable and the other organizational properties will be maintained if we simultaneously control for all four of the contextual variables. To put it another way, we want to know if our results are a consequence of organizational arrangements or a consequence of the environmental situations.

The partial correlation analysis is reported in Table 11-4. If this table is compared with Table 11-2, it will be noted that the correlations remain approximately the same when size, age, auspices, and function are controlled, except for two measures: the number of occupational specialties and the hierarchy of authority. Function has a very high correlation with the number of occupational specialties, while size and auspices have moderately high correlations. The more time the client spends in the organization, the greater the number of occupational specialties ($r = .67$). If the organization is public, there are likely to be more occupational specialties than if it is private, suggesting different availability of funds ($r = .39$). Similarly, larger organizations have more occupational specialties ($r = .41$). When function, size, and auspices are held constant, the relationship between number of occupational specialties and rate of change disappears. This suggests a process when the time ordering of these variables is considered.

The function of the organization, its size, and its auspices affect the number of specialties it has; this in turn is associated with the rate of program change. The partial correlation analysis makes clear, however, that the number of occupational specialties has little independent effect in explaining the variation in rate of program change once auspices, size, age, and function are held constant.

In contrast, the partial correlation between rate of program change and hierarchy of authority, holding constant the four contextual factors, has the predicted negative relationship with rate of program change. In fact, the relationship is stronger after controlling for these contextual factors.

In general, the observed relationships between rate of program change and the organizational properties remain, even after simultaneously controlling for these contextual factors. That is, even though the context or environment affects the organization, most of the organizational properties examined are still related to the rate of program change.

Table 11-4

Rate of Program Change and Other Organizational Properties When Size, Auspices, Age of Organization, and Function Are Controlled

Organizational Properties	Partial Correlations with Rate of Program Change*
Structural variables:	
Degree of complexity:	
Measure of the number of occupational specialties†	.00
Measure of the amount of professional activity	.11
Measure of the amount of professional training	.14
Degree of centralization:	
Measure of the degree of participation in decision-making	.46
Measure of hierarchy of authority	—.37
Degree of formalization:	
Measure of the degree of job codification	—.33
Measure of the degree of rule observation	—.02
Performance variable:	
Degree of satisfaction:	
Measure of job satisfaction	.27
Measure of expressive satisfaction	—.19

*These are fourth-order partial correlations, i.e., the partial correlation coefficients between each factor listed and the rate of program change, controlling for size, auspices, age of organization, and function.

†This is the number of occupational specialties as of 1959, before the program changes discussed in this study were introduced.

Another way of determining the generalizability of these findings is the examination of other studies of organizations to see if they found similar results. In a study of large business firms in the United States, Chandler suggests that increases in complexity as measured by product diversification led to the decentralization of decision-making.[38] This was especially likely to occur after the introduction of professional managers. These firms were also more likely to allocate a much larger proportion of their budget to research, indicating a higher rate of program change.

Woodward's study of some ninety industrial firms in South Essex, England, suggests that those firms that made small batches of products or custom models were more likely than the assembly-line manufacturers to have professional managers, skilled labor, decentralized decision-making, higher job satisfaction, and less routinization of procedures.[39] While this study does not have a direct measure of the rate of program change, both of these studies are at least supportive of the findings reported here.

CONCLUSIONS AND DISCUSSION

Our findings suggest the following two stories about the rate of program change. One line of reasoning is as follows: Given that there is a high rate of program change, there is likely to be relatively decentralized decision-making because of the necessity for discussions about the problems of change. There is a variety of decisions involving the allocation of personnel and funds attendant to the addition of new programs. In addition, the implementation of programs inevitably indicates contingencies not considered and engenders conflicts that must be resolved. Similarly, the high rate of program change will necessitate the relaxation of rules in order to solve the problems of implementation. There will be conflicts between the demands of the new program and previous regulations that will make rule observation difficult. The addition of new programs is likely to attract better-trained and active professional personnel who will like the challenge of change. And new programs can require, in many cases, new skills or areas of expertise relative to the organization. The high rate of job satisfaction can flow from the satisfaction of being a member of a dynamic organization. But the high rate of change creates strain in interpersonal relationships.

Another line of reasoning is as follows: If an organization is relatively decentralized, it is likely to have a variety of information channels which allow the consideration of both the need for new programs and their appropriateness. The sheer number of occupational specialties also increases the diversity of informal channels of communication. This is likely to lead to conflict among competing ideas for organizational resources. In contrast, the amount of job codification reduces the diversity of informal channels of information by circumscribing the occupants' perspectives, including the recognition of needs and the choice of remedies. Given that an organization is complex, decentralized, and non-formalized, then it is likely to be high in rate of program change. Such an organization is also likely to have high job satisfaction but low satisfaction with expressive relations. High job satisfaction evidently facilitates the introduction of changes, but the changes themselves are evidently disruptive of interpersonal relationships. The structural arrangements that facilitate change seem to generate conflicts among staff members. The diversity of occupational specialties, the power struggles in a decentralized arrangement of decision-making, and the lack of clear work boundaries—consequences of the lack of formalization—are all conducive to organizational conflicts that are manifested in dissatisfaction with expressive relationships.

The nature of our data does not allow us to choose between these two lines of reasoning. It is our belief that both are correct and reflect again the system nature of organizations. However, future research should be directed to verifying which line of reasoning is more pervasive, but this will require longitudinal studies. Our analysis indicates that rate of program change is associated with configurations on other organizational properties, supporting the basic assumption that an organization is best viewed as a system of variables. While program change is only one kind of change within the system, future research should be directed to the question of whether other changes within the system, such as changes in rules as opposed to changes in degree of job codification, changes in who makes decisions as opposed to changes in emphasis on hierarchy, changes in techniques as opposed to changes in technology, can be analyzed in the same way. We feel that this study provides an illustration of how change within the system and change of the system can be differentiated.

Our analysis indicated that different empirical indicators of the three structural properties of organizations, that is, centralization, complexity, and formalization, are related differently to the rate of change in new programs, at least among the sixteen organizations in this study. The number of occupational specialties in the organization, an indicator of complexity, is a better predictor of program change than professional training or professional activity. Participation in agency-wide decision-making is a more powerful predictor of organizational change than the degree of hierarchy of authority. Finally, the degree of job codification, an indicator of formalization, is a more powerful predictor of program change than the rule observation.

A partial correlation analysis simultaneously controlling for size, auspices, age of organization, and function demonstrated that most of the organizational properties have associations with rate of program change which are independent of variations in these contextual factors. However, function and auspices, to a lesser extent, were so strongly related to the number of occupational specialties that the relationship between number of occupational specialties—one indicator of complexity—and rate of program change disappears. Future research should attempt to consider additional contextual variables besides the ones included here.

A major theme contained in this chapter is that it is important to view organizations from a sociological viewpoint. Our method for drawing the sample and the procedure for computing scores for organizational properties conceive of organizations as a collection of social positions (or jobs), not simply as an aggregate of individuals. Several different collective properties of organizations were found to be related to the rate of change. When individual orientations toward change were measured, they were found to be relatively unrelated to the rate of organizational change, at least as we have defined it. Our findings are supportive of Durkheim's famous phrase that "social facts must be explained by other social facts." That is, we were able to explain the rate of organizational change better with other organizational properties, such as degree of centralization, degree of complexity, or degree of formalization, than with measures of attitudes of organizational members toward change. Certainly this does not constitute definitive proof, but it does suggest that emphasis on structural and performance variables in organizations may be a more fruitful way to study organizational change.

Notes

1. See Jerald Hage, "Organizational Response to Innovation" (unpub. Ph.D. diss., Columbia University, 1963), ch. 3, for a discussion of several different kinds of change.
2. Amitai Etzioni, in intro. to "Organizational Change," *Complex Organizations: A Sociological Reader,* ed. Etzioni (New York: Holt, Rinehart & Winston, 1961), pp. 341–343.
3. Talcott Parsons, *The Social System* (Glencoe, Ill.: Free Press, 1951), ch. 12.
4. Executive directors were asked: "How many new programs or services have you added in the last five years?" In many cases the new programs did not involve the addition of new personnel or new funds but, instead, represented re-allocation of existing resources. The question used a standard interval of time so that the rate could be expressed as a number. It might also be noted that the choice of an interval of time is not an easy one. We selected an interval of five years as a minimum because any shorter period is too likely to be subjected to random or episodic fluctuations.
5. In other words, all hypotheses are reversible; see Hans Zetterberg, *On Theory and Verification in Sociology* (rev. ed.; Totowa, N.J.: Bedminster, 1963), p. 11.
6. We are presently engaged in the second logical step of research, namely, the attempt to predict the future rate of program change on the basis of organizational properties measured prior in time.

7. For a discussion of why these properties should be related as hypothesized, see Jerald Hage, "An Axiomatic Theory of Organization," *Administrative Science Quarterly* 10 (Dec. 1965): 289–321.
8. A very common error in statistical analysis is the failure to realize that assumptions must be made not only about the unit of analysis, usually the individual, but also about the time and place. Few studies systematically examine these three factors together, yet each is important. Most studies should be qualified with reference to a specific time and place.
9. For a discussion of some of the basic differences between individual and collective properties, see Paul Lazarsfeld and Herbert Menzel, "On Individual and Collective Properties," in *Complex Organizations,* ed. Etzioni, pp. 422–440; and James S. Coleman, "Research Chronicle: The Adolescent Society," in *Sociologists at Work,* ed. Phillip E. Hammond (New York: Basic Books, 1964).
10. One advantage of this procedure is that it allows for the cancellation of individual errors made by the job occupants of a particular position. It also allows for the elimination of certain idiosyncratic elements that result from the special privileges a particular occupant might have received as a consequence.

    An alternative procedure for computing organizational means is to weigh all respondents equally. These two procedures yield strikingly similar results for the variables reported in this paper. The product moment correlation coefficients between the scores based on these two computational procedures were as follows for the variables indicated:

    Hierarchy of Authority .70
    Actual participation in decision making .90
    Job codification .68
    Rule observation .88
    Job satisfaction .89
    Satisfaction with expressive relations .88
    Professional training .90
    Professional activity .87
    Index of self-interest and anti-change .87
    Index of values and pro-change .74

11. D. S. Pugh et al., "A Scheme for Organizational Analysis," *Administrative Science Quarterly* 8 (1963): 289–316.
12. Emile Durkheim, *The Division of Labor in Society* (New York: Macmillan, 1933), pt. 1; also preface to 2d ed.
13. See Victor Thompson, *Modern Organization* (New York: Knopf, 1964), ch. 3.
14. See Hage, "An Axiomatic Theory," p. 303.
15. Durkheim, *Division of Labor,* pp. 267–270.
16. It should be noted that our count of occupational specialties is not based on the number of specific job titles. Instead, each respondent was asked what he did and then this was coded according to the kind of professional activity and whether it was a specialty. This procedure was used for two reasons. First, it allows for comparability across organizations. Second, it avoids the problem of task specialization where one activity might be divided into many specific and separate tasks (see Thompson, *Modern Organization,* ch. 3).
17. The index was scored as follows: (*a*) An absence of training beyond a college degree and the absence of other professional training received a

score of 0; (*b*) an absence of training beyond college degree and the presence of other professional training received a score of 1; (*c*) a presence of training beyond a college degree and the absence of other professional training received a score of 2; (*d*) a presence of training beyond a college degree and the presence of other professional training received a score of 3.

18. The index of professional activity, which ranged from 0 to 3 points, was computed as follows: (*a*) 1 point for belonging to a professional organization; (*b*) 1 point for attending at least two-thirds of the previous six meetings of any professional organization; (*c*) 1 point for the presentation of a paper or holding an office in any professional organization.

19. See Victor Thompson, "Bureaucracy and Innovation," *Administrative Science Quarterly* 10 (June 1965): 10–13.

20. Durkheim, *Division of Labor,* pp. 267–270; although he was discussing the characteristics of city life, the argument is that much more compelling in the context of an organization where interaction is facilitated.

21. Max Weber, *The Theory of Social and Economic Organization,* trans. Henderson and Parsons (Glencoe, Ill.: Free Press, 1947), pp. 334–340.

22. The classic study is, of course, Lester Coch and John French Jr., "Overcoming Resistance to Change," *Human Relations* 1 (1948): 512–532. For a review of the literature and organizational experiments reflecting this dilemma between satisfaction and production, see Nancy Morse and Everett Reimer, "The Experimental Change of a Major Organizational Variable," *Journal of Abnormal and Social Psychology* 52 (1955): 120–129.

23. The index of actual participation in decision-making was based on the following four questions: (1) How frequently do you usually participate in the decision to hire new staff? (2) How frequently do you usually participate in in the decisions on the promotion of any of the professional staff? (3) How frequently do you participate in decisions on the adoption of new policies? (4) How frequently do you participate in the decisions on the adoption of new programs? Respondents were assigned numerical scores from 1 (low participation) to 5 (high participation), depending on whether they answered "never," "seldom," "sometimes," "often," or "always," respectively, to these questions. An average score on these questions was computed for each respondent, and then the data were aggregated into organizational scores as described above.

24. Thompson, "Bureaucracy and Innovation," pp. 13–18.

25. The empirical indicators of these concepts were derived from two scales developed by Richard Hall, namely, hierarchy of authority and rules (see his "The Concept of Bureaucracy: An Empirical Assessment," *American Journal of Sociology* 69 [July 1963]: 32–40). The index of hierarchy of authority was computed by first averaging the replies of individual respondents to each of the following five statements: (1) There can be little action taken here until a supervisor approves a decision. (2) A person who wants to make his own decisions would be quickly discouraged here. (3) Even small matters have to be referred to someone higher up for a final answer. (4) I have to ask my boss before I do almost anything. (5) Any decision I make has to have my boss's approval. Responses could vary from 1 (definitely false) to 4 (definitely true). The individual scores were then combined into an organizational score as described above.

26. Robert K. Merton, "Bureaucratic Structure and Personality," in *Complex Organizations,* ed. Etzioni, pp. 48–61.

27. Hall, "Concept of Bureaucracy." The index of job codification was based on the following five questions: (1) I feel that I am my boss in most matters. (2) A person can make his own decisions without checking with anybody else. (3) How things are done here is left up to the person doing the work. (4) People here are allowed to do almost as they please. (5) Most people here make their own rules on the job. Replies to these questions were scored from 1 (definitely true) to 4 (definitely false), and then each of the respondent's answers was averaged. Thus, a high score on this index means high job codification.

The index of rule observation was computed by averaging the responses to each of the following two statements: (1) The employees are constantly being checked on for rule violations. (2) People there feel as though they are constantly being watched, to see that they obey all the rules. Respondents' answers were coded from 1 (definitely false) to 4 (definitely true), and then the average score of each respondent on these items was computed. Organizational scores were computed as previously described. On this index, a high score means a high degree of rule observation.

28. Coch and French, "Overcoming Resistance to Change."

29. We used a satisfaction scale developed by Neal Gross, Ward Mason, and Alexander McEachern, *Explorations in Role Analysis* (New York: John Wiley & Sons, 1958), Appendix B. When factor analyzed, this battery provided the following scales: job satisfaction, satisfaction with expressive relations, satisfaction with salary, and satisfaction with time. The index of job satisfaction was computed on the basis of responses to the following six questions: (1) How satisfied are you that you have been given enough authority by your board of directors to do your job well? (2) How satisfied are you with your present job when you compare it to similar positions in the state? (3) How satisfied are you with the progress you are making toward the goals which you set for yourself in your present position? (4) On the whole, how satisfied are you that (your superior) accepts you as a professional expert, to the degree to which you are entitled by reason of position, training, and experience? (5) On the whole, how satisfied are you with your present job when you consider the expectations you had when you took the job? (6) How satisfied are you with your present job in light of career expectations?

The index of expressive satisfaction was computed from responses to the following two questions: (1) How satisfied are you with your supervisor? (2) How satisfied are you with your fellow workers?

30. See Floyd C. Mann and Lawrence Williams, "Observations on the Dynamics of a Change to Electronic Data-processing Equipment," *Administrative Science Quarterly* 5 (Sept. 1960): 217–257; and Floyd Mann and T. Hoffman, *Automation and the Worker* (New York: Henry Holt, 1960). The same point is made in several other studies of organizational change; see, for example, Harriet Ronken and Paul Lawrence, *Administering Changes* (Cambridge, Mass.: Harvard Graduate Business School, 1952); and Charles Walker, *Toward the Automatic Factory* (New Haven, Conn.: Yale University Press, 1957).

31. Philip Selznick, "Critical Decisions in Organizational Development," in *Complex Organizations,* ed. Etzioni, pp. 355–362.

32. See Mann and Hoffman, *Automation.*

33. George Homans, "Bringing Men Back In," *American Sociological Review* 29 (Dec. 1964): 809–819.

34. Four scales that purport to measure attitudes toward change developed by Sister Marie Augusta Neal, *Values and Interests in Social Change* (Englewood Cliffs, N.J.: Prentice-Hall, 1965), were used.

35. See Michael Aiken and Jerald Hage, "Organizational Alienation," *American Sociological Review* 31 (Aug. 1966): 497–507, for a discussion of this relationship.

36. Pugh et al., "Scheme for Organizational Analysis." See Hage, "An Axiomatic Theory," pp. 304–306, for hypotheses concerning these contextual variables.

37. Size was based on a rank order of all salaried employees. Rank ordering was used because we had an extremely skewed distribution. Auspices is a natural dichotomy between tax-supported and non-tax-supported. Age was treated as a trichotomy because all the organizations were founded either prior to 1900, between 1919 and 1923, or after the Great Depression period. Function was measured by creating a dummy variable based on the amount of contact per week between the agency and the client. An hour or less per week, the typical casework interview, was treated as low client involvement. The sheltered workshops, the rehabilitation agencies, and the total institutions were categorized as high-involvement agencies. Ideally more distinctions would be describable, but with only sixteen organizations additional refinement becomes impossible.

38. A. D. Chandler, Jr., *Strategy and Structure* (Cambridge, Mass.: M.I.T. Press, 1962).

39. Joan Woodward, *Industrial Organization: Theory and Practice* (London: Oxford Press, 1965), ch. 2, pp. 23–25.

Part III   Models for Action in Organizational
Change

The preceding chapters have focused on theoretical perspectives for understanding the organizational context of service and models for analyzing and anticipating resistance to change activities undertaken to reduce dysfunctions in service delivery. The emphasis in Part III will be on organizational change models that have been developed in the last decade or two to deal with such dysfunctions. To conclude this part, a study of the types, frequency, and outcome of organizational change activity is also reported. These models in one way or another reflect the typical activities associated with effective planned change—that is, goal development (problem and goal selection), resource mobilization (the organizing and focusing of the supportive forces available to an action system within and external to an organization), and strategy and tactical planning (the thinking through of general and specific plans to guide behaviors of organizational change agents).

These three elements of organizational change are implicitly and explicitly discussed, analyzed, and illustrated by the chapters of Part III as part of the organizational change process. The lead selection, "Patterns of Organizational Change," advances a model of organizational change by focusing on the development of action systems as one aspect of mobilization of resources. It explicates three patterns in which an action system may be convened and by so doing highlights the crucial role of a staff member–leader or a change catalyst in organizational change. Resnick implicitly suggests a framework for thinking about organizational change that contains five components: a change catalyst, an innovation or a change, an action system, a problem to be worked on, and a plan for acceptance and widespread diffusion of an innovation by decision-makers. These components are arranged into a sequence that, while varying with each of the three patterns, is necessary for the successful completion of an organizational change project.

The emphasis in Chapter 13, "Tasks for Changing the Organization from Within," is on mobilizing resources, strategy, and tactics selection. Resnick focuses in detail on the major tasks that need to be performed by action system members, such as goal selection, predicting resistance, and selection of strategies. In addition, two of the essential interaction tasks—developing action systems and meeting with decision-makers—are discussed and illustrated.

Chapter 14, "Changing the Agency from Within," which develops the authors' model of organizational change, addresses the three elements of effective change by stressing their interrelatedness—that is, the goal of the change project is modified by the resources available, which in turn influences the strategy and tactics selected. It is the authors' contention that "the change agent is more likely to select an effective strategy if he/she bases his/her choice on a deliberate assessment of the goal and the resources available to the action system." Two other aspects of this model are also discussed: the utilization of an action system of low- and middle-echelon staff as a vehicle for the original change process, and the specification of four environments or contexts within which intervention (or preparation for intervention) can take place.

Chapter 15, developed from the innovation literature as well as the social sciences, also emphasizes the strategy question but in a different way. Rothman develops guidelines that encourage practitioners to initiate a small change in an organization and then, either through spontaneous action or the offices of a decision-making unit, to seek to spread the change to other parts of the system: "Practitioners wishing to promote an innovation in a general target system should develop it initially in a partial segment of that target system." Rothman's focus is on the activity needed to spread the innovation or change throughout the system, whereas Patti and Resnick's model focuses more on the problems involved in helping a change project get started and completed. They emphasize the early activities of organizational change in contrast to Rothman, who stresses the widespread diffusion of practitioner innovations. A major contribution of Rothman's material is that its utility has been demonstrated by a number of practitioners who have participated in organizational change projects using this model.

Chapter 16, "Tinkering with the Organization," is included because it focuses on tactics—those specific guidelines to behavior necessary for effective action. Pawlak suggests *when* to engage in organizational tinkering (during periods of organizational transition or change), *what* might be changed (rules), and, finally, *how* to effect change (the use of reports on specific subjects, demonstration projects or bypassing channels, and the like). He concludes that human service workers "as a condition of employment and as a professional right and responsibility should have the opportunity to bring their insights into the plans and programs of the organization they work for."

Segal's "Planning and Power in Hospital Social Service" presents an interesting variant on Patti and Resnick's model of organizational change.

In Segal's approach, the action system is a hospital social service department, not an individual or staff group. As such, it is a formal, integral part of the larger organization with legitimation, reward, punishment, and expertise sources of power to support its organizational change activities. Segal focuses on power in the change process and the necessity for planning as hospital departments become "more partisan" in hospital life and governance. Central to his planning model is determining a need or dissatisfaction on the part of patients or staff. This is followed by establishing a clear purpose for the change plan to address the need or reduce the dissatisfaction. A final step in the planning process is organizing for action where required tasks are allocated to individuals and groups based on expertise, power, feasibility. Segal does not deal with the question of the unity of the department in the face of potential resistance, nor is the role of the administration made clear. It is fair to say, however, that for given issues a department can become unified sufficiently under effective leadership to carry out needed organizational changes.

The action models presented in Part III represent guidelines and suggestions for worker activity that stem either from a particular author's experience or from some analysis of relevant social science literature. But rarely is this material derived from, or based upon, empirical data about organizational change in social agencies. The last selection, "Internal Advocacy and Human Service Practitioners: An Exploratory Study," is one such effort, designed to begin an organized, systematic collection of information about organizational change in "the real world." In particular, Patti's study was directed toward learning more about the frequency of organizational change activity, the goal of such activity and the extent to which these goals were attained, and the techniques utilized.

One major finding was that organizational change "seems to be a fairly pervasive activity among the practitioners involved in the study." A number of other findings emerged from this study, such as the apparent association between education and frequency of change efforts, the high rate of success experienced by practitioners in their organization change efforts, and the central role, at the outset at least, of the administrative superior in the organizational change scenario. All of this suggests that a call for further research is not merely a response to custom, but rather a realistic, necessary step that, if taken, could yield much to benefit the profession in general and the field of organizational change in particular.

Supplementary References

Feinstein, Norman and Susan. "Innovation in Urban Bureaucracies: Clients and Change," *American Behavioral Scientist* 15, no. 4 (March-April 1972): 511–531.

Hallowitz, Emanuel. "Innovations in Hospital Social Work," *Social Casework* 53, no. 7 (July 1972): 89–97.

Kami, M. J. "Planning for Change with New Approaches," *Social Casework* 51, no. 4 (April 1970): 209–215.

Lee, A. M. "Institutional Structures and Individual Autonomy," *Human Organization* 26, no. 1/2 (Spring-Summer 1967): 1–5.

McCormick, M. "Social Advocacy: A New Dimension in Social Work," *Social Casework* 51, no. 1 (Jan. 1970): 3–11.

Needleman, M. C. *Guerrillas in the Bureaucracy: The Community Planning Experiment in the U.S.* New York: John Wiley & Sons, 1974.

Patti, Rino J., and Herman Resnick. "The Dynamics of Agency Change: An Analysis of One Agency's Transformation," *Social Casework* 53, no. 4 (April 1972): 243–255.

Resnick, Herman. "The Professional: Pro-Active Decision Making in the Organization," *Social Work Today* 6, no. 15 (March 1975): 462–467.

Rice, Robert M. "Organizing to Innovate in Social Work," *Social Casework* 54, no. 1 (Jan. 1973): 20–26.

Specht, Harry. "Disruptive Tactics," *Social Work* 14, no. 2 (April 1969): 5–14.

Wax, John. "Power Theory and Institutional Change," *Social Service Review* 45, no. 4 (Sept. 1971): 274–288.

Weiner, Hyman J. "Toward Techniques for Social Change," *Social Work* 6, no. 2 (April 1961): 593–603.

Chapter 12 **Effecting Internal Change in**

Human Service Organizations

Herman Resnick

Within human service organizations there are two groups that could be seen as entitled and motivated to seek improvement in organizational functioning: administrators,[1] one of whose tasks is very often to change the organization as well as administer it; and practitioners and supervisors, whose motivation and legitimation to promote innovations in the organization rest on their commitment to quality service for their clients, but whose job descriptions rarely call for improving the organization's functioning. Whereas the administrator has long been recognized as an organizational changer, the second group, composed of low- and middle-echelon personnel, has only recently been perceived as a changer of or innovator in its organization.[2] It is to this latter group and its purposes that this chapter is addressed, in the hope that it may serve to encourage human service staff members engaged in organizational change. The chapter is also an attempt to add to the beginning literature on organizational change and, more specifically, to codify some of the existing practice wisdom in this subfield by focusing on the avenues or patterns through which changing the organization from within (COFW) may be initiated. It is, therefore, an attempt to contribute to a systematically developed body of knowledge in this variant of planned change.

Although COFW as a subfield in the human service professions has been described in the literature,[3] it might be useful to define COFW briefly and to discuss some of its basic assumptions, as well as the four major elements that are essential to its conception of organizational change.

Reprinted from *Social Casework* 58, no. 9 (Nov. 1977): 546–553, with the permission of the Family Service Association of America.

DEFINITIONS AND ASSUMPTIONS OF COFW

COFW can be defined as a series of activities occurring inside an organization that are designed to improve delivery of services to clients and that are carried out by low- or middle-echelon members of human service organizations. These change activities usually focus on modifications of agencies' policies, programs, procedures, or administrative arrangements.[4] Four major elements essential to this conception of organizational change are the change catalyst, the action system, the innovation proposal, and the action plan. A *change catalyst* is one or more organizational participants who have sufficient motivation and capacity to initiate action to improve the organization. Organizational members who are stimulated by a change catalyst to form a group and carry out a plan to improve organizational functioning and services represent an *action system*. An *innovation proposal* is some new mechanism, process, or idea that would, from the staff member's perspective, improve a particular policy, program, procedure, or administrative arrangement, which the action system develops and brings before administrative or official decision-makers. A thought-through series of steps designed to increase the probability of a decision-maker's acceptance and widespread utilization of an innovation is an *action plan*.

As a variant of planned change, COFW rests on four basic assumptions:

1. Social welfare organizations adversely affect staff or clients at some time.[5]

2. Decision-makers will either support or resist change proposals, depending on how they perceive the value of such proposals to them and their organization.[6]

3. Organizations can be improved by the focused and sustained activities of their low- and middle-echelon staff members.

4. Staff morale can be improved through their activity in COFW.[7]

PATTERNS

Having defined and made explicit some of the assumptions upon which COFW is based, we can describe its three basic patterns. Each of the patterns and the basic features that differentiate them from each other will be specified and described. The patterns will be illustrated with case studies drawn from a school of social work, a university, and finally a voluntary counseling agency. In addition, some of the advantages and disadvantages of each of the patterns will be discussed. Prior to discussing the three patterns, however, it is necessary to comment briefly on the role of the change catalyst.

The Change Catalyst

Common to all three patterns is the presence of an organizational member with a range of attributes and interests who, when activated by some stimulus, may begin the process of organizational change from below. This member, a change catalyst, may urge the formation of, and give convening leadership to, a group of staff generally dissatisfied with the current state of affairs. Alternatively, he or she may specifically propose an idea for improving the organization as a way to organize an action system, or pull a group of staff together because the change catalyst and others suddenly experience some particular policy or procedure as especially onerous. In all these patterns, the role and status of the change catalyst may be crucial. He or she will have to be a respected member of the staff, whose functioning in both the organization and with clients is satisfactory. Professionals are highly sensitive to organizational members who are continually complaining and calling for change but do not have the substantive, consistent behaviors, relationships, or professional acceptance to implement their interests or expressions.[8]

Pattern A

A logical, if not typical, way for the change catalyst to begin an organizational change project is to become active after perceiving that a certain problem indirectly or directly causes poor client services. In this pattern, the activity he or she undertakes might consist of calling together a group of colleagues to form an action system, which would then, as a unit, formulate innovations for the problem that drew them together. Or the activity might be to find an innovation that could solve the problem and then convene an action system to consider both the problem and solution.

The following case example illustrates the first approach, where the change agent convenes a group of concerned colleagues to examine the problem.

A school social worker noticed that some of the foreign students at a local high school were getting into trouble at school and doing more poorly in their grades than would be expected, judging from their school records. As she obtained information as to the nature and extent of the problem, she discovered that there was no provision made for the fact they spoke or understood little English. She felt that their problems in school could easily be related to this deficit, and she enlisted the aid of a community worker and three teachers whom she felt would be as concerned as she was about the plight of these students.

After a series of evening meetings and lunchtime sessions, this newly formed action system decided on a simple innovational proposal (as well as an action plan to implement that proposal). Both the proposal and the plan are outlined below. They would: establish an English-speaking class for the eighteen students involved; involve administrators, parents, teachers, and students to consider their ideas and gain their support; organize the project so that costs, financial and psychological, would be minimal; and feel their job was done only when the school system had incorporated this kind of class into their budget requests for the following year.

The action system members then initiated contacts with the parents (of these young people), who were quite enthusiastic and who were able to provide some funds for this project and, more importantly, a volunteer who would take responsibility for teaching the class twice per week after school. At the same time, they met with the building administrators, who, while reluctant to start such a program in mid-year, did provide a room in the basement of the school.

Two meetings with the teachers were held to inform them of the project and the reasons behind it. The students themselves were approached individually and in groups to obtain their commitment and willingness to participate in this class after school during their leisure time.

The above activities took place over a six-week period, and by the seventh week the students were installed in the class, beginning their work on the English language taught by an instructor who came from the same ethnic background.

The action system then met with the administrators to plan how the course, its finances, legitimation, and instruction would be taken over by the school system next year.

The school social worker, after perceiving the problematic behavior of the foreign students and linking their language limitations with that behavior, organized an action system of interested persons to address the problem. It is important to note that in this variant of Pattern A, the school social worker did not come to the action system with an innovation proposal in hand. Instead, she brought the problem to their attention and left the finding of a solution to their ingenuity. She played a crucial role in one other respect in that she demonstrated her practicality by adding to the total plan a phase that would ensure the inclusion of such a class into next year's school budget. She knew full well how difficult it is to have new ideas permanently implanted in the system.

The distinguishing feature, then, of Pattern A is the way the change project begins—by the change catalyst focusing on a specific, delimited problem in the agency. Change catalysts can either use this problem as a stimulus around which an action system can be formed, as is illustrated in the case example, or can generate ideas to solve the problem. In the latter instance, the action system (which would be formed because of its interest in the problem as well as the solution) would be able and willing to put most of its energy into developing a plan for acceptance by relevant decision-makers of the proposed solution—the action plan. Figure 12-1 outlines the steps in Pattern A.

Pattern B

The second mode of beginning an organizational change project also requires a change catalyst to surface, but in this case the catalyst will seek to organize a group of staff members known to be generally dissatisfied with agency functioning and with whom he or she enjoys a relatively good working relationship. Once the action system (in this

FIGURE 12-1
Pattern A

Step 1	Change catalyst emerges	
Step 2	Change catalyst identifies problem	
Step 3 Change catalyst develops action system	or	Change catalyst identifies innovation
Step 4 Action system identifies innovation	or	Change catalyst develops action system
Step 5 Action system develops a plan for acceptance and maintenance of an innovation by decision-makers.		

pattern) has started, it agrees to work on a specific problem to improve the organization (for example, poor communication between administration and staff) or agrees on an innovation it wants the organization to utilize (for example, group treatment technique).

In both cases the action system will (or should) move either from focusing on a specific problem to working on an innovation to solve the problem[9] or from an innovation (generally agreed to be of interest to the action system members) back to the problem for which the innovation is a solution. A final step will be the creation of an overall plan to guide the action system in its activities to help the innovation achieve acceptance and utilization. The following case example illustrates the first version of Pattern B.

An informal action group, composed of administrators and faculty generally critical of the way their university was run, was started by a young faculty member trained in group dynamics in a large midwestern university during the mid-1960s. Its purpose, implicit at first, was to work against the competitive, bureaucratic, and noninnovative orientation of the university. Experimentation in the classroom, more collaboration, and interdisciplinary activities among the faculty were some of its positive goals. The action group also hoped to improve relationships among administration, faculty, and students.

After it had been formed, its major activity was to introduce a series of innovation projects: (1) training high school students to conduct research and publish their findings and (2) organizing a course for 200 students that included two lectures a week, once-a-week participation in a six-person study group, and involvement in a group representing the students in a course-planning council for making changes during the remainder of the semester. Often projects included management innovations to revitalize the university council—the academic policy-making group of the university.

Later on, as the group became more formal and increased its size, it widened its scope to include participating in long-range planning sessions with university administrators, as well as working with formal committees in their respective departments to improve education.

Its operating procedures were quite informal and relationships were personal and friendly. Meetings were held in members' homes at the end of a working day and every planned meeting was scheduled for at least two hours to ensure that sufficient time was given to issues and to each other.[10]

Although in the above example the action system had "failures" as well as "successes," it made a distinct contribution to the well-being of its own membership and to students and faculty, who benefited from the new approaches advocated and utilized.

As is clear in the university example, Pattern B differs from Pattern A in the manner in which the action system is created; that is, the action system in Pattern B is developed because of the members' long-standing critical posture toward the organization. Once the action system begins meeting in some regular way, a range of problems and potential solutions will surely emerge to be worked on by this action system in some long-range way. Pattern A tends to be an ad hoc action group that might disband at the end of the change project. Pattern B might conceivably become a quasi-permanent, albeit informal, part of the organization. Figure 12-2 outlines the steps in Pattern B.

Pattern C

In the third possible pattern, the change catalyst is also a significant figure in the organizational change project. He or she advances an innovation that, at least on face value, would be seen as having interest to others and appears to be a solution or a help to some generally felt problem in the agency. The change catalyst could then either work to establish an action system that could (and should) focus on and seek

FIGURE 12-2
Pattern B

Step 1	Change catalyst emerges	
Step 2	Change catalyst convenes action system	
Step 3 Action system identifies problem	or	Action system identifies innovation
Step 4 Action system identifies innovation	or	Action system identifies problem
Step 5 Action system develops a plan for acceptance and maintenance of an innovation by decision-makers.		

to understand the problem that the innovation proposal is designed to ameliorate, or the change catalyst could link the innovation and the problem as the means by which an action system could come together and work for change. Thus, in Pattern C, the major activities of the action system are related to increasing its understanding of a problem and innovations in which it has interest and formulating a plan to help the innovation be accepted. Pattern C is reflected in the following case example.

A team of social caseworkers were impressed by their experience in a training workshop where small groups were used for problem-study and problem-solving purposes. Upon their return to their agency, they succeeded in persuading four of the nineteen staff members to form an action system that would plan ways and means to encourage the agency to increase the use of small group techniques (*a*) with clients and (*b*) for organizational and administrative issues. Because of the positive "publicity" given to group approaches in the social work community at that time, and the fact that other community agencies were already experimenting with group techniques, it was not difficult to involve the action system in a series of evening and weekend meetings focused on the advantages of group intervention in a human service organization. Readings were passed around, and informal seminars were held and conducted by practitioners and faculty who had experience in different modes of group work.

After a few of these meetings, when enthusiasm was high, the action system decided to submit a plan to the agency administrators to start groups with clients and for staff. The plan included a schedule for training staff in group approaches, a list of group consultants who might help, and a program for reeducating the board of directors to group conceptions of social work.

The administrators, after considering the plan, felt it had merit but raised questions as to cost of training and effectiveness of group approaches with clients.

The action system recognized that it had not done its homework on these important issues and went back for more planning and thinking. At a meeting with the administrators three weeks later, they came up with the following responses to the questions and issues raised:

1. Staff would pay 25 percent of training costs and agency 75 percent.
2. Group treatment had certain advantages over casework treatment: Some clients functioned better in groups, and the agency could serve more clients through the use of groups; in addition, staff could learn

more about this model of helping, which would widen their skill repertoire.

3. The research regarding effectiveness of group approaches generally indicated that groups were effective with some clients but not with others. They were prepared, however, to recommend that the agency go ahead with increased group activity and evaluate its success in this agency vis-à-vis client outcome and staff morale.

The administrators (to the surprise of the staff) supported the recommendations of the staff action system and helped implement group approaches in the agency.

Pattern C, then, is characterized by an action system coming together in response to some innovative idea that seems useful, that is, that will improve the organization in some way. Unlike the other two patterns, where the change catalyst relies on the action system's interest in reducing a problem, the activity here explicitly focuses on a solution. In this pattern, the action system comes together because of its potential interest in an innovative proposal that seems to advance the agency, its members, or its purposes. In the other patterns, the action system is pulled together by a change catalyst who either senses the intensity of staff's anger or is upset at a specific problem in the organization (Pattern A) or who identifies and convenes a group of dissatisfied staff members who might be generally interested in working to improve the organization (Pattern B). An outline of the steps in Pattern C is given in Figure 12-3.

All three patterns have certain limitations as well as advantages, some of which are discussed below.

ADVANTAGES AND DISADVANTAGES OF THE PATTERNS

Pattern A

In Pattern A the process of problem identification, that is, the problem to be worked on as one of the steps in organizational change, is probably easier to accomplish successfully because only one person, the change catalyst, is involved. Too narrow a view of the relevant and deeply felt problems of the organization as the staff sees them, however, may also occur when only one person begins an action project this way.

FIGURE 12-3
Pattern C

Step 1	Change catalyst emerges		
Step 2	Change catalyst identifies innovation		
Step 3	Change catalyst develops action system	or	Change catalyst identifies problem
Step 4	Action system identifies problem	or	Change catalyst develops action system
Step 5	Action system develops a plan for acceptance and maintenance of an innovation by decision-makers.		

The development of the action system in this pattern is sometimes most rapid because the selection of members is based on interest in a common specific problem to be solved: the group has high commonality of purpose,[11] an ingredient that facilitates solution of a new group's socioemotional problems. A further advantage of Pattern A is that its focus on a specific problem encourages the action system to take a more rational problem-solving approach; that is, problem identification precedes problem solution, a sequence not always utilized in groups seeking change.

Pattern B

Probably the major advantage of Pattern B compared to the others is the size,[12] representativeness, and potential power of the action system. To start with a general problem that, one can presume, is of interest to staff members clearly generates a commitment and involvement in the action system among a larger number of people than starting with a more narrowly focused problem whose adherents would be fewer. As most social reformers will realize, however, this situation has two potential attrition difficulties. One is that as the action system develops and works to select a specific, and therefore manageable, problem to focus upon, members will drop out as a result of not having their original interests met. In other words, the problem chosen now may be far different from the general problem that originally served to attract and bring together those members. The size of the initial group causes the second problem of attrition, for the problems and complexities found in organizing a large new group often prevent members from having their individual or more personal needs met.

A predictable consequence of Pattern B is a change in group composition of the action system, which makes that action system less stable unless steps to remedy this situation have been taken in advance.

Pattern C

The distinguishing feature of Pattern C is its approximation to reality; that is, it is probably true that many persons are "recruited" to a change project because of the attractiveness of a particular solution (or innovation) to them. Pattern C is probably the most frequently used method of initiating an action project. A main limitation of this pattern, however, is that when the action system begins to discuss the reasons for, or origins of, the agreed-upon innovation, an examination of these reasons may lead to suggestions of other innovations that then may split or destroy the group, because some members may feel their commitment to the group is based on their interest in a particular innovation and not on solving a problem in the organization or on different innovations suggested by other members.

SUMMARY

In an effort to stimulate intraorganizational change activity in human service agencies, three approaches to promoting organizational innovations have been described. The first approach, Pattern A, is characterized by the change catalyst, a respected organization member, convening an action system whose members are, or seem to be, concerned about an immediate problem in the organization. Pattern B, a second way to bring an action system together, has the change catalyst recruiting and selecting organizational members known to be generally dissatisfied with the organization's functioning to form an action system to work for the betterment of the organization. A third mode, Pattern C, has the change catalyst pulling an action group together because of its members' interest in some innovation that they feel would be beneficial to the agency.

These three patterns illustrate the variety of ways by which the COFW process could be initiated and maintained. They represent the activities and thinking of low- and middle-echelon personnel in health, education, and welfare organizations who are pro-actively responding to organizational dysfunction, and who have learned that staff innovations, properly formulated and supported, can be accepted by administrators who value improving service delivery and staff morale. Thoughtful utilization or selection of the three patterns by staff action systems could help in the attainment of these desired organizational outcomes. All the patterns, whatever their advantages and disadvantages, are effective ways of introducing and achieving organizational change from within.

Notes

1. See Leonard R. Sayles, "Accommodating for a Change," in *Policies, Decisions and Organizations*, ed. Freemont J. Lyden, George A. Shipman, and Morton Kroll (New York: Appleton-Century-Crofts, 1969), pp. 228–39, for a description of the processes by which administrators identify the need for change in an organization and the action steps that could be taken to facilitate changes; see Alvin Zander, "Resistance to Change—Its Analysis and Prevention," in *Social Work Administration*, ed. Harry Schatz (New York: Council on Social Work Education, 1970), for an account of the variety of ways resistance develops in organizations and how administrators can act to decrease it; and Benjamin R. Sprafkin, "Impact on Agency Administration of Staff Concern for Social Change," *Child Welfare* 50 (Feb. 1971): 82–85.
2. See Hyman J. Weiner, "Social Change and Social Group Work Practice," *Social Work* 9 (July 1964): 106–111, for an early description of changing the organization from within in a medical setting; George A. Brager, "Institutional Change: Perimeters of the Possible," *Social Work* 12 (Jan. 1967): 59–69; and Rino J. Patti and Herman Resnick, "Educating for Organizational Change," *The Social Work Education Reporter* 20 (April/May 1972): 62–66. For a case description of organizational change from below, see Harold Weissman, *Overcoming Mismanagement in the Human Service Professions* (San Francisco: Jossey-Bass, 1973), and Edward J. Pawlak, "Organizational Tinkering," *Social Work* 21 (Sept. 1976): 376–380.
3. Ibid.
4. Rino J. Patti and Herman Resnick, "Changing the Agency from Within," *Social Work* 17 (July 1972): 48–51.
5. See for example, Fred Goldner and Richard Ritti, "Professionalization as Career Immobility," *American Journal of Sociology* 72 (March 1967): 459–502; Irving Piliaven, "Restructuring the Provision of Social Services," *Social Work* 13 (Jan. 1968): 34–41; Richard Cloward and Frances Piven, "The Professional Bureaucracies: Benefit Systems as Influence Systems," in *The Role of Government in Promoting Social Change*, ed. Murray Silberman (New York: Columbia University, School of Social Work, 1966). For a

vivid account, see David Wineman and Adrienne James, "The Advocacy Challenge to Schools of Social Work," *Social Work* 14 (April 1969): 23–32.

6. For a discussion of decision-makers' inclination to resist or support changes, see Rino J. Patti, "Organizational Resistance and Change: The View from Below," *Social Service Review* 48 (Sept. 1974): 367–383.

7. See Herman Resnick, "The Professional Pro-active Decision Making in the Organization," *Social Work Today* 6 (Oct. 1975): 462–467.

8. See Patti and Resnick, "Educating for Organizational Change," for a brief discussion of the role of the action system participant and his or her general relationship to the organization.

9. It is recognized that many change groups work on an explicit action plan without being aware that the plans are implicitly trying to solve a problem. These groups often do not specify the problems for which the plan is a solution. This chapter emphasizes the necessity for understanding the reciprocal relationship between problem and action plans to reduce or solve those problems.

10. Sherman Grinnel, "The Internal Action Group: One Way to Collaborate in a University," *Journal of Applied Behavioral Science* 5 (Jan.-March 1969): 75–103.

11. See George Theodorson, "Elements in the Progressive Development of Small Groups," *Social Forces* 31 (May 1953): 311–320, for a perceptive look at the dynamics of task groups over time. He illustrates most clearly the importance of commonality in early stages of group life.

12. See Edwin Thomas and Clinton Fink, "Effects of Group Size," in *Small Groups: Studies in Interaction*, ed. A. Paul Hare (rev. ed.); (New York: Knopf, 1966), for a summary of the findings of studies on size of small groups.

Chapter 13 Tasks In Changing the Organization from Within

Herman Resnick

In response to the attacks on bureaucratically admin-istered organizations in the human services field in the last two decades,[1] a variety of change strategies were mounted to improve them.[2] One of these strategies, changing the organization from within (COFW), is based on the use of staff-developed action systems that operate in the informal and formal system of organizations to reduce the effects of either inhumane or inadequate policies or administration.[3] This model is described in the present chapter, with an eye toward more specificity as to its procedures and practices.

The first section of the chapter serves as a brief review of the COFW framework and introduces the reader to a definition of the model as well as some major elements and patterns of COFW. The second and major section focuses on the specific tasks associated with this model of or-ganizational change but heretofore not discussed in the literature.

REVIEW OF COFW FRAMEWORK

Definition

COFW is a series of activities carried out by lower or middle-echelon staff in human service organizations to modify or alter organizational conditions, policy, program, or procedures for the ultimate improvement of service to clients. The activities engaged in are legitimized by profes-sional purposes as well as by organizational norms.[4]

Three major elements of COFW are a change catalyst, an action sys-tem, and a change goal. A change catalyst is an organizational partici-

Reprinted from *Administration in Social Work* 2, no. 1 (Spring 1978): 29–44, with the permission of the publisher. © 1978 by The Haworth Press. All rights reserved. Appreciation is expressed to Benson Jaffee for his help in editing the manuscript.

pant who has sufficient motivation and capacity to initiate action to improve services.[5] An action system or team is a group of organizational members stimulated by or working with a change catalyst to carry out an organizational change project. A change goal is some specific mechanism, process, or idea that would improve a particular policy, program, procedure, or administrative arrangement for the purpose of improving service to clients.

Patterns of COFW

Staff in human service organizations engaged in organizational change may utilize two basic modes. The first is a "go it alone" style.[6] The human service worker sees some aspect of the organization that adversely affects clients and decides to try to remedy it. He or she assesses the situation, decides on a realistic goal, collects and organizes needed information, selects a strategy, and puts together a change project. The major advantages of this style are speed of the accomplishment and minimal upset of the organizational equilibrium. On the other hand, improvements are usually small and temporary. In addition, the organization may label and isolate the worker as a troublemaker, and thus limit or curtail subsequent pro-active behavior.

A second mode, advocated in this chapter, involves a change catalyst joining with a group of fellow social workers who have interest in changing some aspect of their organization. There are at least three patterns in this mode. First, a change catalyst, seeing a problem in the organization, pulls together an action system, which in turn selects goals, establishes a change project, and then carries the project out. Alternatively, an action system already engaged in carrying out a change project at some point selects (from outside of itself) a leader who is seen as a change catalyst to help attain its changed goals. A third pattern involves an action system meeting over time to effect some change in the organization, deciding upon a specific goal and a change project, and, in the process, producing its own emergent change catalyst.

These three patterns that link the change catalyst to a potential action system can be illustrated by three possible versions of Fletcher Christian's role in *The Mutiny on the Bounty*. In the first pattern, Christian, angered at the brutality of Captain Bligh, would have organized the men into an action system, which in turn would have planned and carried out the mutiny. In the second version, the men would have planned the mutiny without Christian but, fearful that they lacked the strong leadership to see it through, would have selected Christian to be their change catalyst. In the third pattern, Christian and the other men would have participated equally in planning the mutiny, and, as time went on, Christian's leadership capacity would have pushed him to the fore.

Having defined COFW and its major elements, and described some patterns that human service practitioners may employ while engaging in COFW, I will now turn to the specific tasks that have to be undertaken by action system members.

TASKS OF ORGANIZATIONAL CHANGE

It is possible to identify two categories of tasks that need to be engaged in COFW, namely, analytical tasks and interactional tasks. Early analytical tasks are: (*a*) the determination of a goal for the action system, and (*b*) analysis of possibilities of resistance that may be elicited by the movement toward the goal. Completion of these tasks is usually followed by a third task, namely, the choice of a strategy to be used in the change project. Two crucial interactional tasks to be discussed are: (*a*) developing the action system, and (*b*) presenting proposals for change to relevant administrators.

Analytical Tasks of Organizational Change

GOAL SELECTION

The goal sought by an action system or a change catalyst is any specific mechanism or suggestion that is intended to reduce the adverse effects of some policy, program, procedure, or organizational condition. Each goal typically has at least two major characteristics: it is a response to a problem directly or indirectly affecting client service, and it is specific —that is, it represents concrete ideas about how to change those undesirable conditions. Examples of goals may range from the establishment of regular meeting times for physicians, social workers, and nurses in a hospital to discuss cases, to the shifting of the program focus of a social work department from individual services to a group or community service. A goal may be as minute as designing a new face sheet on a case record or as major as establishing a workshop to improve administration-staff relationships.

Selection of a goal, then, is a process clearly linked to some problem in the organization and emerges from the consideration of, hopefully, the best or most realistic proposals for resolving or reducing the problem. The goal selection process consists of two parts: problem identification and analysis, and consideration of goals.

Problem Identification and Analysis

Action systems often come into existence around a problem felt to be intolerable to staff or clients. Identifying a problem for attention is usually not a rational process of selecting from a range of problems the one that would have most salience to action system members. Rather, the process is more like an emotional pulling together of a group of people who desire to right some wrong in the organization. Discussion of the problem subsequently reveals its nature and extent. Analysis of this sort, held usually at a lunch meeting or evening session after work, often results in heightening the solidarity and commitment of the change team.

If the action team is working effectively, the very discussion of the problem occasionally causes a shift in the way it is conceived.[7] For example, the group may have come together because of frustrations about the way staff meetings in the agency have been conducted. But as the group discussion delves more deeply into the nature of the problem, it becomes clear that staff relationships are the problem. So much tension exists between two factions of the staff that any decision at a staff meeting becomes a cause around which the two rival groups act against each other, making it difficult for the meeting to be conducted effectively. The first conception of the problem might have led to the selection of a change project goal such as recommending training for the entire staff in group decision-making. This type of solution might have missed the basic dynamics of the problem and therefore might be ineffective at worst, or minimally effective at best. The analysis of the problem therefore directly affects possible solutions.

Consideration of Goals

Whereas the identification of a problem can help unify a new action system, the decision-making process involved in the selection of a single realistic goal can cause conflict and pull apart the team. The group dynamics of an action system can therefore influence this goal selection process. For example, new action systems lack a tradition of conflict resolution or successful decision-making and are especially vulnerable to these strains. They need to work to find a compromise goal that somehow enables them to stay together and yet is sufficiently on target to warrant continued activity. In addition, an untried action system should recognize its inexperience and possibly reduce the scope and magnitude of its goals because resistance often increases with more ambitious change goals.[8]

Three other variables should be mentioned as contributing to the process of selection of goals: the concept of impermanence, the multiplier effect, and integration. With respect to impermanence, some change projects are successful only temporarily. Organizational change goals that have greater possibility of being permanently internalized (to the extent that this can be predicted) should be given greater priority over other goals.[9] Goals that have multiplier effects, that is, goals that potentially influence or modify more than one subsystem of the organization, stand a better chance of being internalized in the organization, since their impact is positively felt by more than one unit. Similarly, goals that are easily managed stand a better chance of being kept by the system. The reason for this is that goals that require continuous input from the administration are harder to integrate and tend not to be permanent. Consideration of one or more of these three variables does not, of course, guarantee the effectiveness of the change effort or its durability, but discussion of these variables enhances the rationality of the deliberations and enables the action system to better predict the results of its efforts.

PREDICTION OF RESISTANCE

"Never fight a battle if there is a chance of losing it" is a guideline for insurgent groups that has relevance for action systems in organizations. It implies that analysis should precede action and possibly that some analyses should lead to no action. In other words, the action system's prediction of resistance to a change project is a crucial determinant of the nature of its action. More specifically, if the action system predicts substantial resistance, and if it perceives itself as having inadequate resources (time, commitment of members, its own solidarity, or community support) to overcome this resistance, it might decide to postpone a given change project. Alternatively, the analysis might help the action system to decide to change the goal or its strategy, or indeed the very problem it wants to address—all this in order that the action system may increase the possibility of never fighting a battle if there is a chance of losing it.

Scholars and practitioners studying the phenomenon of resistance have identified four systems or processes that affect the success or failure of a change project and that may be of help to the action system in predicting resistance. They are: the organization in which organizational change takes place; the decision-makers relevant to the change project goal; the members of the action system; and the stages of resistance to change efforts.

The Organization

The organizational context of a change project may affect the reactions of relevant decision-makers and staff to the project. For example, an organization that has recently experienced a number of major changes imposed by external forces will probably be resistive to any new change efforts. An organization highly dedicated to its purpose and emotionally identified with its methods will also tend to react negatively to most attempts to alter its methods or purposes.[10] Finally, an older organization whose staff are more concerned with relationships and status will be likely to resist projects impacting on organizational social structure but might be more receptive to efforts directed at changing the organization's purpose or methods.[11]

Relevant Decision-Makers

The receptivity of upper-echelon decision-makers to organizational change efforts may be viewed through a number of analytic lenses. They may be "cosmopolitans," that is, persons identified primarily with the purpose of the organization, or "locals," individuals identified mostly with the organization itself and its interests.[12] Decision-makers who are more local in orientation might resist change efforts if such efforts threaten organizational interests.

Decision-makers may also be described in terms of style or personal goals.[13] Some are conservers and resist most change. Others are client advocate types and tend to be supporters of changes if those changes promise the improvement of service to clients. A third group might be called climbers, characterized by a commitment not to the organization or its goals but rather to their own advancement. They are probably unpredictable as regards potential reactions to a given change project, but it could be fair to say that the climber types would resist change project goals not currently in vogue in the profession or upon which their superiors might frown.

Personalities of decision-makers also play a role in anticipating resistance to change efforts. Some decision-makers have strong needs for control and respect, whereas others value relationships more. When these needs are not met, these decision-makers may veto innovative proposals even if these innovations might be in their own or their organizations' best interests. Action system members are often quite aware of these personal dynamics and consciously direct themselves, while interacting with respect-and-status-minded decision-makers, to act deferentially and appropriately (without, of course, demeaning themselves). Similarly, when interacting with decision-makers whose needs are greater in the relationship area, members of the action team can carefully cast their proposals in terms that will not be personally rejecting of the decision-maker and, by so doing, reduce the risk of irrational and possibly negative responses.

Of course, accurate analysis of these factors may not lead to the acceptance of a proposal for change, but the very process of assessment provides support and confidence to action system members. By classifying a decision-maker's probable responses, the action system member might be more able to withstand pressures emanating from the heat of the organizational change interaction. These "diagnostic categories," then, contribute to the rationality of the organizational change process, making it a more predictable phenomenon.

Action System Members

Organizational members participating in an action system are part of an interpersonal social network within the organization that includes colleagues not on the action team and middle- and upper-echelon administrators. This informal network is based on a friendship and respect pattern that influences the change process. Organizational members who are not respected by their colleagues or administrators because of their inexperience, incompetence, personality, or point of view will probably be less successful in persuading decision-makers than will other, more highly regarded staff members. The principle at work here is that organization decision-makers will be more likely to support more radical change project goals if the members of the action system advancing these proposals are themselves seen by the decision-makers as conformist. An effective action team must be willing to evaluate its own members in these terms and to allocate roles accordingly. For example, staff respected by administration should be more visible and active when proposals are surfaced for decision-making in meetings with administrators. Other staff should make their contributions and achieve their satisfaction in the earlier phases and in other aspects of the project.

Stages of Resistance to Change Efforts

Practice experience with innovating in systems reveals patterns in resistance to innovation that can be divided roughly into four sequential stages.

The first stage of resistance to a change effort is usually a massive and undifferentiated one. Reaction seems to be overwhelmingly negative, with few supports emerging: Potential allies do not speak up, and the critics seem especially effective. Participants in the change project can feel overwhelmed and may be inclined to withdraw because of the lack of positive reaction and the apparent hopelessness of the cause.

However, persistence on the part of the changers may enable them to carry the process to a second stage, which is characterized by a more selected and differentiated response. In this stage, supporters and critics emerge more distinctly, and action team members are now in a position to reassess their early predictions. They now can more accurately evaluate their chances of success than they could in the first stage of resistance, when the wide range of different interests in the organization was masked. With time and persistence on the part of the action system, these interests tend to surface and play their part.

The third stage might lead occasionally to a showdown, as resistance and support are mobilized. If the action team has planned well and properly evaluated the strength of the supportive and resistive forces in relation to the change goal, that goal may now be achieved.

However, a fourth stage still "lurks in the wings." Although the change goal has been accepted, forces of resistance to it are still there, operating to sabotage its widespread utilization. The action team must not rest on its laurels at this point but must continue actively to reduce residual resistance.

An example from a university setting of the four steps of resistance will clarify them:

A curriculum change was advanced by a small group of faculty and students to reduce the amount of time spent in the field during the first year of a two-year graduate training program in social work. The faculty on the whole seemed negative or indifferent, and critics were easily able to postpone discussion of this proposal at meetings for many months (Stage 1). The action team, however, was persistent and succeeded in getting the proposal discussed at a faculty meeting. Enough faculty members saw value in this proposal, as a result of the discussion, to warrant the establishment of a major task force composed of faculty and students to study the question and bring back recommendations (Stage 2). In the next three months, acting in the informal and formal network, the action system convinced large numbers of faculty that this curriculum would meet their own needs and those of the organization. Therefore, when a vote came on the recommendations from the task force, the innovators won (Stage 3). However, implementing the new curriculum was a complicated task and required much expenditure of energy and time. A few faculty members were still unconvinced about the efficacy of the new curriculum and/or were angry at losing the battle and continued to attempt to undermine the innovation (Stage 4). Ultimately, however, they were not successful in their efforts.

STRATEGY SELECTION

A third major task in organizational change is the choice of a general strategy or overall plan, once the problem and related goals have been determined and the resistance factors assessed. The action team is now ready to decide how it will generally move forward toward the attainment of its goals.

Selecting a strategy requires an analysis of the organization as it relates to the goal of the change project. Will attainment of that goal lead to concomitant attainment of the goals of colleagues and administrators in the organization? Or will success benefit only the interests of the action system, at the expense of these others? If the latter is true, a situation results in which rewards are to be distributed in a win/lose manner. If, on the other hand, both parties win, an integrative situation is at work. In the world of games and sports, a poker game represents a distributive situation—one or more persons win at the expense of another (or others). But the members of a football team, on the other hand, are in an integrated situation with each other, since the scoring of a goal by one player benefits the team as a whole and each of its members individually.

Similarly, in organizations, change situations can be logically analyzed to determine the extent to which they are integrative or distributive. This is illustrated in the following example:

A change project was carried out by a group of social workers and teachers to develop a volunteer, after-school English-speaking class for recently arrived Oriental children who were having behavioral difficulties in school. The action team achieved some support and success not only because the project was conceived and designed to benefit clients but also because it had payoffs for the school administrator, whose prestige was enhanced by the presence of an innovative program in his school and whose difficulties with these youths were decreased by the success of the program. The change project, then, not only added resources to the school in the form of the English-speaking class for Oriental children, it also contributed to the administrator's position in his network (and, it might be added, to a positive climate for subsequent change efforts in the organization). The action system then used an integrative strategy where both the action team and the decision-maker won. The action team's assessment that the attainment of the change project goal represented an integrative situation was a correct one, and a strategy based on that analysis was consequently also successful.

However, other change situations exist that are more distributive in nature, as in the following example:

The board of directors of a voluntary social work agency refused to recruit ethnic minority members to fill three existing vacancies on the board. The board had sixteen members, two of whom were minority persons, and the board felt that this number was sufficient to represent the ethnic minority community. Some of the staff believed that the board was too traditional in its outlook and was responsible for policies and programs serving primarily white, middle-class clients. This staff formed an action system to achieve a specific goal of filling the board vacancies with three ethnic minority persons. They reasoned that, if appointed, minority members would support the existing coalition of minority persons and whites on the board working to increase the number of low-income and nonwhite clients served by the agency. The action system correctly analyzed its goal and determined that it should ultimately be aimed at reducing the power of the white conservative sector of the board of directors, thus enabling the minority community and staff to assume some of that power. This meant that a situation was emerging where either the action system won and the board of directors lost or vice versa, that is, a classical distributive situation. Since the action system was highly committed to its goal and felt it had sufficient resources to deal with the anticipated resistance, it was willing to develop and carry out a distributive strategy.

The tactics used by the action systems in the two examples above differed fundamentally, as would be expected. In the first example, the social worker–teacher action team, after determining that, given the team goals, an integrative strategy was possible, then chose tactics that would guide their interaction with their administrator. They decided to provide information about the problem and about the details of the program they hoped to establish. No coercion was utilized, and the decision-making meeting went quite smoothly, despite some initial reservation expressed by the administrator about starting a new program so late in the year. When the action team spokesperson said she thought the new program could be implemented in six weeks, the administrator raised no further objections.

Different tactics were necessary, however, in the ethnic minority situation. A series of disruptive interactions were employed, including threatening letters, confrontations with the board of directors, and finally a strike by action team personnel, minority board members, and concerned community persons. The board, faced with such harassment and embarrassment, first threatened to close the agency and then sought to reduce the number of minority members needed to fill the vacancies from three to two. When newspaper accounts identified board members opposing increased minority representation, those board members capitulated and a settlement was achieved.

The tactics of the two strategies differ in other ways as well. Integrative strategies allow honesty in looking at the situation, a collaborative approach to rational problem-solving, and a belief in building organizations that value innovations. Distributive strategies, on the other hand, require secrecy, threats, bluffs, manipulation of data, and use of coercion. They probably achieve greater change than do integrative strategies, but they also require greater solidarity and more resources than do integrative strategies. Analysis of the consequences of each strategy in relation to goals and resources is, of course, essential.

In summary, three analytical tasks of organizational change have been specified and discussed: goal selection, prediction of resistance, and strategy selection. The following section will focus on two interactional tasks of organizational change: developing the action system and meeting with the decision-makers.

Interactional Tasks

DEVELOPING THE ACTION SYSTEM

When an action system is considered necessary for the attainment of a change project goal, careful attention to its composition is important. Unless the action system is planned, events set off by the action project themselves may lead to the development of an ineffective group.[14] An action system is not only a mechanism through which the change project is conceived and/or carried out, it is also one of the major and renewable resources of energy and motivation for action system members to continue their participation in the face of resistance. Its stability and capacity to change are crucial to effective organizational change activity.[15]

Some of the essential elements to be considered in developing action systems are composition, understanding of and commitment to purpose, and group leadership and participation skills.

Composition

There are two aspects of composition that need to be considered: size and selection.

Size.[16] The dilemma for the change catalyst is to recruit as large an action system as possible without giving it too many members in its early stages of development. Starting with a smaller group may facilitate decision-making and communication at a time in a group's life when the establishment of such processes is crucial for its development. However, too small a group risks insufficient representativeness and inadequate power. Up to five members ought to work adequately: there are enough differences in a five-person group to provide representativeness as well as sufficient numbers of members to provide some influence. Larger beginning groups require well-worked-out mechanisms and traditions for effective work. This, of course, is not possible early in an action group's life. However, as the action system progresses in carrying out its change plan, new members can be more easily incorporated.

Selection.[17] Bringing together the right staff members who fit with each other is a task often difficult to implement. Attention to socioemotional variables can very often spell the difference between action systems that stay together and those that dissolve in the face of adversity or hard work. For example, staff members who are long-term enemies in the organization may have difficulty reconciling their personal differences in an action group despite a strong commitment to its particular purpose. Also, very high- and very low-power persons will probably be incompatible action system members because of the differences in rank. For example, assistant directors and social work trainees, or administrators and students, may have great difficulty in working with each other as co-participants.[18]

In recruiting action system members, the change catalyst should give clear information about the system purposes, potential group membership, and the extent of the possible time commitment that will be demanded of action system members. There will be some people who, because of limited time and risk restraints, will be able to participate in only a limited way. The resourceful change catalyst will provide the opportunity for them to do so. Permanent or hard boundary lines between action and nonaction system members should be avoided. Secret

meetings, whispered remarks, and criticism of nonaction members contribute to an undesirable separation between staff members.

Understanding of and Commitment to Purpose

The change catalyst who effectively communicates the purpose of the
action system to potential members not only screens out disruptive
members but also creates a group that from the beginning has a high
commonality of interests and purpose. New groups need this solidarity
to provide them with sufficient energy to deal with the many complex
and sticky problems of moving beyond the beginning stages, where
socioemotional issues are paramount, to later stages where effective
work can be done.

Group Leadership and Participation Skills

Social change groups often experience difficulty at the onset of their
work because they tend to underestimate the complexity of the tasks
they must undertake. The new change unit has to perform the difficult
manifest task of thinking through a problem and the strategy for its
solution. The group must also simultaneously engage in the latent task
of transforming itself into a viable working group to perform the manifest tasks rationally and effectively. Either one of these tasks is difficult
at any one time, but both together at the same time represent a formidable obstacle to success. Two possible ways of overcoming this obstacle
might be: the use of existing informal staff leaders whose charisma
could help the action system work on its dual tasks successfully; and
obtaining agreement among the action system members to participate
in a brief group training workshop aimed at helping them to build their
action system. Facilitators sympathetic to the group's purpose from outside the organization might prove useful in conducting such workshops.

MEETING WITH THE DECISION-MAKERS

After the action system has been developed and has given attention to
the three basic analytical tasks (goal selection, prediction of resistance,
and strategy selection), it is now ready for one of the final and most
difficult tasks: the presentation of its proposal to relevant decision-
makers in the organization at a formal meeting. All previous work of
the action system was in preparation for this formal event, and in at
least one fundamental way was quite different from the forthcoming
meeting. Interaction prior to this event was with friendly sources whose

values and experiences were probably similar to those of action system members.

Role Allocation

Persons chosen to meet with decision-makers should be those whose interpersonal styles, prestige in the organization, and skill in formal debate would facilitate the attainment of the goal. Further, these staff members need to know who will play what roles in the meeting—who, for example, will open the discussion, present the problem, respond to queries, lay out the proposal, summarize the issues and points of difference between the action and target systems, and close the discussion.

Such decisions, taken in advance and consistent with the agreed-upon integrative or distributive strategy, help rationalize the action group–decision-maker interaction and provide a source of discipline for the action system participants. Finally, the selection of and commitment to a spokesperson for the action group in the discussion is often very helpful.

Reaffirming Overall Strategy and Tactics

Decision-making meetings between action teams and decision-makers can easily become heated confrontations, since few precedents for this kind of interaction exist in social work organizations. Tensions may be high, and communication in such a situation may tend to be distorted and subject to misinterpretation. The action system is especially vulnerable since this may be its first formal effort. By contrast, the administration has worked together as a team many times before, albeit in different contexts and with different purposes. Action system members may get drawn into angry and attacking behaviors that predictably elicit the same reaction from the decision-makers. The interaction, originally designed as collaborative, may then escalate into a distributive situation that could be counterproductive to the interest and goals of the action system.

A useful preparation for the action system would consequently be to explicate and reaffirm whether the overall strategy is integrative or distributive and link such commitment to a plan for consistent behavior in the meeting. This clarification could help the action system members adhere to their plan despite emotional reactions.

Conducting a Simulation of the Anticipated Meeting

It can often be useful for the action team members to design and conduct for themselves a simulation of the anticipated meeting prior to its actually taking place. Team members would be given roles of specific persons expected to be at the meeting. They would then play these roles as realistically as possible. The resulting interaction could then provide clues as to the possible tactics that might be used by the decision-makers, as well as flaws in the action team's proposed tactics. The administration's tactics might include a range of reasonable reservations and objections about the proposal's lack of funds, the wrong time of year, a requirement that the proposal be made in writing, previous failures of similar attempted changes, and so on. Occasionally, the persons advancing the proposals are queried as to their "real" motivations. These reservations could then be studied and specific responses prepared for each one. The simulation would then be repeated with action team members now equipped with detailed responses to potential objections and questions. The potential for improvement in the action system's performance is immediately evident in the actual meeting as a result of this procedure (technique) potential for increased effectiveness in achieving its objectives at that meeting.

CONCLUSION

This chapter, after introducing the reader to some basic components of COFW, has attempted to provide for the potential change catalyst in the human service organization more specific guidelines for action than are found in previously published material in this subfield. These guidelines are in the form of tasks—analytical and interactional. Three analytical tasks have been discussed: goal determination—what the change shall be; resistance assessment—who and what may be potential obstacles to this change; and strategy selection—which guidelines or strategies may be utilized to achieve the change goal. Of the many interactional tasks in an organizational change project, two major ones have been presented and explored: developing the action system, and meeting with the administrators for decision-making.

Notes

1. A variety of studies and writings could be cited of which the following is a sample: Fred H. Goldner and R. R. Ritti, "Professionalization as Career Immobility," *American Journal of Sociology* 72 (March 1967): 489–502; Irving Piliaven, "Restructuring the Provision of Social Services," *Social Work*

13, no. 1 (Jan. 1965): 34–36; Richard Cloward and Frances Piven, "The Professional Bureaucracies: Benefit Systems as Influence Systems," in *The Role of Government in Promoting Social Change*, ed. Murray Silberman (New York: Columbia University School of Social Work, 1966). For a vivid account, see David Wineman and Adrienne James, "The Advocacy Challenge to Schools of Social Work," *Social Work* 14, no. 2 (April 1966).

2. A partial listing of these strategies is: organizational development; consumer- or client-directed change; community control; ombudsmanship.

3. For early formulations of this strategy see Hyman Weiner, "Towards Techniques for Social Change," *Social Work* 6, no. 2 (April 1961), and George Brager, "Institutional Change: Perimeters of the Possible," *Social Work* 12, no. 1 (Jan. 1967). For more recent formulations, see Rino J. Patti and Herman Resnick, "Changing the Organization from Within," *Social Work* 17, no. 4 (July 1972), and Harold Weissman, *Overcoming Mismanagement in the Human Service Professions* (San Francisco: Jossey-Bass, 1973).

4. For a discussion of the boundaries between professionals and organizations, see Robert Vinter, "The Social Structure of Service," *Issues in American Social Work*, ed. Alfred Kahn (New York: Columbia University Press, 1959).

5. See C. Jones, *The Planning of Organizational Change* (Washington, N.Y.: Praeger, 1969), for an early and different use of the term "change catalyst."

6. Although this paper advocates a group mode of organizational change, this individualistic approach was also included since it is also a pro-active one. This model has been documented by Weissman, *Overcoming Mismanagement.*

7. There is often a strong tendency in such groups to talk about solutions to the problem before there is a full understanding of the nature and scope of the problem. It is important that the group recognize that problem analysis should precede consideration of solutions. If this happens, the result is more likely to be better understanding of the problem's nature and severity, and therefore more effective remedies for that problem may emerge.

8. See Rino J. Patti, "Organizational Resistance and Change: The View from Below," *Social Service Review* 48, no. 3 (Sept. 1974).

9. The question of permanence or retention of change is rarely discussed in the human services professional literature. A noteable exception is Ronald Lippit, Jeanne Watson, and Bruce Westley, *The Dynamics of Planned Change* (New York: Harcourt, Brace, 1958).

10. See W. H. Starbrook, *Organizational Growth and Development* (Middlesex, Eng.: Penguin, 1971).

11. Ibid.

12. See Alvin Gouldner, "Cosmopolitans and Locals," *Administrative Science Quarterly* 2 (1957–1958), for a full discussion of this concept.

13. See Patti, "Organizational Resistance."

14. See Robert Vinter, "An Approach to Group Work Practice," in *Individual Change through Small Groups*, ed. P. Glasser, Rosemary Sarri, and Robert Vinter (New York: Free Press, 1974), for a discussion of the influence potential of group composition.

15. For a vivid account of the power of a group to sustain members' morale and ideality in the face of threat, see R. Lifton, *Thought Reform and the Psychology of Totalism: A Study of Brainwashing in China* (New York:

Norton, 1961), pp. 75–178. Especially relevant is his description of the all-European group placed in the same cell with eight Chinese prisoners.

16. See Edwin Thomas and Clinton Fink, "Effects of Group Size," in *Small Groups: Studies in Interaction*, ed. A. Paul Hare, E. Borgotta, and R. Vale (rev. ed.; New York: Knopf, 1966), for a summary of the findings of studies on size of small groups.

17. See Vinter, "Approach," for his discussion of the influence potential of member selection on group processes.

18. See Dorwin Cartright and Alvin Zander, "Leadership and Performance of Group Functions: Introduction in Group Dynamics," in *Group Dynamics*, (2d ed.; New York: Harper and Row, 1960), for a discussion of the goal achievement and socioemotional functions of groups. For a discussion of roles played by group members that are socioemotional or goal achievement in orientation, see Kenneth Benne, and P. Sheats, "Functional Roles of Group Members," in *Group Development* (Washington, D.C.: National Training Laboratory, NEA, 1961). See B. Berleson and G. Steiner, *Human Behavior* (Burlingame, N.Y.: Harcourt, Brace and World, 1964), ch. 8, pp. 348–349, for a brief discussion of communication patterns and rank in small groups.

Chapter 14 Changing the Agency from Within

Rino J. Patti and Herman Resnick

Although the rhetoric of social action in the 1960s sensitized social workers to the negative consequences of agency practices and policies, practitioners have not been particularly active in pressing for change from within their agencies. This is attributable in part to their lack of knowledge and skills in working with large systems. Equally important, however, is the fact that schools and professional associations have been far too timid about challenging inequitable and injurious agency practices. This situation should change as the knowledge and skills needed to undertake organizational change are considered an integral part of the practitioner's training.

As yet efforts to provide an informed and systematic conceptual framework for intraorganizational change are still in the embryonic stage.[1] "Intraorganizational change" refers to the systematic efforts of practitioners to effect changes in policies or programs from within their agencies, when they have no administrative sanction for these activities. The legitimation for these efforts is derived from the practitioner's ethical obligation to place professional values above organizational allegiance —that is, he has the responsibility to become actively engaged in promoting an organizational environment that enhances the welfare of the agency's clients and staff.

This chapter discusses three phases of the intraorganizational change component in social work practice—formulation of goals, mobilization of resources, and intervention. In describing each phase, the authors provide some organizing concepts that will help the practitioner plan his change efforts more systematically. In addition, they illustrate how a careful assessment of goals and resources can help the change agent choose a rational intervention strategy.

Reprinted from *Social Work* 17, no. 4 (July 1972): 48–57, with the permission of the publisher. The authors wish to thank Professors Benson Jaffee, Sid Miller, Naomi Streshinsky, and Ted Teather for their critical comments on an earlier version of this paper.

GOAL FORMULATION

Once the practitioner has identified the organizational problem he wishes to address, he must specify the changes he wants to bring about —that is, the goal he seeks.[2] Although this task may seem implicit in identifying the problem, the change agent must keep in mind that formulating a goal involves not only a consideration of what should be done to alter or eliminate the undesirable situation, but what can be done under existing circumstances—that is, he must separate what he would like to achieve from what he can reasonably expect to achieve.

In determining what goal to pursue, the practitioner must consider two important factors. First, he must examine the agency's decision-making process to determine who exercises both formal authority and informal influence on the outcome of his proposal. In other words, how are decisions made in the organization on the specific issue in question, and who is in a position to influence this process? Clearly an administrator does not make his decisions in a vacuum. He is substantially influenced by the information and perceptions provided by subordinates, as well as his own evaluation of how his decision will be received by those who will carry it out. For example, if a change agent's proposal can be distorted, discredited, or delayed by someone before it reaches the ultimate decision-maker, that person must be considered central to the decision-making process. In other instances, the decision-maker may reject a proposal, despite his inclination to accept it, to avoid embarrassing or threatening someone whose favor he wishes to retain. The number of persons who may influence the decision-maker on a particular matter will, of course, vary with the nature of the proposal.

Second, the change agent must consider whether those who exercise formal authority or informal influence in the decision-making process are likely to agree or disagree with his proposal. This kind of analysis is important because it enables the change agent to anticipate how much resistance or support his proposal is likely to encounter.

In refining the discussion on agreement and disagreement, Warren's formulation of issue consensus, issue difference, and issue dissensus is useful.[3] Originally, this scheme was proposed in the context of community organization practice, but it seems equally applicable to intraorganizational change. Warren posits an agreement-disagreement continuum between the change agent and the power configuration (those who directly influence or actually make decisions). This continuum is defined by the extent to which these parties have common values and interests with regard to a specific issue. Thus when both parties basically agree on how an issue should be resolved, or are likely to reach an agreement once it has been explored, there is *issue consensus*. When the decision-makers do not recognize the problem or do not understand the substance of the proposal, *issue difference* exists. In this situation the change agent is confronted with either refusal to acknowledge that an issue exists or opposition to his proposal. In either case, however, he believes that through education and persuasion he can tap some mutual values or interests that will serve as a basis for acceptance of his proposal. In situations involving issue dissensus, decision-makers also refuse to recognize the issue or oppose the proposal, but the values or interests of those involved are so divergent that mere persuasion or education is unlikely to bring about consensus.

By utilizing this scheme as an analytic aid, the change agent can estimate the resistance, obstacles, or support he is likely to encounter before he attempts to pursue his proposal. This estimate, however rough, will help him to choose the resources and strategies needed to accomplish his goal. Most important, it will help him decide whether he wants to make the personal commitment required.

It has been suggested that the practitioner may not always be able to apply this scheme readily because he lacks direct access to decision-makers, especially in large organizations.[4] Yet he can often determine much about the values and interests of those in authority by carefully assessing how they have reacted to similar proposals in the past. Although administrators do change their views over time, one can expect more continuity than discontinuity on matters that touch their vital interests. In addition, a careful assessment of the functions an organization serves for groups that legitimate and support it frequently provides important clues as to how a change proposal will be received.

Too many change efforts founder because change agents fail to consider in advance the kind and intensity of opposition their proposals will encounter. Often change agents are so certain that their goal is inherently right that they assume others will agree. Thus an analysis of the sort just described can help the practitioner determine whether his goal is feasible.

A goal's feasibility is only partially determined after an analysis of the decision-making process and the extent to which the decision-makers will agree or disagree with the proposal. As Morris and Binstock suggest, the change agent's capacity to overcome the resistance to it is also extremely important.[5] This leads to a discussion of the resources available to the intraorganizational change agent.

RESOURCE MOBILIZATION

Assessment and mobilization of resources for intraorganizational change have not been adequately considered by theoreticians or practitioners.[6] In part this may reflect a pervasive tendency to assume that organizational change is solely the responsibility of those officially vested with the authority to effect changes in agency structure and operation. As a result, the focus is usually on how decisions can be implemented rather than how the decision-making process can be influenced.

The concern here is with identifying the sources of power that *may* be available to the change agent who has no legitimate authority for his activities.[7] This is crucial because one of the major obstacles confronting the change agent is his apparent lack of power.[8]

Practitioners frequently complain about some aspect of their agency in one breath and proclaim in the next that there is little or nothing they can do about it because their superiors are resistant to change. This sense of powerlessness is caused in part by their failure to recognize that the legitimation for change efforts is derived from one's professional commitment to client service—a commitment that is independent of a person's position in an agency. Another factor, however, is the general inability of practitioners to assess rationally the resources within an organization that can be marshaled on behalf of change efforts.

Obviously, the change agent must first assess his own qualities and characteristics as they relate to the change being contemplated. For example, if he seeks to reform some aspect of the agency, he will have more credibility if he is competent in his job. Nothing is quite so damaging to a cause as a leader who is professionally vulnerable. Consequently, the change agent must consider his standing in the agency so that the action system's agenda will not be undermined by charges of professional irresponsibility, unethical behavior, substandard performance, and the like.[9]

The change agent should also evaluate his ability to engage in interpersonal conflict. If he is unable to function effectively in such encounters, he should let someone who is skillful in handling situations involving confrontation, disagreement, and negotiation assume primary responsibility. If a practitioner equates his commitment to the change effort with his capacity to engage in confrontation, he may avoid becoming involved. Thus the action system is deprived of talents that could be utilized in other facets of the change effort. For example, some groups adopt a public stance of uncompromising militancy to create conditions in which private negotiations can occur. Since it is difficult for one change agent to carry on both tactics simultaneously, it is most efficient to allocate persons with different skills to these respective areas of activity.

The worker who lacks official authority to change agency policies or procedures must also attempt to identify and mobilize the sources of power that are available to the action system. In most instances, his fellow workers are his greatest source of power. Although they do not represent the only resource he can draw on, they are vitally important if the action system is to be credible.

The following framework, adapted from the work of Raven and French, is useful in relating workers' attributes to potential sources of power.[10] It suggests five types of power and the sources from which they are derived:

1. *Coercive power*—the capacity to reward and punish.
2. *Referent power*—the ability of a person or group to attract others —that is, to serve as a role model with whom others wish to identify.
3. *Expert power*—the possession of knowledge in some area that the agency considers important.
4. *Legitimate power*—the capacity to invoke authority that is officially vested by the agency.
5. *Value power*—the ability to articulate values to which other people are drawn.

Assuming that these sources of power are available to the change agent, then what observable personal characteristics or attributes, found among potential members of the action system, could be translated into the kinds of power just mentioned? The following list of attributes is offered as a point of departure:

Cosmopolitan Orientation. Staff members who are committed to professional values and norms and seek affirmation from individuals and groups espousing similar values have a cosmopolitan orientation. This includes practitioners who strongly identify with social causes; have allegiances to outside organizations that seek to protect or advance the interests of exploited, oppressed, or powerless groups; or have made personal or professional sacrifices to meet client needs. Such persons can influence others, including administrators, by pointing out agency practices that diverge from professional principles. They can also serve as liaisons with outside groups (e.g., schools, associations, client groups) that the action system may turn to when seeking support or coalitions.

Informal Leadership. Informal leadership is provided by staff members who are sought out by peers and superiors for advice, counsel, and support; influence the tone and direction of informal group interaction; or have linkages with several subgroups in the agency. Such persons are a potential source of power to the extent they can attract others who are ambivalent about engaging in organizational change. Sometimes they can also serve as intermediaries with administrators or bring some legitimacy to the change effort.

Educational or Experiential Qualifications. Staff members with special educational or experiential qualifications are a potential source of coercive power because they perform specialized or highly skilled tasks in the agency, their professional judgment and knowledge are valued by peers and administrators, or their professional reputation lends prestige to the agency and is likely to attract other talented practitioners. Thus the agency needs them because of the specialized nature of their work or their prestige. Since they are also highly desirable in the employment market, their threats to resign are likely to be believed.

Specialized Information or Knowledge. Staff members who are knowledgeable about the problem under consideration are a potential source of expert power because they can withhold, selectively utilize, or marshal their knowledge to help the action system make its case.

These attributes do not represent an exhaustive list. Nor is it implied that one person could not possess some or all of them in combination. They are presented to illustrate potential sources of power that may be available within an agency.

The relationship between practitioners' attributes and types of power can be illustrated graphically as Table 14–1.

TABLE 14-1
Practitioner Attributes and Types of Power

	Workers' Attributes			
Types of Power	Cosmopolitan Orientation	Informal Leadership	Education and Experience	Specialized Knowledge
Coercion	X		X	X
Referent		X		
Expertise			X	X
Legitimacy		X		
Value	X			

This analysis suggests that, other things being equal, an action system is likely to be more powerful in influencing agency policy if it includes workers who possess these attributes.[11] In addition, it appears that an action system's chances of success are increased to the extent that it mobilizes the kinds of power that are salient to its goals and strategies.

Again it must be mentioned that these attributes and their power equivalents are only potential resources. They are of little value to the action system unless they are committed to the change effort, and this seldom occurs in the absence of personal energy and willingness to take risks.

INTERVENTION

Selecting and implementing a strategy are, of course, central to the process of intraorganizational change. In this phase the action system chooses a course of action that initially defines the parameters of its efforts to effect the desired change. In situations involving complicated change processes, the action system may use more than one strategy in combination at a specific time or sequentially over a period of time. Seldom, if ever, is an action system able to anticipate all the consequences of its interventions or foresee all the forces that will come into play as the scenario unfolds. Consequently, it is artificial to suggest that the strategy an action system chooses and implements is final and irreversible. Indeed, probably the most characteristic activity of the intervention phase is evaluating the effects of the chosen strategy and making necessary adjustments, alterations, and so forth.

Nevertheless, choices must be made, and the change agent is more likely to select an effective strategy if he bases his choice on a deliberate assessment of the goal and the resources available to the action system.[12] The following discussion deals with the relationship between these two variables and strategy.

A number of useful schemes for conceptualizing the range of strategies that are available to the change agent can be found in the literature.[13] Generally, these schemes are based on an underlying continuum, ranging from fundamental agreement to fundamental disagreement between the action system and the "target system" with regard to the substance of the proposed change.[14] The following dichotomy of strategies is useful in discussing the change agent's options.

Collaborative Strategies

The adoption of a collaborative strategy is based on the notion that the best way to induce change is to work with the target system. In other words, if the target system is aware of the problem or sees the merits of the action system's proposal, it will voluntarily try to make changes in the organization. A collaborative strategy also rests on the assumption that the target system is rational, open to new ideas, and acting in good faith. Since collaboration implies reciprocity, this stance necessarily implies that the action system is willing to modify its goals to accommodate the needs and interests of the target system.

Activities. Operationally, a collaborative strategy may involve the following activities: (1) providing information about the nature of the problem, (2) presenting alternative courses of action (programs, procedures, and the like), (3) requesting support for experimentation with new approaches to the problem (e.g., new forms of service delivery), (4) seeking to establish a committee to study and make recommendations on alternative approaches to the problem, (5) creating new opportunities for interaction between members of the action system and target system to express ideas and feelings, build trust, and learn better ways to communicate with one another, (6) making appeals to conscience, professional ethics, and values, (7) persuading by logical argument, selective presentation of data, and (8) pointing out the negative consequences of continuing a specific policy.

Adversary Strategies

If the action system adopts an adversary strategy, it believes that to bring about the desired change it must work against the target system. Thus it tries to coerce the adversary into adopting some or all of the changes proposed. It assumes that the target system operates from a relatively fixed position and resists the proposed change because it has an investment in the existing scheme of things, is afraid of unanticipated consequences or financial constraints, or is concerned about losing the support of groups or constituencies that sanction it. In any case, the action system is convinced that it must be made more costly for the target system to adhere to the existing arrangement than to adopt the proposed change and that the organization's failure to respond will be more dysfunctional in the short or long term than any negative consequences that may result from instituting the plan.

Activities. If the action system chooses an adversary strategy, it might be involved in the following activities: (1) submitting to the administration petitions that set forth its demands, (2) confronting the target system openly in agency meetings and public forums, (3) bringing sanctions against the agency through external funding, standard-setting, and professional agencies, (4) engaging in public criticism and exposing organizational practices through the communications media, (5) encouraging deliberate noncompliance with agency policy or interference with agency procedure, (6) calling strikes, (7) picketing, (8) engaging in litigation, and (9) bargaining for the purpose of negotiating differences and developing compromise solutions.

In practice it may be difficult to distinguish whether a collaborative or adversary strategy is being used because action systems often utilize elements of both strategies simultaneously or sequentially over time. It is also not uncommon for practitioners to follow a collaborative course of action, although their assumptions about the target system would suggest an adversary strategy. Frequently this occurs because members of the action system recognize that they lack the resources and skills necessary to sustain an adversary approach. In other instances, the choice simply reflects their discomfort about violating organizational norms, fear of losing colleagues' support or approval, or unwillingness to risk their jobs, promotions, and so forth. In any case, the action system is not always able to translate its analysis of the desired strategies into action.

Nevertheless, having set forth the assumptions that underlie collaborative and adversary strategies and some of the activities that tend to be associated with each, it is possible to illustrate how the action system might relate the selection of strategies to goals and resources.

A collaborative strategy is most effective when there is consensus between the action system and target system on the issue in question. Because both systems basically agree on how the issue should be resolved and the major problems are technical in nature, the action system needs the power of expertise. Therefore, it should draw on practitioners who have specialized substantive knowledge about the problem, are able to collect and analyze data in a systematic manner and present it cogently, and have demonstrated some competence in dealing with the problem.

A collaborative strategy is also appropriate, at least initially, in situations that involve issue difference—that is, when the action system must persuade or educate the target system to recognize the problem's existence or importance and the necessity for action. Although the importance of utilizing change agents who are knowledgeable about the problem cannot be overemphasized, this may not be sufficient. To activate dormant value commitments, the action system may find it advantageous to recruit a change agent with a cosmopolitan orientation—for example, a person who is identified with social causes or strongly committed to client interests. Because a change agent with these attributes can point out the discrepancy between agency policy and professional values such as racial equality, he often has as much impact on decision-makers as the most carefully executed study. Finally, if the action system wants to promote agreement with the target system by increased communication and attitudinal change, it should recruit change agents who are trusted and respected by the target system, have the skill to facilitate communication and understanding between the interested parties, or are sensitive to the administration's need to maintain agency stability.

When the action system's goals conflict sharply with those of the target system, an adversary strategy is most appropriate. Because there is little possibility of achieving consensus, the action system must pose some credible threat to the agency's operation if compromise and exchange are to occur.

To sustain an adversary strategy, the action system must mobilize members with attributes that can produce coercive power—for example, workers who are important to the agency because of their experience or educational qualifications, are capable of and willing to engage in disruptive activities, or have links with outside groups that can bring negative sanctions against the agency or support the change effort. In addition to coercive power, the action system engaged in an adversary strategy must be attentive to its own need for stability. This is true to some extent for any group attempting intraorganizational change. But it is particularly crucial when an adversary strategy is used because of the strain and uncertainty involved. Therefore, the system should deliberately try to involve practitioners who are informal leaders—for example, those who can help group members articulate their fears and frustrations; resolve the internal conflicts that so often occur during intensive change efforts; and provide support, counsel, and encouragement to colleagues who experience feelings of uncertainty or futility.

In general, then, the chances of inducing organizational change are maximized when the action system consciously relates its strategy to its goals and the resources available. Conversely, when strategies, goals, and resources are mismatched, the chances of success are considerably reduced.

Whether strategies for intraorganizational change will be properly implemented depends on many factors; some have not been identified, let alone studied systematically. Nevertheless, one specific factor should be considered, that is, how the change agent uses the various contexts of action—the environments within and around the organization that may serve as the locus of change activity. In the general sense, two loci can be identified: those within the organization's boundaries and those in the field of influence or power that surround the organization. It is helpful to relate these loci of action to the types of groups that engage in change activities. Again, in the general sense, there are two kinds of groups: informal groups (those that arise from the unofficial interactions of the persons involved in change activities) and formal groups (those that are officially created and sanctioned by the organization).

In their experience with organizational change, the authors have observed that agency workers usually think of change activities as occurring in formal contexts, both internal and external to the organization. Thus practitioners often believe that the only way to attempt change is to present their plan of action to decision-makers through memos, letters, special meetings and conferences, or the development of formal relationships between the organization and professional associations, educational institutions, and the like. As a result, the plan of action surfaces prematurely, and the change effort languishes for lack of support. Informal contexts are used, but usually in an unsystematic way.

The authors suggest that informal contexts can and should be exploited more carefully. For example, if the agency is not prepared to recognize or act on a problem, the worker may find it necessary to utilize the informal-internal context to develop awareness among his colleagues and recruit members to the action system before he brings the matter into the internal-formal context.

Informal-external activities may involve development of coalitions between members of the action system and selected informal allies outside the agency. These coalitions are often crucial because change agents, especially if they are attempting to bring about major changes in agency structure or purpose, are highly susceptible to being co-opted or isolated by those in authority. Such relationships serve at least two important functions: (1) Informal-external relationships can provide socioemotional support and affirmation to change agents involved in unpopular and perhaps conflict-oriented change efforts. (2) Intraorganizational change agents often benefit from discussing strategies with someone outside the system. An outside peer-consultant frequently gives the change agent a rational innovative perspective that he would otherwise not have because he is caught up in agency norms and procedures and the exigencies of day-to-day operations.

CONCLUSION

Some critics of American social welfare agencies argue that agency demands conflict with professional values to such a degree that the practitioner who wishes to preserve his ethical commitments must do so outside the context of an agency.[15] The authors believe that the professional can work within an agency and retain his primary commitment to client welfare. Although organizational expectations frequently constrain workers to behave in ways that are deleterious to clients and workers have been victims of dehumanizing organizational practices as often as they have been the perpetrators, the vast majority of social workers will continue to be employed by agencies in the foreseeable future. It is comforting to think of a delivery system in which workers can function as autonomous professionals, unfettered by bureaucratic constraints. But until that occurs, there is an alternative—intraorganizational change.

The development of an intraorganizational change component in social work practice does raise an ethical dilemma. Social workers traditionally seek to counteract an increasingly controlling, manipulative environment by encouraging trust and open communication among people, maximizing the range of choices available to the individual, and promoting rationality in problem-solving. But much of the change that occurs in the world (particularly at the organizational level) results from the exercise of power and from calculated exchanges among parties with selfish interests, rather than through mutual understanding and rationality. Thus the practitioner who wishes to engage in organizational change will in some instances have to decide whether to become involved on these terms. Some will argue that using tactics such as deliberate confusion, threats, unrealistic demands, and disruption—regardless of how worthwhile the goal—seriously compromises the professional's humanizing function and contributes to the very dehumanization he seeks to reduce.

No matter how the practitioner resolves this issue, he should be aware of the potential costs involved. If he attempts to effect organizational change through mutual understanding and rational problem-solving, he is likely to be ineffective or irrelevant in some important contexts. If he uses tactics associated with the exercise of power, he runs the risk of being considered unethical by others.

The authors believe that the intraorganizational change agent should use the full range of strategies available to him—selecting those that are likely to be most effective, based on an informed assessment of organizational dynamics. Whether he should use marginally ethical means depends on how grave the problem is. Considering the number of agency policies or practices that do serious harm to the well-being of clients or staff, the authors are inclined to agree with Alinsky that "the most un-ethical of all means is the non-use of any means."[16]

Notes

1. A number of important theoretical contributions have helped lay the founda-tions for the ideas presented here. See Hyman Weiner, "Toward Techniques for Social Change," *Social Work* 6, no. 2 (April 1961): 26–35; Weiner, "Social Change and Group Work Practice," *Social Work* 9, no. 3 (July 1964): 106–112; George Brager, "Institutional Change: Perimeters of the Possible," *Social Work* 12, no. 1 (Jan. 1967): 59–69; Robert Morris and Robert Binstock, *Feasible Planning for Social Change* (New York: Columbia Uni-versity Press, 1967); Harry Specht, "Disruptive Tactics," *Social Work* 14, no. 2 (April 1969): 5–15; and Roland Warren, "Types of Purposive Change at the Community Level," in Ralph Kramer and Specht, eds., *Readings in Com-munity Organization Practice* (Englewood Cliffs, N.J.: Prentice-Hall, 1969), pp. 205–222.
2. Goal formulation rests on identifying the problem and analyzing the factors within and outside the organization that cause it. Force field analysis can be productively employed to help social workers with widely varying knowledge about organizational behavior translate their discomfort about agency situa-tions into explicit, cogent statements of the problem. For a fuller discussion of this instrument and its application in an organizational context, see David H. Jenkins, "Force Field Analysis Applied to a School Situation," in Warren Bennis, Kenneth Benne, and Robert Chin, eds., *The Planning of Change* (New York: Holt, Rinehart & Winston, 1964), pp. 238–244.
3. Warren, "Types of Purposive Change," pp. 207–210.
4. Conversation with Benson Jaffee, Associate Professor, School of Social Work, University of Washington, Seattle, June 1971.
5. Morris and Binstock, *Feasible Planning,* pp. 25–31.
6. A major exception is the excellent discussion in ibid., pp. 113–127. See also Brager, "Institutional Change," pp. 66–68.
7. The term "power" denotes "a capacity to overcome part or all of the resis-tance, to introduce changes in the face of opposition (this includes sustaining a course of action or preserving a status quo that would otherwise have been discontinued or altered)" (Amitai Etzioni, "Power as a Societal Force," in Marvin Olsen, ed., *Power in Societies* [New York: Macmillan, 1970], p. 18).
8. There is increasing recognition of the power possessed by nonadministrative personnel in organizations. See, for example, David Mechanic, "Sources of Power of Lower Participants in Complex Organizations," *Administrative Science Quarterly* 7, no. 3 (Dec. 1962): 349–364; and Jan Howard and Robert Somers, "Resisting Institutional Evil from Within," unpub. paper, undated (mimeo.).
9. The term "action system" means those persons or groups that consciously join in planned collective activity to change some aspect of the organization's policy or practice.

10. See Warren Bennis, *Changing Organizations* (New York: McGraw-Hill, 1966), p. 168.

11. An action system composed of workers with few of these attributes might generate considerable power if its numbers and commitment were high or if it engaged in tactics that were disruptive to the agency. Other sources of power that do not depend on the individual attributes of members of the action system can be mobilized through alliances with other organizations such as funding and standard-setting agencies, professional associations, professional schools, and so forth.

12. Other relevant variables include the nature and magnitude of the problem that prompted the change activity, whether the change process is considered finite or part of a long-range effort involving several subsequent interventions, the secondary consequences sought by the action system as a result of the change process, the ethical boundaries within which the change agent feels constrained to operate, and the probable effects of a specific strategy on the action system's morale and commitment.

13. See, for example, Brager, "Institutional Change," pp. 68–69; Warren, "Types of Purposive Changes," pp 210–218; Specht, "Disruptive Tactics," pp. 378–386; Richard Walton, "Two Strategies of Social Change and Their Dilemmas," in Kramer and Specht, eds., *Readings,* pp. 337–345; Arthur Blum, Magdalena Miranda, and Maurice Meyer, "Goals and Means for Social Change," in John Turner, ed., *Neighborhood Organization for Community Action* (New York: National Association of Social Workers, 1968), pp. 106–120; and Morris and Binstock, *Feasible Planning,* pp. 113–127.

14. The term "target system" refers to those persons who directly influence or are formally responsible for making decisions on the changes proposed by the action system.

15. See, for example, Irving Piliavin, "Restructuring the Provision of Social Services," *Social Work* 13, no. 1 (Jan. 1968): 34–41.

16. Saul Alinsky, "On Means and Ends," in Fred Cox et al., eds., *Strategies of Community Organization* (Itasca, Ill.: Peacock, 1970), p. 200.

Chapter 15 **Promoting an Innovation**

Jack Rothman

The human service professions generally, and the area of community organization in particular, have often been characterized as change-oriented fields. For this reason the process of the diffusion and adoption of innovations invites our attention. Practitioners are constantly involved in promoting new programs, new techniques, new tactics, and new ideas that they wish to propagate in working with target and client systems of various kinds. In many cases these new programs are already well established elsewhere and are only "new" in terms of being transposed to that particular situation. On the other hand the innovation is sometimes an entirely unique creation of the practitioner and the people he is associated with (for example, the "teach-in" as a tactic or Mobilization for Youth as a program). In either case, the process followed in promoting the idea and the problems to be encountered is apt to be similar.

Often a practitioner is overwhelmed or immobilized in introducing an innovation because the task seems so large, the obstacles so disarming, and the time available so restrictive. One of the participants in the field study discussed her situation in the following terms:

> I had been working on an individual basis with a number of pregnant girls who attended programs at our community center. Because of this activity I was asked to serve on the advisory committee of the board of education School-Age Parent Program. It became obvious to me that the girls were having a very limited educational experience. I saw the need to help them think through what they intended to do and what alternatives were available to them. Many seem to have given up on the idea of any kind of future after high school. Not only would they need help in planning for themselves, but they would need special skills that would help them proceed with their intentions.

Reprinted from *Promoting Innovation and Change in Organizations and Communities,* edited by Jack Rothman et al. (New York: John Wiley & Sons, 1976), pp. 22–57, with the permission of John Wiley & Sons, Inc.

After analyzing all this, I became convinced a more substantial guidance program was necessary for them. However, taking into account the usual kinds of attitudes that prevail in the public schools I knew that I would be facing a lot of resistances to an intensive high quality service. Because of all the time I knew would be involved in trying to set up such a program—while still performing all my other duties—I merely thought about this from time to time but took no specific steps.

RESEARCH ON INNOVATION

Fortunately, a fairly comprehensive and systematic literature exists on the subject of diffusion of innovations. Much of the early research was conducted by rural sociologists interested in agricultural extension problems—how new farming methods and materials came to be adopted by farmers. Other fields that have contributed to this area include anthropology, medical sociology, education, and industry. The planned parenthood and public health areas have also stimulated a great deal of interest in recent years.

From a number of these studies by different disciplines and professions we have drawn the following generalization: Innovations that are amenable to trial on a partial basis will have a higher adoption rate than innovations that necessitate total adoption without an anticipatory trial.[1]

Generally, an innovation is any program, technique, or activity perceived as new by a population group or organization. An innovation, as the term is most often used in the research literature, refers to new technical, professional, and commercial ideas and practices, such as contraceptive devices, new medical equipment, and farming techniques. These are typically legitimate, conventional, and within the normative consensus of a community and its elites. The promotion of broad and radical political change is not usually defined in the diffusion literature, though it seems likely that some applications can be made to this area.

This concept of partialization can be applied in two ways, for which Everett Rogers uses the terms "observability" and "trialability." That is, an innovation is more likely to be adopted by an individual or group if there is an opportunity, first, to see the innovation in action and witness its results ("observability") or, second, to employ a portion of an innovation before having to employ the total innovation ("trialability"). In observability one typically divides the target population; in trialability one divides the innovation itself. Both approaches may be combined in a given episode. Studies also emphasize the importance of "opinion leadership." According to research, the likelihood that an innovation will be adopted by a larger population is increased if the innovation is first utilized by a smaller group of opinion-leaders. This smaller initiating group may be characterized as style-setters, information-disseminators, key communicators, sparkplugs, or gatekeepers, among other descriptions. Thus innovations frequently take place in a two-step sequence, from a small subsystem of early adopters and opinion-leaders to adoption by a larger population or system. The subsystem may use only part of the innovation at the outset.

A useful illustration of these findings is provided by Carlson's study of how the new math became part of the curriculum of schools in Allegheny County, Pennsylvania.[2] Five superintendents who were closely associated with one another introduced the new approach in 1959. As a result of their example and their contacts with other superintendents, an additional ten schools adopted it in 1960. Then twelve more schools tried it in 1961. By the end of 1963, thirty-eight schools were employing this altogether different method of teaching mathematics. This is a good example of the sequential, snowballing pattern that is found in the dissemination of many innovations.

From this concept of partialization found in the research, we have derived the following action guideline: *Practitioners wishing to promote an innovation in a general target system should develop it initially in a partial segment of that target system.*

Although the generalization permits partializing either the target population or the innovation, for purposes of systematic and consistent treatment the guideline focuses on the target population. A target system is defined as a particular group, organization, community, or society toward which an innovation is directed. In the context of our guideline we are dealing largely with the organizational and subcommunity level. Adoption of the guideline implies an incremental, stepping-stone process; success on a small scale with a limited group is used as the basis for promoting a new idea, or having it spread spontaneously, across a wider population. There are many familiar analogues: the demonstration project, the pilot program, the modeling of new roles or behavior, and the free sample. In their book on innovations in organizations Zaltman and his associates support this action principle: "The more obvious the innovation is, the more likely it is to be adopted. This suggests still another factor. The more amenable to *demonstration* the innovation is, the more visible its advantages are, and thus the more likely it is to be adopted."[3]

Rogers' writings contain concepts from which we can infer some attributes of a partial target system that are conducive to communication and linkage. Communication appears to be facilitated when two groups possess similar outlooks, values, social status, or education. There is more comfort and trust when people are similar; messages are more likely to be sent and received accurately. For some types of situations, then, similarity of the partial and general target systems may be advisable.

On the other hand, Rogers notes that this similarity may also serve as a barrier to communication. New ideas usually enter a system by way of higher-status, more cosmopolitan opinion-leaders. Characteristics of opinion-leaders as determined in mass communications and diffusion studies include higher social status, more education, greater media exposure, more contact with the change agent, and more openness to innovative ideas. Typically, opinion-leaders have slightly more of these traits than other individuals at the same social level. These characteristics suggest attributes to be sought in selecting target populations for some types of innovations, particularly those using mass communications as the medium of transmittal.

As we noted earlier, radical ideas, or a context of intense political conflict, would not provide a suitable setting for this guideline. The strategy is most useful when the innovation is reasonably legitimate and conventional, and when the following conditions are present:

> The cost of large-scale application is high while the cost of a limited demonstration is small.

> There is little or no information about the value or cost of a large-scale application.

> The process is not easily reversible once it is begun.

> A large-scale application might alert and mobilize opposition, but a small-scale one would not.

> The larger system has little or no receptivity to the innovation.

This incremental, partialization notion can be connected with the idea of *proximate* goals. These are moderate, tangible objectives that can be attained in the short term. Looking at the new math illustration, we find that a partial target system of five superintendents initiated the innovation. A proximate general target system of ten additional schools had accepted this method in the next year. A practitioner who was attempting ultimately to reach the thirty-eight schools that adopted the innovation by the end of the study as a general target system, would have performed in a reasoned way by starting out with the $5 \rightarrow 10$ formulation as a lead-in to implementing the guideline. This 15 now constitutes a new *aggregate* partial target group that can be used as the basis for impacting the next-stage proximate general target system. One can visualize a rippling effect resulting from casting a pebble into the water. A given proximate general target system is intermediate to where the pebble lands (partial target system) and the farthest-out ripple (general target system). The implementation of this guideline, then, may usefully be conceptualized as a series of *incremental stages*.

OPERATIONALIZING THE GUIDELINE

The selection of an appropriate, facilitative partial target system is crucial in carrying out the guideline. That is, the partial system chosen should enhance the probability of the innovation's success on a limited scale. An organizer in a welfare workers union, for example, wanted to introduce a system of implementing the union's programs at the individual building level. He took into account many factors in selecting an initial target building:

> The basic consideration for the successful application of this
> guideline, at least in my case, was the selection of the target sub-
> population. I was able to employ the following factors:
> Geographic location, history of organizational activity leading
> to cohesiveness (how long had the folks been relating to each
> other organizationally), leadership (both actual and potential)
> within the partial target population, level of skill and experience
> within the target population.

Figure 15–1 illustrates other instances of innovation promotion in order to show the range of innovations to which this guideline has been applied, as well as to demonstrate how other practitioners have applied the concepts of a general target system and partial target system. The chart also indicates the mechanisms by which the transfer was made from the smaller to the larger target system.

PATTERNS OF IMPLEMENTATION

There were two important variations in the patterns of implementation of the guideline in the field test. In the first pattern, which we call a

FIGURE 15-1   Elements of the *Innovation Guideline Operationalized*

Setting	Innovation	General Target	Proximate (short-run) Target	Partial Target	Transfer Mechanism
A community mental health center in a semi-rural county	Stimulate local unions to accept the function of community care givers for their members	All 200 local unions in the county	50 unions from around the county	A limited number of union members and leaders participated in a workshop on community care giving—including 10 unions	The country-wide (all-inclusive) AFL-CIO Labor Educational Committee voted sponsorship of a follow-up workshop to be offered to all county locals
Traditional settlement house serving a largely black population	Introduce an intensive educational focus into a program that had been essentially recreational	Entire school-age membership of the settlement house	The same as general target	A group of 20 teen members were involved in two educational counseling sessions	Board of directors voted an allocation for hiring an educational director to serve the membership
A regional planning council serving several counties	Have the planning council gain responsibility for advising HUD on housing applications from all regional municipalities	All 30 municipalities in the region	12 municipalities with whom practitioners have had positive previous contact	With HUD approval, reviewed and assessed trial applications from four municipalities	HUD approved review procedure for all municipality applications
A social welfare employees union in a metropolitan community	Decentralize program implementation through building-level unit committees	All 25 building-level units in the union: the total membership	6 units in a contiguous area	Shop stewards at a single building location were involved successfully in union program implementation functions	The union executive board instituted a policy of building-level program implementation

"spontaneous" contagion model, the action proceeds from the practitioner (P) to the partial target system to the general target system. This pattern is typical of the agricultural extension approach in which one farmer uses a new seed and is successful; his neighbors see the results and then plant the same seed. It can be depicted as follows:

$$P \rightarrow \text{Partial Target System} \rightarrow \text{General Target System}$$

In the second pattern, the action moves from the practitioner to the partial target system, and then to a relevant decision-making unit and from there to the general target system. In other words, a decision-making unit intrudes as a necessary pass-through point between the partial and general target systems. This process typically is used in organizational situations.

$$P \rightarrow \text{Partial Target System} \rightarrow \begin{array}{c} \text{Decision-} \\ \text{Making} \\ \text{Unit} \end{array} \rightarrow \text{General Target System}$$

In the spontaneous contagion process the general target system accepts the innovation directly. In the decision-making unit arrangement a transfer mechanism or agent authorizes the carryover from the smaller to the larger group. The authorization may involve carrying out the program either with or without the prior explicit acceptance of the general target system.

Variations on the pattern of Practitioner → Partial Target → Decision-Making Unit → General Target are many. Sometimes the practitioner needs initial approval from a supervisor or the agency director. Occasionally he first receives approval from the Decision-Making Unit to carry out the demonstrations, completes it, and returns to the Decision-Making Unit for authorization to spread to the general target. In some instances there are two Decision-Making Units involved. Some practitioners arrange to have the Decision-Making Unit experience the demonstration directly as, for example, attending a conference at which a new technique or medium is employed.

Practitioners in the field study followed both of the basic patterns. An illustration of the spontaneous contagion model is taken from the experience of a president of a social workers union who wished to institute a training program for his executive board, using a method by which case examples and sharing personal experiences are used to enhance effectiveness in dealing with grievance problems. He obtained approval from the board before he began the process.

I then contacted a select group of four board members, requesting them to participate on the committee. I asked them to present a case example for the meeting and scheduled a committee time with them.

I chaired the committee meeting, suggested the rationale for the model to be used, and assumed responsibility for following up on specific tasks. The committee decided to conduct the training session in front of the board following the format of the committee meeting. Individual contacts were made to publicize the training session. The model was used at the training session, and the response was most favorable as the board had directly seen and experienced what I was trying to get across.

The general target system, the executive board, participated with interest in the training session with positive evaluative comments ("we were really able to share problems in a new way"; "it was really helpful to know that other people had some of the same problems"; etc.).

The key suggestion—at the training session—was that a next target system, for the future, could be the general membership with the same model being applied.

The decision-making unit pattern was followed by a community worker in a traditional family service agency who was attempting to develop the concept of outreach services. She believed the agency should work directly with clients in a low-income housing project, rather than expecting them—or, more likely, middle-class substitutes—to come to the agency offices. The problem was to convince the agency board to provide this type of service and the housing manager to clear the way for it to operate within the project.

My use of the guideline involved a small group of residents living on a court in a low-cost housing project. We were able to convince the Housing Authority that social work intervention could make a difference in the social problems in the housing project; reduce the social causes for eviction. A sub-goal was the introduction and sustaining of an out-reach program by our agency to housing project residents. We selected one court (5 families) out of the entire project as a demonstration; set up a time limit for evaluative purposes; promised progress reports at specific intervals; and met with the residents regularly as well as just "dropping in." This plan was submitted in writing to the board along with my periodic progress reports.

The plan worked almost too well in that it was constantly referred to in agency Board meetings; the out-reach idea was new
here but it really impressed the Board and the Housing Director,
and was accepted as a legitimate and appropriate agency program.
The results with the residents were not as spectacular, but represented at least a beginning, and we gradually expanded to
other courts.

In the great majority of cases in our study a formal decision-making
unit was necessary to foster or legitimize the transfer and broadening of
the innovation. This is of particular importance because in much of the
diffusion literature such mechanisms are not acknowledged. This may
be partly true because many diffusion studies deal with agricultural extension and similar enterprises, in which a single practitioner or change
agent deals with a geographically limited and homogeneous population
of individuals or families. In such work diffusion can take place more
informally, either through a demonstration by the change agent followed
by social contagion throughout the target population, or by means of
opinion-leaders who are encouraged to adopt the innovation and through
the examples they set to influence others to try some new approach or
procedure. Clearly, most human service practitioners are organizationally based, and this means that they require more formal and structured
procedures in order to execute processes similar to those carried out by
extension agents.[4]

Another difference in implementation concerned the amount of effort
expended by the practitioner in diffusing the innovation from the partial
to the general targets. In some instances the practitioner was very active
in promoting the diffusion. For example, the community center worker
quoted earlier demonstrated an intensive guidance program for unwed
mothers in one high school. She then set out to have the same format
introduced throughout the school system:

> I now had to involve additional individuals and groups. I pro-
> ceeded to develop a proposal and arrange for meetings with the
> following: my Center's Board of Directors, School Age Parents
> Advisory Board, Episcopal officials (for funds), school adminis-
> trators, teachers and students. After a number of meetings and a
> month and a half, we were able to gain administrative approval
> and a verbal commitment for funding of the program so all rele-
> vant students might benefit.

In other instances, such as with the social work union training program,
the partial group did the "selling."

These patterns might be identified as a spontaneous process on the one hand and a directed process on the other. In the spontaneous process, the practitioner is active in securing the adoption of the innovation by the partial target, but leaves the diffusion of the innovation to the general target in the hands of the partial target. The diffusion is thus carried out by the partial target, either by active promotion or by "inactive" modeling or example. Looked at another way, the spontaneous process might be the result of a naive practitioner's belief that upon reaching the partial goal he could sit back and allow the guideline to do the work, or it might be the result of a not-so-naive practitioner's recognition of the isomorphism between the practice problem and population on which the research on diffusion of innovations was based.

By contrast, the directed process involves the practitioner both in the adoption phase of the partial target and in the diffusion phase to the general target system. It may involve the practitioner's "supervision" or encouragement of the partial target system in the diffusion to the general target system, or it may involve the practitioner as the sole "line of communication" between the partial and general target systems. Again, viewed another way, it may be the act of a skeptical practitioner, doubting the validity of the guideline, or it may be the act of a practitioner who recognizes a lack of exact correspondence between the practice problem and the population on which the research was based.

The innovations being promoted by the practitioners fell into two categories. First, some of the practitioners had a fairly concrete detailed "product" to promote—a policy or program for adoption:

> The development of a policy statement calling for an increase in the number of psychiatric beds for children in the metropolitan area.

> To establish the Poverty and Social Problems Curriculum in six schools in the tri-county area.

> A rotating toy library for use by six child care facilities.

Second, some practitioners had a more fluid "process" of participation or involvement as an innovation to be promoted:

> A subcommittee or task force of the eight private agencies in Wayne and Oakland Counties involved in institutional work with children to work cooperatively with three representatives of the public sector.

> Small groups of black and white students who will meet together in one junior high school.

There were also differences in the practitioners' attitudes toward the innovation. Some practitioners were convinced of the validity of the new program. Others, however, were less certain and saw the guideline as a basis for "testing" rather than "selling." We have seen the first attitude expressed in several of the previous examples. In this illustration a mental health worker describes what can be considered a feasibility study:

My first experience involved a program designed for mentally retarded adults to prove that such services could be delivered with volunteer help, and that response from volunteers would be forthcoming. Up until that time the agency had resisted using volunteers to any extent. Two small groups of adults were selected initially by using some Department of Social Services community care homes and their residents. Eventually we had other home operators asking that their residents be allowed to participate, and ultimately we used our experiences in this program to write a proposal to the public school's Adult Education Department for a weekly socialization program for 200 mentally retarded adults. All of this took planning in great detail initially because we could not afford for those first few programs to fail.

We recruited and trained volunteers; we selected the initial group with some care; and tried to monitor everything constantly.

Through demonstrating with a small portion of the target population, we could then open up the program to the larger target population—which we did. If we had not limited the group initially we would have had disaster, because we did not have the volunteers, the space, the equipment nor the "know how" to handle a large group. In addition we did not have the acceptance of the agency that this was a viable way to proceed in this program.

In the discussion thus far we have spoken of dichotomous categories —for example, a decision-making unit or the lack of one, spontaneous or directed diffusion—but the processes of social change are more complex. If we trace the steps of a practitioner in action, we may correct any tendency to oversimplify. Here the director of a mental health association lists the steps he followed in getting the county mental health board (the general target) to endorse a policy statement calling for the provision of more psychiatric beds for emotionally disturbed children (the partial target was the Children and Youth Committee of the board):

1. Collect basic data identifying the scope of the problem;
2. Renew active support of my own organization by presenting

the problem to the Board of Directors at its December 2nd meeting;

3. Discuss the problem informally with Mental Health Act staff;
4. Discuss the problem informally with selected members of the Children and Youth Committee;
5. Present the issue formally to the Children and Youth Committee;
6. Discuss the problem informally with representatives of the State Department of Mental Health;
7. Encourage suggestions to meet the problem from members of the Children and Youth Committee, and from Mental Health Act and State Department staff;
8. Encourage site visits to prospective facilities;
9. Elicit a formal recommendation from the Children and Youth Committee to the full Mental Health Act Board;
10. Move to secure support of the full Mental Health Act Board.

Excerpts from his final report convey some of the flavor of this activity:

> I first discussed the need for additional beds informally with several Committee members and with the Committee staff person. These contacts were with people whom I did not feel were resistive on doctrinaire grounds. These people encouraged me to bring the issue to the Committee for general discussion.
>
> During the following two weeks, I again talked informally with several Committee members, and also spent some time meeting personally with mental health board staff in an effort to help them understand the nature of the need and the more desirable options available. The key staff person agreed that it would be helpful for me to present basic information to the Committee at its next meeting, and informed the Committee Chairman that I was going to prepare some helpful information.
>
> With staff assistance from my own agency, I researched some of the issues related to in-patient care. . . . It was possible to prepare materials that provided valid answers. . . .
>
> Prior to the actual Committee meeting, I again discussed the matter informally with several Committee members. I discussed the data I was collecting and asked them for their thoughts and suggestions.
>
> At the December 15 meeting I presented the information that had been collected. Surprisingly (to me) there was general agreement about the validity of the data, and little support for the notion that there were alternatives to hospital care for the children

in question. Inasmuch as the time seemed right to suggest a formal policy statement, I did so. After some discussion, the policy statement was adopted.

The Committee, through its chairman (a member of the full Board), made its recommendation to the Mental Health Board at its late December meeting. The Board adopted the policy statement and directed the Committee to work for its implementation.

QUANTITATIVE FINDINGS FROM PRACTITIONER'S LOGS

Of the staff of twenty-two practitioners who participated at the onset of the second-year main field test, twenty actually implemented the action principle of the guideline (that is, developed the innovation in a partial target system). Fifteen practitioners were judged by our panel of raters to have completely or almost completely attained their stated goal, and our discussion below of individuals and groups contacted and facilitating and limiting factors in implementation is based on the experiences of this group.[5]

The experience of practitioners in contacting important community groups and individuals while implementing this guideline is summarized in Tables 15–1 and 15–2. Forty-seven percent of the practitioners contacted between one and five important community groups, while 27 percent contacted none. The largest number contacted was twenty. Fifty-three percent indicated public agencies as important mainly for legitimation and participation. One-third indicated private agencies, generally to seek immediate participation. Forty percent indicated voluntary associations most frequently for public relations or information and guidance.

Practitioners considered from one to over thirty individuals important, with 27 percent indicating over thirty.

Agency executives were most frequently considered important by the successful practitioners (67 percent). The following types of individuals, although not considered important by a large percentage of practitioners, were contacted in large numbers by those who so viewed these categories: board members (7.6) (line over figures indicates mean score) and committee members (8.3), agency peers (6.2), community people (6.7), and clients (14.8).

Key agency executives were contacted primarily to obtain future participation (10 percent), immediate participation (17 percent), or legitimation (17 percent). In addition, legitimation was sought from key board members (17 percent), and immediate participation from relevant community people (10 percent).

TABLE 15-1
Key Community Groups Contacted*

Type of Group	Percent of Practitioners Who Considered This Group Important	Major Reasons Contact
Public agency	53	Legitimation Participation, immediate and future
Private agency	33	Immediate participation
Voluntary association	40	Information and guidance Public relations

*Refer to the logs in Appendix B [of *Promoting Innovation and Change*] for full range of variables from which those cited here are reported. Number of groups considered important: Range was 0–20. Between 1 and 5 groups were indicated by 47 percent of the practitioners, with 27 percent indicating none.

TABLE 15-2
Key Individuals Contacted*

Types Most Frequently Considered Important	Major Reasons for Contact
Agency executives	Future participation Immediate participation Legitimation
Board members	Legitimation
Board committee members	No trends
Agency peers	No trends
Community people	Immediate participation
Clients	No trends

*Number of individuals considered important: Range was 1–over 30; mode (27%) over 30.

Certain tentative practice implications may be inferred from this information. Probably a moderate number of important community groups will be contacted during implementation of this guideline (perhaps between one and five) depending on the nature of the particular situation. We found that less successful practitioners tended to contact a larger number of groups. The time and energy required to work with very many groups may not be efficient in relation to your objectives. Contacts with different types of organizations (public, private, voluntary) are likely to be useful. Such organizations will probably be contacted for a variety of reasons, public agencies in particular for legitimation and immediate participation.

More contacts with important individuals than with groups may be anticipated. While some readers may not make *any important organizational* contacts, at least minimal contact with such *individuals* is necessary. Approximately a quarter of the contacts are with fairly large numbers of these individuals (thirty or more).

There are many different reasons for making such contacts; obtaining an individual's participation was the most common. Participation is likely to be sought from agency executives and community people. Agency executives are also a logical source of legitimation or formal approval. The use of much time in soliciting participation of various types of individuals may be expected. Not much effort in the field test went into seeking financial or other material resources. This suggests that it may be efficacious to select an innovation for which there are already existing resources (especially in short-run situations).

When practitioners listed the factors that facilitated and limited their progress, they tended to put greater stress on the facilitating factors. (The facilitating and limiting factors, and the practitioners' evaluation of their importance, are listed in Table 15–3). Personal sources of facilitation were particularly emphasized by practitioners, perhaps because these are the most accessible and subject to immediate practitioner control.

Certain tentative practice advice may be inferred from this information gathered from practitioners in the field study. First, there are several ways in which you may use personal resources. For example, (1) develop and rely upon good relationships within the agency; (2) select a program to which you are committed and which is logically related to your position or role in the agency; (3) take advantage of your prior experiences in a deliberate way—select a program and setting in which your experience will be an asset.

In addition, you should consider fostering support for the program at all levels within the agency, particularly at upper levels of the agency, as this was reported to be an important facilitating condition. If the program is consistent with your other assignments and tasks in the or-

TABLE 15-3

Facilitating and Limiting Factors—Scores from Intensity Scale
(0 = None, 4 = Great Deal)

Facilitating Factors (General Intensity $\overline{3.2}$)	Limiting Factors (General Intensity $\overline{1.2}$)
Personal ($\overline{3.6}$) *	*Personal ($\overline{1.6}$)*
1. Good relationships with agency, staff, board members, administrators	1. Lack of time 2. Overinvolvement 3. Lack of commitment to agency
2. Commitment to program 3. Position or role 4. Prior experience 5. Commitment to agency and 6. Knowledge of community, guideline clients, programs, and ideology 7. Good reputation, self-confidence	
Client ($\overline{2.5}$)	*Client ($\overline{1.1}$)*
1. Participation	1. Lack of knowledge of organization
2. Interest in program	2. Competition from other activities
3. Receptivity	3. Lack knowledge and skills
Agency ($\overline{2.7}$)	*Agency ($\overline{1.8}$)*
1. Administration support and involvement	1. Hindering structure
2. Staff support	2. Lack of power
3. Supervisor support and involvement	3. Lack of funds and resources
4. Board support	4. Unclear or shifting goals, programs, assignments
5. Staff involvement	5. Lack of staff
6. Assignments and tasks consistent with effort	
Community ($\overline{2.7}$)	*Community ($\overline{1.1}$)*
1. Support of organization	1. Competition from other activities
2. Support of practitioner	2. Lack of knowledge of organization
	3. Lack of knowledge or skills

*These figures represent mean scores.

ganization, this can serve to legitimize the activity and allow a concentration of energy as well as an interpenetration of contacts, resources, and other factors.

Both community and client factors may be of assistance. Community participation and community support of your organization and yourself may be significant—build such support or select groups to work with in which such support already exists. Client participation may be important. Their interest in and receptivity to the program or organization are also considerations. Select a program in which clients are interested, or work hard to develop such interest.

You are likely to experience limiting forces most intensely within your own agency situation. Such agency limitations frequently result from lack of clarity or instability, so that the clarification of goals, programs, and assignments may be a useful tactic. Since internal lack of funds or staff may be a problem, it would be advisable to plan a program realistically within the means of the agency, or think of tapping available external resources. To a lesser extent, the agency's structure may be hindering, or its lack of power or authority may be limiting. Both of these factors suggest strategic considerations in the choice of a program.

The need to manage time and energy efficiently was emphasized in the field study by the frequent mention of lack of time and overinvolvement as major personal limitations. Within the client population and the larger community, the biggest limitations are likely to be competition from other activities and lack of knowledge. This calls attention to the educational functions of the practitioner's job (interpretation, communication, public relations) and the need to formulate programs that are meaningful and interesting enough to compete with the many other forces that demand the attention of clients and community people.

We have attempted to put the findings to use in a variety of ways. The implications, however, are no stronger than the data upon which they are based. Like many prescriptions, the material above should be labeled, *Caution, Use with Care*. The findings are tentative and suggestive. Your own good judgment should influence your evaluation and use of them. Some of the more narrative, direct comments by practitioners that follow amplify and qualify the data that were reported.

PRACTITIONERS' VIEWS OF PROBLEMS AND PROSPECTS

General support for the principle underlying the guideline was expressed by a number of practitioners. As two of them noted:

There is a universality about the application of the principle of spreading innovation from a small group of "converts" to a wider clientele. The key to it is the "experiencing" of the innovation by the small group. The guideline works because it reflects truth about the way people learn anything.

I feel the guideline itself is sound. If meetings of black and white students are ever to become a regular part of the curriculum in my school the worth and feasibility of the innovation will first have to be demonstrated with a small group. It would be too risky to the system to initially implement on a large scale without any demonstration of the innovation's worth.[6]

Several practitioners commented that the guideline helped them to be more systematic in their work, and some of them found the guideline easy to understand and apply. For example:

The guideline serves the purpose of breaking down in concrete terms a specific method for initiating and implementing change. I think it is useful to be specific, purposeful, and sequential in pursuing a goal. This guideline suggests such an orientation.

Given some clarity as to support for its use, the guideline is sensible, practical, do-able, and realistic.

It is one that I can put into use in a number of situations with little or no difficulty on my part.

Other practitioners noted that it is useful for long- (and medium-) range planning because operational problems can be seen on a small scale before the innovation is attempted on a large scale. They also felt that the initial experience by a limited portion of the target system was helpful in determining the potential success or failure of the innovation itself.

You do have an opportunity to work out problems of the innovation and to test its value before trying it on the total target system.

It allows for a test of the idea or change for the practitioner as well as a strategy for gaining acceptance.

While the practitioners expressed enthusiasm for the ideas behind this mode of action, they also pointed out a wide range of problems related to its execution.

1. The perennial problem of time was noted (already indicated also on the quantitative checklist), as was the related factor of the need to select a feasible, moderate-sized proximate goal.

> I had little time to do the implementation of the guideline.

> I guess it was having to be patient before things started happening. Assessment had to constantly take place along with the incredible amount of public relations. At first the pay off is small but it makes the professional more credible.

> The guideline is still valid but there has to be a caution of thinking small and clearly—and limiting the goal sufficiently.

> I would not advise one person to try to work in as many communities as I have attempted to do. It's too much of a workload if responsibilities are not delegated to other leaders and organizations.

2. The selection of the partial target system was described as both a very important and a difficult task.

> The most difficult thing is defining the appropriate "limited portion" of the target population.

> It is important to choose a partial target system that will carry the innovation out with the total target.

> I found the most problematic aspect to be getting the larger community involved in the effort.

The experience of a health planner who attempted to establish a preventive patient education program by working first with part of the agency staff illustrates some hazards involved in selecting the partial group:

> In some ways, the partialization of staff "backfired" in this situation. In that there was little experience of staff being involved in planning and carrying out such a piece of agency work, those involved became extremely ego-involved and those not directly involved developed a real we-they attitude as though they had no role whatsoever, even though they were needed to help carry out contacts. Apparently in this particular situation, this type of

partialization in relation to this particular staff grouping did not work, given the previous experience, attitudes, and total situation.

Another practitioner, a particularly sophisticated and skilled professional, experienced success even in a political and controversial setting, because he had successfully chosen the partial target:

> I believe that the guideline's use produced a favorable result in that the organizations represented in the partial target system were not able to block the Planning Council's housing review system. I think that had we confronted all elements of the target system simultaneously—particularly if we had dealt with all the local governments without first gaining agreements with HUD—we would have been defeated before we were even ready to begin.

Two general recommendations regarding the selection of a partial target group can be drawn from the experiences of the field test. First, the group should be so constituted as to ensure the success of the limited demonstration. That is, it should have some of the following characteristics: receptive to the innovation, generally accepting of change, good relationship with or willingness to work with the practitioner, good motivation, special qualifications such as education, and skills or experiences that would facilitate a successful demonstration.

Second, the partial group should be respected by the general target population (or least not be a deviant, disapproved segment). There should be strong linkages and good means of communication between the partial and general targets. (This second recommendation would not apply when one wanted the demonstration to be a *fait accompli* before diffusing, so as not to arouse a known opposition.)

The size of the partial target, and its *proportional* size relative to the general target should have a bearing on both these matters. In our limited study we were not able to find any discernible patterns regarding proportional size and outcome.

3. The following action implications are suggested from other practitioner comments:

Give attention to interpersonal factors. The narrative comments reinforced the high intensity rating given to personal factors.

Practitioners stressed the degree to which this guideline called for the exercise of interpersonal skills with board members, clients, the agency executive, and other people.

One needs to be clear about the nature and quality of interpersonal relationships involved in the process of trying to reach the goal.

This suggests that the guideline entails modes of influence such as persuasion, example, and communication. It does not typically involve manipulation of power or the use of conflict and contention. (In the familiar French and Raven[7] terminology, referent and expert power receive emphasis; coercive power is in low key.) As one practitioner puts it, "This approach is useful for getting new ideas accepted that do not have major implications for the existing power relationships."

Determine the amount of environmental support-opposition and obstacles.

Nothing in the guideline itself would automatically alert you to consider very strong influences in the environment. It seems to me that the successful implementation of any innovation would generally require a substantial support in the environment.

The most problematic aspects was for me securing the resources to conduct the demonstration properly in the first place.

The guideline is a natural approach to innovations which have some support by those who control resources enough to conduct the demonstration. In my situation there are generally enough actors that support can be found for most anything if the timing is right.

My mistake was that I overestimated the need for a program without assessing whether parents really wanted it before having some other needs met.

It may, in some ways, presume an administrative structure predisposed to giving sanction to experimentation and trying out new ideas. It requires that the practitioner trying to use it must be very clear about the realities of his authority to effect change, or even do his basic every-day job.

The guideline did not help achieve my goals. The following events occurred that prevented this from happening:
The board president resigned and delayed appointment of board members to committee.

The board was delayed for over a two month period in electing a new president.

Some board members disagreed with the person selected as the new president.

Conflict between board members over the goals of the agency began to come into the open.

Some board members began to work toward a change in staffing of the agency.

Try the strategy first on a less important issue; after this experience expand to a larger scale or to more significant innovation.

I feel that working through the goal formulation and operationalizing elements aspects on the initial log was the most problematic of the guidelines. Although the examples given were of great value, I still feel one had to have the experience of working it through before it could be understood and of future use.

Perhaps a good way to end this general discussion of the guideline, and to form a bridge with its actual implementation in the field, is to heed the words of one practitioner:

Once one determines how the innovation can be experienced initially by the partial group there is little problem in carrying it out.

GETTING STARTED

In attempting to use this guideline for the first time you might follow this thought-action process:

1. Think of some new program, technique, or other activity that you have been planning to carry out, or that ties in with general tasks and objectives of your current position or assignment.

2. Attempt to set this down as a goal, but of moderate scope and of short-range time dimension—something that could be completed in a minimum of about five and a maximum of twenty-three weeks.

3. Conceptualize the general or "total" target system at which this innovation is directed: who are the people collectively who would be benefiting from utilizing or participating in this innovation?

4. Think through a smaller segment of that target system, a more delimited subgroup: (*a*) who might relatively easily be drawn into a trial or demonstration of the innovation; (*b*) with whom there is high likelihood of success in an initial trial; (*c*) whose success would be likely to have an impact on the larger target system, or on a relevant Decision-Making Unit that could legitimate or authorize transfer of the innovation to the larger target system.

5. Our review of patterns of implementation suggests that, early in the game, authorization or legitimation is often needed in order to proceed. This may be obtained from an administrative superordinate (supervisor, agency director, and so on) or from the agency board. Also quite early in the process, persons or organizations may need to be approached who can provide resources to carry through the small-scale demonstration, or can offer access to the smaller target system. Make a determination of the individuals, groups, or organizations whose acceptance needs to be gained.

6. When you have worked the issue through in your mind to this point, begin to fill out the Initial Log. This is meant to assist you to formulate (put down on paper) some tentative early steps that you might take in starting to carry out this guideline.

INITIAL LOG FORM

As a further step toward getting started, we suggest that you put down your tentative thoughts regarding implementation of the guideline. The Initial Log Form we developed for the field test was helpful to practitioners in that connection. The Initial Log is a tool for organizing your thinking in a systematic way. It is geared especially to helping you think about your goal, ways of operationalizing the guideline, the key individual and community groups to involve, and the facilitating and limiting factors in the situation (personal, agency, client, community).

Following the Log Form you will find illustrations of key sections that were completed by project practitioners.

INITIAL LOG

A Preliminary Guide for Action

1. Date of Preparation of Guide for Action ＿＿＿＿＿＿＿.

2. In relation to using the guideline, what is your goal (i.e., the innovation)? Be as specific and concrete as possible. Keep a short-term time perspective (5 to 12 weeks).

3. Describe the circumstances (conditions, events, assignments, requests, etc.) that led you to use this guideline to achieve the goal above.

4. Look back at the intervention guideline. How would you begin to define or concretize *each* element of the guideline in your immediate practice situation (i.e., how might you operationalize these components)? Keep in mind the delimited innovation goal stated in question 2.

    (*a*) What is the *General Target System:*

    The *Proximate Target:*

    (*b*) What is the *Partial Target System* (specifically):

(*c*) Is a Decision-Making Unit involved? Describe it. How will its members be encouraged to accept the innovation?

(*d*) How will you foster diffusion from the partial to the larger target—for example, forms of linkage, communication, promotion?

5. List the *major* steps you anticipate going through to utilize this guideline. Describe specific behaviors in the order in which you expect they will occur.

6. What *key* community groups will you probably involve (if any)?

GROUP: REASON FOR CONTACT:

_____   _____
_____   _____
_____   _____
_____   _____
_____   _____

7. What *key* individuals will you probably involve (if any)?

| | TITLE AND/OR | |
| INDIVIDUAL(S): | AFFILIATION: | REASON FOR CONTACT: |

_____ _____ _____
_____ _____ _____
_____ _____ _____
_____ _____ _____
_____ _____ _____
_____ _____ _____

8. Facilitating and limiting factors in guideline implementation.

As an aid to implementation you should consider factors that will affect your progress. We have provided checklists of common *facilitating factors,* those that will assist you to carry out the guideline, and typical *limiting factors,* those that may inhibit your success. In the checklists we have included conditions that were frequently indicated by practitioners in the field study. Others may be important in your own situation, and space is provided for you to note these.

Following the itemized checklists, you are asked to estimate the relative importance of various facilitating and limiting factors.

Personal Factors

FACILITATING:

- ☐ Good personal relationship with administrator.
- ☐ Good personal relationship with supervisor.
- ☐ Good personal relationships with staff.
- ☐ Personal commitment to the agency.
- ☐ Personal knowledge of clients.
- ☐ Personal position or role.
- ☐ Good personal reputation.
- ☐ Self-confidence.
- ☐ Other: _____

_____

LIMITING:

- ☐ Poor personal relationships with board (members).
- ☐ Lack of personal knowledge of the community.
- ☐ Poor personal reputation.
- ☐ Personal loss (demotion, job title, etc.).
- ☐ Overinvolvement.
- ☐ Fatigue.
- ☐ Lack of time.
- ☐ Other: _____

_____

Agency Factors

FACILITATING:

- [ ] External authority requires your organization to support your effort.
- [ ] Affiliated organizational support.
- [ ] Board involvement.
- [ ] Administration support or involvement.
- [ ] Administration disinterest.
- [ ] Supervisor involvement.
- [ ] Supervisor disinterest.
- [ ] Physical facilities aid the effort.
- [ ] Other: _____

_____

LIMITING:

- [ ] Lack of power or authority of your organization.
- [ ] Unclear or shifting goals, programs, or assignments.
- [ ] Lack of agency knowledge of clients or community.
- [ ] Lack of agency support, or hindering action of affiliated organizations.
- [ ] Lack of agency support, or hindering action of supervisor.
- [ ] Other: _____

_____

Client Factors

FACILITATING:

- [ ] Voluntary client participation in your organization or program.
- [ ] Client participation in your organization or program through a legal or administrative ruling.
- [ ] Client is generally interested in your organization.
- [ ] Client shows receptivity to your organization or program.
- [ ] Other: _____

_____

LIMITING:

☐ Client shows a general negative response to your organization.
☐ Client is disinterested or dissatisfied with your organization or program.
☐ Client lack of knowledge of your organization, its purposes, programs, or activities.
☐ Other: _____

_____

Community Factors

FACILITATING:

☐ Voluntary community participation in your organization or program.
☐ Community support of clients.
☐ Other: _____

_____

LIMITING:

☐ Community disinterest or dissatisfaction with your organization or program.
☐ Community lack of knowledge of your organization, its purposes, programs, or activities.
☐ External influences make the community unsupportive of your organization or program.
☐ Community residents are specifically disinterested in your program.
☐ Other: _____

_____

9. Facilitating factors—relative importance.

In general, to what degree do you think *personal factors related to yourself* may be facilitating in implementing this guideline? (These factors might include good relationships with staff, good relationships with community people, personal knowledge of community, and positive effects of skill.)

Rate the degree of facilitation:

None ___ ___ ___ ___ ___ Great deal
      0   1   2   3   4

In general, to what degree do you think *agency* factors may be facilitating in implementing this guideline? (These factors might include administration support, supervisor support, staff support, and physical facilities aid effort.)

Rate the degree of facilitation:

None ___ ___ ___ ___ ___ Great deal
      0   1   2   3   4

In general, to what degree do you think *client* factors may be facilitating in implementing this guideline? (These factors might include client participation in organization or program receptivity to organization of program, client receptivity to organization or program, and client support of practitioner.)

Rate the degree of facilitation:

None ___ ___ ___ ___ ___ Great deal
      0   1   2   3   4

In general, to what degree do you think *community* factors may be facilitating in implementing this guideline? (These factors might include: community supports organization generally, influential and other community groups support organization or program, changes in community tend to support organization or program, and community supports practitioner.)

Rate the degree of facilitation:

None ___ ___ ___ ___ ___ Great deal
      0   1   2   3   4

10. Limiting—relative importance.

In general, to what degree do you think *personal factors related to yourself* may be limiting in implementing this guideline? (These factors might include poor relationships with staff, poor relationships with community people, lack of personal knowledge of community, and negative effects of insufficient skills.)

Rate the degree of limitation:

None ____ ____ ____ ____ ____ Great deal
      0   1   2   3   4

In general, to what degree do you think *agency* factors may be limiting in implementing this guideline? (These factors might include unclear or shifting goals, programs, and/or assignments; lack of funds, facilities, and other resources; lack of support or hindering action of supervisor; and lack of support or hindering action of staff.)

Rate the degree of limitation:

None ____ ____ ____ ____ ____ Great deal
      0   1   2   3   4

In general, to what degree do you think *client* factors may be limiting in implementing this guideline? (These factors might include negative response to organization generally, clients' interference with organization activities, and dissensus among clients.)

Rate the degree of limitation:

None ____ ____ ____ ____ ____ Great deal
      0   1   2   3   4

In general, to what degree do you think *community* factors may be limiting in implementing this guideline? (These factors might include negative response to organization generally; lack of knowledge of organization purposes, programs, or activities; influential community groups or leaders that do not support organization or program; and competition by other activities with community residents' time and interests.)

Rate the degree of limitation:

None ____ ____ ____ ____ ____ Great deal
      0   1   2   3   4

ILLUSTRATIONS OF INITIAL LOGS
COMPLETED BY PRACTITIONERS

Example of Outreach Programs in Housing Project

GOAL STATEMENT

To establish outreach services for tenants in a housing project served by a traditional family service agency. (A broader goal, beyond the application to the guideline in this particular instance, is related to a desire for the agency to establish outreach services in the community generally.)

CONCRETIZATION (OPERATIONALIZATION) OF
GUIDELINE ELEMENTS

General Target System: All tenants of the housing project (20 courts).
The Proximate Target: Tenants in six courts.
Partial Target System: One court made up of six families. This court will be selected fairly randomly, because there is little basis for knowing which court offers the best potential for successful initial implementation.

Example of Social Welfare Employees Union

GOAL STATEMENT

To establish a pattern of implementation of union programs at the building level through building committees at each work location.

CONCRETIZATION (OPERATIONALIZATION) OF
GUIDELINE ELEMENTS

General Target System: All building units (25 in all).
The Proximate Target: Six units contiguous to one another and to the partial system.
Partial Target System: One building-level committee structure where staff has already expressed an interest in operating in this way. (This interest can be built on to bring about an initial successful trial.)

Notes

1. Everett Rogers of the University of Michigan has codified much of the research on innovation in his two books, *The Diffusion of Innovations* (New York: Free Press, 1962), and the revised edition with F. Floyd Shoemaker, *The Communication of Innovations* (New York: Free Press, 1971). Pertinent research in this area includes: Johan Arnt, "A Test of the Two Step Flow in Diffusion of a New Product," *Journalism Quarterly* 45, (1968): 457–465; Marshall H. Becker, *Patterns of Interpersonal Influence and Sources of Information in the Diffusion of Two Public Health Innovations* (Ann Arbor: University of Michigan, Pub. Health Practice Res. Program, Rept., 1968); James Coleman et al., *Medical Innovation: A Diffusion Study* (New York: Bobbs-Merrill, 1966); Frederick C. Fliegel and Joseph E. Kivlin, "Farm Practice Attributes and Adoption Rates," *Social Forces* 40 (1962): 364–370; Frederick C. Fliegel and Joseph E. Kivlin, "Attributes of Innovations as Factors in Diffusion," *American Journal of Sociology* 72 (1966): 235–248; Eugene A. Havens and Everett M. Rogers, "Adoption of Hybrid Corn: Profitability and the Interaction Effect," *Rural Sociology* 26 (1961): 409–414; E. Hruschka and H. Rheinwald, "The Effectiveness of German Pilot Farms," *Sociologia Ruralis* 5 (1965): 101–111; Elihu Katz and Paul F. Lazarsfeld, *Personal Influence: The Part Played by People in the Flow of Mass Communications* (New York: Free Press, 1955); Joseph E. Kivlin and Frederick C. Fliegel, "Differential Perceptions of Innovations and Rate of Adoption," *Rural Sociology* 32 (1967): 78–91; Edwin Mansfield, "Technical Change and the Rate of Imitation," *Econometrica* 29 (1961): 741–766; Herbert Menzel and Elihu Katz, "Social Relations and Innovation in the Medical Profession: The Epidemiology of a New Drug," *Public Opinion Quarterly* 19 (1955): 337–352; Stephen Polgar et al., "Diffusion and Farming Advice: A Test of Some Current Notions," *Social Forces* 41 (1963): 104–111; Everett M. Rogers and George M. Beal, "Community Norms, Opinion Leadership and Innovativeness among Truck Growers," *Wooster, Ohio Agri. Exp. Sta., Res. Bul.* 912 (1962); Everett M. Rogers with Lynne Svenning, *Modernization among Peasants: The Impact of Communication* (New York: Holt, Rinehart and Winston, 1969).

2. Richard O. Carlson, "School Superintendents and Adoption of Modern Math: A Social Structure Profile," in *Innovation in Education,* ed. Matthew B. Miles (New York: Teachers College, Columbia University, 1964).

3. Gerald Zaltman, Robert Duncan, and Jonny Holbek, *Innovations and Organizations* (New York: Wiley-Interscience, 1973), p. 39.

4. In his revised book with Shoemaker, Rogers includes a section on "Authority Innovation Decisions," which considers the effects of decision-making units in organizational settings.

5. We will not attempt a full summary of field-test findings here. We have found that such a summary in all its detail and complexity has impeded the use of the manual for specific intervention purposes. Some highlights and tendencies will be presented in a highly succinct fashion. The methodology note in the Appendix A [of *Promoting Innovation and Change*] spells out limitations of these data. Any reader wishing a detailed treatment of the research design and findings will find it in the forthcoming publication cited earlier: *Research and Development in The Human Services: Constructing Effective Systems Intervention Strategies* (Englewood Cliffs, N.J.: Prentice-Hall, 1980).

6. Because this was the first guideline that was implemented in our field test, unfamiliarity with approaches and procedures may have influenced the practitioners' reactions. Half of the practitioners rated the guideline 5 (most useful) on the 1 to 5 continuum of usefulness; the average rating was 4.0.

7. John R. P. French, Jr., and Bertram Raven, "The Bases of Social Power," in *Studies in Social Power,* ed. Darwin Cartwright (Ann Arbor: University of Michigan, 1959), pp. 150–167.

Chapter 16 Organizational Tinkering

Edward J. Pawlak

To tinker means to work at something in an experimental or makeshift way. Although the clinician's position and role in many social welfare organizations preclude him from pursuing ambitious organizational change, he still may be able to work at change in modest, makeshift ways. And, despite the fact that clinical social work is usually practiced in an organizational and policy context, many clinicians are uninterested in acquiring the knowledge and skills that might facilitate intraorganizational tinkering on behalf of their practice or their clients. Others are overwhelmed, cynical, or disillusioned by their dealings with bureaucracy.[1] Some front-line practitioners, however, have learned to tinker effectively.[2]

To help clinicians improve their talent in dealing with organizations, this chapter identifies tactics they can use to tinker with organizational structure, modes of operation, rules, conventions, policy, and programs. The specific tactics discussed are tinkering with bureaucratic succession and rules, the white paper or position paper, demonstration projects, modification of board composition, bypassing, influencing grant reviews, leaking information, and protest by resignation.

Although the author takes a partisan stand on behalf of clinicians, it does not follow that managers are necessarily the villains. However, some of the tactics identified here are directed toward those administrators who cause clinicians to harbor severe misgivings about the organization.

This chapter stems not only from the author's observation of and experience with organizational tinkering, but also from the contributions of others who have addressed similar themes.[3] It warns clinicians to bear in mind the pitfalls and dilemmas of organizational tinkering—that it takes

Reprinted from *Social Work* 21, no. 5 (Sept. 1976): 376–380, with the permission of the publisher. A version of this article was presented at the NASW Twentieth Anniversary Symposium, Hollywood, Florida, October 1975. The author is appreciative of the helpful advice given by Roger Nooe, Kate Mullins, and Roger Lohmann in the preparation of this manuscript.

place in a political climate and in a structure of authority, norms, and sanctions.[4]

BUREAUCRATIC SUCCESSION

Bureaucratic succession usually refers to a change in leadership at the highest levels of an organization. Here, however, the author uses the broader concept that includes changes in leadership at all levels in the hierarchy.[5] Bureaucratic succession must be called to the attention of clinicians because it is an opportunity to influence intraorganizational change. For the clinician to exert influence during this phase of organizational transition, it is essential that he understand certain features of organizational life that frequently accompany succession.

Prior to an administrator's departure, organizations usually go into a period of inaction. Most staff members are aware of the lame-duck character of this phase of organizational life, when any major change is avoided until the new administrator takes office. There are, however, ways in which clinicians take advantage of this period. They can, for example, (1) suggest criteria for the selection of a successor, (2) seek membership on the search committee, (3) prepare a position paper for the new administrator, (4) propose a revision in the governance structure to enhance participatory management, (5) organize fellow subordinates to propose changes that had been unacceptable to the outgoing administrator, or (6) propose the formulation of a task force to facilitate transition.

The "first one hundred days" is another critical phase of bureaucratic succession that should be examined for the opportunities it offers. Although new administrators tend to be conservative about implementing changes until they are more familiar with the organization, they still are interested in development and in making their own mark. This three-month period, therefore, provides opportunities to orient and shape the perceptions of the new administrator, who, until he acquires his own intelligence about the organization, is both vulnerable and receptive to influence.

The following case illustrates how practitioners can tinker with organizational hierarchy by taking advantage of a resignation.

The resignation of a clinician who had served as director of staff development in a child welfare agency provided the staff with an opportunity to influence the transformation of the position into that of administrative assistant. The agency had recently undergone rapid growth in staff size, resources, and diversity, without an accompanying increase in the administrative staff. Thus, the clinician's resignation became the occasion for examining whether the position should be modified to serve such administrative staff functions as program development and grant management.

Bureaucratic succession, therefore, provides an opportunity for an organization to take pause; to examine its mission, structure, policies, practices, accomplishments, and problems; and to decide what it wants to become. It is incumbent upon practitioners to participate in these processes and to take advantage of the structure of influence during that vulnerable phase.

RULES

Rules are features of organizations that, by their nature, invite tinkering. They act as mechanisms of social control and standardization, provide guidelines for decision-making, limit discretion, and structure relationships between persons and units within the organizational structure and between separate organizations.[6] There are two types of rules—formal and informal. Formal rules are derived from law or are determined administratively or collectively. Informal rules—which may be as binding as formal ones—are practices that have been routinized so that they have become organizational conventions or traditions. Rules vary in specificity, in their inherent demand for compliance, in the manner in which compliance is monitored, and in their sanctions for a lack of compliance.

Clinicians can tinker with rules either by the kind of interpretations they apply to them or by using their discretion, as is permitted with an ambiguous or general rule. Rules do not necessarily eliminate discretion but they may eliminate alternatives that might otherwise be considered.[7] Gottlieb describes them as follows:

> Rules are not necessarily static. They appear to be a controlling force working impersonally and equally, but they vary both in adherence and enforceability and are used variously by staff in their adaptation to the "welfare bind."[8]

Hanlan suggests that "in public welfare there exists an informal system that operates without invoking the formal administrative machinery of rules."[9] The author overheard the director of a community action program encourage new workers "to err on the side of generosity in determining eligibility for programs." A vocational rehabilitation counselor reported that he had had many teeth fixed by liberally interpreting a rule that provided dental care for only those clients whose appearance and dental problems would otherwise have prevented them from being considered for employment involving public contact. This shows that one can tinker with the manner in which rules are interpreted and enforced.

Another way of tinkering with rules is to avoid what Gottlieb calls "rule interpretations by agents of the system alone."[10] She goes on to report that welfare workers encouraged clients to seek help in interpreting rules enforced by the National Welfare Rights Organization (NWRO). It is generally known that legal-aid clinics have been called on to give a legal interpretation of welfare rules and rules governing commitment to mental hospitals.

A supervisor for public assistance eligibility once reported that a thorough knowledge of all the rules enables the welfare worker to invoke one rule over another in order to help clients get what they need. This observation is supported by Gottlieb, who points out that rules allow for exceptions and that many NWRO members know the rules better than the workers and thus can challenge their interpretations.[11] In his study of regulatory agencies, Nader suggests that rules not only are opportunities for action but are potential obstacles as well and that major effort is frequently required to persuade the agency to follow its own rules.[12]

Another way of dealing with rules is to avoid asking for an interpretation. One agency administrator has suggested that personnel should not routinely ask for rulings and urges them to use their own discretion. He commented: "If you invoke authority, you put me in a position where I must exercise it. If I make a decision around here, it becomes a rule."

These ways of tinkering with rules suggest that clinicians should examine the function of rules, discern the latitude they are allowed in interpreting them, and exercise discretion. Although the foregoing examples are primarily taken from welfare settings, the principles outlined can be applied to traditional clinical settings.

INDIRECT INFLUENCE

Too often, clinicians rely on the anecdotal or case approach to influence change in an organization. Such an approach is too easily countered by the rejoinder that exceptional cases do not require a change in policy but should be handled as exceptions. The white paper, or position paper, is a much ignored means of tinkering with organizations.

A white paper is a report on a specific subject that emanates from a recent investigation. A position paper is a statement that sets forth a policy or a perspective. The first is usually more carefully reasoned and documented; the second may be argued instead of reasoned. Both white papers and position papers provide opportunities for social documentation and for formulating a compelling case. Such statements strive for logic and are characterized by their use of both quantitative and qualitative data. As the following example shows, by virtue of their character and quality, both position papers and white papers demand a specific response:

A student social worker wrote a position paper identifying the number of teenage pregnancies, the number of associated medical problems, and the high rate of venereal disease among adolescents. She argued for the redirection of the original planned parenthood proposal from the main office to satellite clinics in public housing developments and schools. The paper was well received and spurred the executive to obtain funding from the housing authority.

Lindblom has characterized decision-making in organizations as "disjointed incrementalism."[13] Simon indicates that organizations "satisfice" —that is, they make decisions that are good enough. Uncertainties in the environment, the inability to scan all alternatives, and the unknown utility of a solution or decision all preclude optimal decision-making. If organizations were to try to comprehend all the information and contingencies necessary before making a rational decision, the complexity would be overwhelming.[14] Thus, organizations are reluctant to make changes on a large scale because this could lead to large-scale and unpredictable consequences. Resistance to change, therefore, may often be attributed to structure rather than to a malevolent or unsympathetic administrator. This calls attention to organizational structure and processes, but does not mean that the values and roles of administrators are to be ignored.[15]

Given this perspective of organizational behavior, clinicians may consider approaching innovation incrementally and on a small scale by first gaining authorization for a demonstration project.[16] A demonstration project may be bounded by the duration of time or the proportion of the budget or staff time that is devoted to it. The problem with demonstration projects is that the people for whom the demonstration is being carried out are not always specified, nor are they always kept abreast of developments. Often there is a failure to articulate the ramifications and consequences of a successful or unsuccessful demonstration. Practitioners must develop a strategy of demonstration—a means of diffusing innovation throughout the organization or into other organizations and of obtaining commitments from the administration when the demonstration is complete. The following is an example of the commitment one social worker obtained:

A social worker met with a group of suspended or expelled junior high school students after class to discuss their problems. Realizing that she needed to have a chance to intervene directly in their school behavior, she persuaded the agency supervisor, the principal, and the classroom teacher to develop a pilot project—"the opportunity class"—to be used as a last resort before expulsion. When the project was organized, the social worker remained in the classroom for several periods at least two days each week. She handled the acting-out behavior problems while the teacher continued classroom instruction. Eventually the teacher acquired skill in handling students who were acting out. The class continued without the social worker's presence, and some students returned to a regular classroom while others were expelled.

Agency board committees are typically composed of elected members and the executive director of the agency. In addition, in some agencies, one or two staff members may also serve on the committee or occasionally attend meetings to make reports. One strategy of tinkering with the composition of the committee and the kind of information and influence it receives is to promote the idea that nonboard and nonstaff members with certain expertise be included on the committee. For example, a psychiatrist and a local expert on group treatment with children might be recruited to join a case services committee in order to provide legitimation to innovations that board members were grudgingly resisting.

Bypassing refers to a process whereby a practitioner avoids taking a proposal for change or a grievance to his immediate superior but seeks instead a hearing or decision from a higher level in the hierarchy. In an enlightened organization, this form of bypassing is acceptable and even encouraged; government workers, in fact, are entitled to it as part of "due process." Bypassing is risky, however, in that it can discredit the judgment of the complainant if the matter is trivial or if it appears that it could have been resolved at a lower level in the hierarchy. Bypassing also places the administration in a vulnerable situation because if the tactic is justified, it reflects poorly on the judgment of the superior and the administrators who hired him. This may lead to questions of non-retention or spur a desired resignation. A successful instance of by-passing is described in the following example:

When a clinician's complaints concerning the physical plant and security of a youth home went unheeded by the director, he demanded to meet with the executive committee of the board. The director admitted that his own sense of urgency differed from that of his staff, but arranged for the meeting. The executive committee approved some of the recommendations for change and authorized that they be implemented as soon as possible.

Agencies often write grant applications for funds to support their programs. A critical phase of the application process occurs at a public review of the grant application when the funding agency invites comment or a letter of support from the agency or from interested parties. If a clinician is dissatisfied with a particular program, and if it is an important matter, he can provide the agency issuing the grant with dissenting information, testify at the review of the grant application, or respond from the standpoint of an "expert witness." In any event, the grant-review process may be an opportunity to voice concern about an agency's program and to influence the advisory group to give conditional approval or disapproval. As is shown in the following example, clinicians may attempt to influence the review process indirectly—by encouraging an expert third party to raise questions about the grant application—or directly:

A social worker was asked to serve as a technical reviewer for a volunteer program for young offenders in a regional planning advisory group. The program was modeled after an existing program in another part of the state. The documents supporting the application contained a manual that described the role of the volunteer. It suggested that a volunteer should report any violations of parole to the corrections authority but should not reveal this action to the offender. In seeming contradiction, it emphasized that the volunteer should be a "friend" of the offender. The social worker informed the advisory group of this provision and of his strenuous objection to it. The director of the program had failed to read the manual thoroughly and was unaware of the statement. The advisory group approved the program on the condition that the volunteer not serve as an informer and demanded that the staff codify the conditions under which it may be morally imperative for the volunteer to reveal the offender's behavior.

Social workers are often asked and frequently do endorse a program or a grant application perfunctorily, without having read the proposal. In other instances, programs and grants are endorsed in spite of strong reservations. Notwithstanding the pressures toward reciprocity that exist among agencies, such exchanges of professional courtesy are questionable.

Social workers should take advantage of requests for endorsement or participation in the grant-review process, particularly if they believe that certain aspects of a proposal or program are questionable. The desire for professional endorsement also underlies agency efforts to recruit clinicians for board membership or as paid consultants. Refusal of such offers is a way of "making a statement" about a program.

RADICAL TACTICS

Leaking information, or the covert release of information about an organization, is a tactic that should be used only in grave matters after all other remedies within the organization have been exhausted. The third party to whom the informant gives the information has to verify it and the credibility of the informant, since he is not willing to put his own character and job on the line. However, until "blowing the whistle" becomes an accepted institutionalized value, and until protections are legislated, it is likely that members of organizations will continue to act like "guerrillas in a bureaucracy."[17]

Clinicians who anticipate the need to leak information would be well advised to seek counsel, for discovery could result in liability damages. They are obliged to have a thorough, accurate, and verifiable account of the objectionable situation. As the ethics of leaking information have not been well formulated, clinicians need to consider carefully the professional, moral, and legal standards that support such action.[18] One way in which the clinician may choose to attack the problem is shown as follows:

The clinician in a foregoing example who was concerned about the physical plant and security of a youth home notified the state monitor about the condition of the home. At the next site visit, the monitor raised questions about the residents' access to balconies and the roof and about the staff-client ratio on weekends.

Resignation in protest, or public defection, is another tactic that should be used only when a clinician experiences unbearable misgivings and finds it both morally and professionally imperative to reveal them publicly. The major problem is that the organization has the financial and operational resources to counter the protest, but the employee has none. Also, with few exceptions, resignation in protest has a history of aversive consequences for the protester.[19]

A resignation in protest may also discredit the agency. Therefore, prospective protesters must be prepared to have their observations and conclusions verified and their judgment subjected to public review and scrutiny. In addition, the protester must realize that future employers will wonder whether such history of protestation will continue. An example follows:

When his concerns went unheeded by the board, a clinician resigned in protest. Moreover, he informed the board and the director that he would discourage any professional worker from accepting employment at the agency. He was effective in discouraging local professionals from accepting employment at the agency unless firm commitments were made to modify policies and practices that were detrimental to clients.

The theory of escalation urges the protester to begin by using conventional and formal means to express grievances and influence change. Only after these have been exhausted, and traditional means have encountered failure and resistance, should he engage in a series of escalations to such unconventional or radical forms of protest as boycotting, "palace revolts," picketing, leaking information, and the like. The essential point of this strategy is that the protester should not begin by engaging in the most radical and abrasive strategy. To document the intransigence of the bureaucracy, change must be approached incrementally. If this is not done, the bureaucracy may point to the failure to follow administrative due process. The protester's etiquette and failure to go through channels then become the bone of contention, and the protester becomes the object of protest.[20]

As a condition of employment and as a professional right and responsibility, clinicians should have the opportunity to bring their insights into the plans and programs of the organization they work for. Such participation requires that clinicians acquire skill in dealing with organizations. It is hoped that the participation of clinicians in organizational activity will promote responsive service delivery systems and satisfactory work climates.

At the risk of appearing to be a "double agent," the author plans to write a second article to advise administrators on how to cope with the tinkering of clinicians. After all, organizational power—whether in the hands of clinicians or administrators—"must be insecure to some degree if it is to be more responsible."[21]

Notes

1. See Scott Briar, "The Casework Predicament," Irving Piliavin, "Restructuring the Provision of Social Services," and Harry Specht, "Casework Practice and Social Policy Formulation," *Social Work* 13 (Jan. 1968): 9–10, 34–36, and 42–43; Archie Hanlan, "Casework beyond Bureaucracy," *Social Casework* 52 (April 1971): 195–198; Lawrence Podell and Ronald Miller, *Professionalism in Public Social Services,* Study Series, vol. 1, no. 2 (New York: Human Resources Administration, 1974); and Naomi Gottlieb, *The Welfare Bind* (New York: Columbia University Press, 1974), p. 34.
2. See Thomas F. Maher, "Freedom of Speech in Public Agencies," *Social Work* 19 (Nov. 1974): 698–703; Joseph J. Senna, "Changes in Due Process of Law," *Social Work* 19 (May 1974): 319–324; and Irwin Hyman and Karen Schreiber, "The School Psychologist as Child Advocate," *Children Today* 3 (March–April 1974): 21–33, 36.
3. Rino J. Patti and Herman Resnick, "Changing the Agency from Within," *Social Work* 17 (July 1972): 48–57; Specht, "Casework Practice," pp. 42–52; George Brager, "Advocacy and Political Behavior," *Social Work* 13 (April 1968): 5–15; Carl Martin, "Beyond Bureaucracy," *Child Welfare* 1 (July 1971): 384–388; Warren G. Bennis, "Post-Bureaucratic Leadership," *Trans-Action* 6 (July–Aug. 1969): 44–52; and Harold Weissman, *Overcoming Mismanagement in the Human Service Professions* (San Francisco: Jossey-Bass, 1973).
4. See Rino J. Patti, "Organizational Resistance and Change: The View from Below," *Social Service Review* 48 (Sept. 1974): 367–383; Edward Weisband and Thomas M. Franck, *Resignation in Protest* (New York: Grossman, 1975); Ralph Nader, Peter J. Petkas, and Kate Blackwell, *Whistle-Blowing* (New York: Grossman, 1972); Irwin Epstein, "Social Workers and Social Action," *Social Work* 13 (April 1968): 101–108, and "Professional Role Orientations and Conflict Strategies," *Social Work* 15 (Oct. 1970): 87–92; and A. D. Green, "The Professional Social Worker in the Bureaucracy," *Social Service Review* 40 (March 1966): 71–83.
5. For a more detailed discussion of bureaucratic succession, see Bernard Levenson, "Bureaucratic Succession," in *Complex Organizations,* ed. Amitai Etzioni (New York: Holt, Rinehart and Winston, 1961), pp. 362–365; and Alvin Gouldner, *Patterns of Industrial Bureaucracy* (Glencoe, Ill.: Free Press, 1954), pp. 59–104.
6. For a detailed discussion, see Charles Perrow, *Complex Organizations: A Critical Essay* (Glenview, Ill.: Scott, Foresman, 1972), pp. 23–32.
7. James D. Thompson, *Organizations in Action* (New York: McGraw-Hill, 1967), p. 120.
8. Gottlieb, *Welfare Bind,* p. 8.
9. Archie Hanlan, "Counteracting Problems of Bureaucracy in Public Welfare," *Social Work* 12 (July 1967): 93.

10. Gottlieb, *Welfare Bind,* p. 8.
11. Ibid., p. 32.
12. Nader, Petkas, and Blackwell, *Whistle-Blowing.*
13. Charles E. Lindblom, "The Science of Muddling Through," in *Strategies of Community Organization,* ed. Fred Cox et al. (Itasca, Ill.: F. E. Peacock, 1970).
14. Herbert A. Simon, *Administrative Behavior* (2d ed.; New York: Macmillan, 1957), and *Models of Man, Social and Rational* (New York: John Wiley, 1957).
15. For a useful discussion on organizational resistance to change, see Rino J. Patti, "Organizational Resistance and Change."
16. For a negative view of demonstration grants, see George E. Pratt, "The Demonstration Grant Is Probably Counterproductive," *Social Work* 19 (July 1974): 486–489.
17. Nader, Petkas, and Blackwell, *Whistle-Blowing,* pp. 15, 25–33; and Martin L. Needleman and Carolyn Emerson Needleman, *Guerrillas in the Bureaucracy* (New York: John Wiley, 1974).
18. For some guidelines on this matter, see Nader, Petkas, and Blackwell, *Whistle-Blowing,* pp. vii, 1–8, 29–30, 225–230.
19. See Weisband and Franck, *Resignation in Protest.*
20. Ibid., pp. 55–94; Needleman and Needleman, *Guerrillas,* pp. 285–289, 335–339; and Nader, Petkas, and Blackwell, *Whistle-Blowing,* pp. 16–25.
21. Nader, Petkas, and Blackwell, *Whistle-Blowing,* p. 15.

Chapter 17 Planning and Power

in Hospital Social Service

Brian Segal

For many years, hospital social work practice was limited to casework methodology. More recently, group work has become a popular method of working with hospitalized patients, and it is slowly being incorporated into social service departments.[1] Community planning, development of extended health care services, and community participation programs in hospitals are also becoming more widespread.[2] Social planning has recently emerged as a force in developing social policy and effecting organizational change within the hospital.

This chapter is concerned with the role of social service in planning for change in the policies and programs in a general hospital in order to improve social conditions relating to patient care.[3] The chapter will first examine the historical realities that have patterned the present status quo of hospital social work. It will then define and explore social planning as a method of social work intervention for planning in the hospital. Finally, it will provide a strategy for the implementation of plans based on an action-oriented model. According to Warren Bennis, Kenneth Benne, and Robert Chin, "Many signs and activities point toward an emerging action role for the behavioral scientist. The manipulative standpoint . . . is becoming distinguishable from the contemplative standpoint."[4]

The development of social work practice in the hospital can be attributed largely to the growing recognition by physicians of the relationship between environmental and social conditions and health. Dr. Richard Cabot of the Massachusetts General Hospital first introduced social service as a paramedical means for aiding medical treatment by exposing and trying to change environmental conditions contributing to

Reprinted from *Social Casework*, July 1970, pp. 399–405, with the permission of the Family Service Association of America. The article is based on a paper presented at the Annual Staff Training Institute, Social Service Department, the Jewish General Hospital, Montreal, November 1969.

ill health. The social worker's secondary role was to make the hospital system less impersonal for the patient, thereby facilitating delivery of health services. In both these activities social service functioned as an adjunct to medical services. All social service action, furthermore, was based on the medical plan of the physician. Social workers were continually trying to prove the value of their services in a setting where they would "undertake service only for those patients referred by the doctors" in such a way that this "assistance should be linked with the medical plan for the patient."[5]

Two factors in the development of medical social work were responsible for its subordinate status. Social service in the hospital gained its impetus from the physician rather than from other social work or charitable organizations. Consequently, hospital social service very early became secondary rather than collateral to medical service, and its structure was based on medical rather than on social work values. Because of this relationship, the social service department organized its function and mode of intervention almost entirely on behalf of the medical staff and medical goals. The result is a dearth of innovation in service and in planning new methods of social work intervention.

At present the major emphasis in hospital planning is on meeting the increased demand for improved medical facilities and on delivery of medical services. The former objective needs no explanation; the latter requires some elaboration as it affects not only the patient population but also paramedical and medical services.

CONTROL POINT PLANNING

The hospital is a highly organized authoritarian system. It is continually trying to regulate the behavior of the patient and to involve him in all aspects of treatment. To do so effectively, the hospital must be able to rely on the operation of all systems or services according to established policies and regulations. To ensure this pattern, hospitals practice what Joseph Eaton has called "control point planning."[6] This term refers to the creation by the administration of a bias in the social system to induce the participants of the system to behave in accordance with the administration's goals. In this way, predictability of behavior, which is essential for effective total planning, is incorporated into the system. For example, although self-discharge by the patient is permissible, actually to discharge oneself without medical sanction involves not being able to obtain X rays, medical reports, or medication. The hospital, therefore, exerts strong control on the patient and can usually predict his behavior.

Examination of control point planning provides a neat, theoretical insight into the role of social service in the hospital. The system of medical referral to the social service department limits the scope of social work activities to the departmental level and further restricts innovation and planning. This effect of control point planning on the social service department can relate both directly and indirectly to its effect on the patient population. For example, one control point of administrative planning is the necessity for all clinic patients to register at the same hour although many will not be seen until much later. From the point of view of medical planning, this arrangement ensures that the patients will be present when the physician who is donating his time is ready to receive them. From the point of view of social work, the bread lines of yesterday are replaced by the clinic lines of today.

The clinic lines are a powerful depersonalizing force in the life of the patient and such disregard for the individual's self-esteem is incompatible with social work values. Must the social service department, therefore, rely solely on medical referrals to help individual patients with such feelings, or does it not have a responsibility to change such social conditions in clinics through broader planning? Although the bureaucracy and high degree of specialization in hospitals contribute to efficient and productive administration, they also result in depersonalized treatment of the patient when he is least able to cope with his environment and tend to widen the communication gap between patient and physician. Raymond Duff and August Hollingshead point out:

> Physicians rarely showed consideration in matters dealing directly with the emotions of the patients. Few of the hospital staff recognized the high anxiety level which patients and family members exhibited. Defective communications with physicians were the most prevalent basis for anxiety-provoking events.[7]

The patient is essentially powerless in such a system. Should social service wait for this condition to be recognized by medical staff or should it intervene to bridge the gap between the patient and staff systems? It is gratifying that steps have been taken in this direction. An "ombudsman" program at Mount Sinai Hospital in New York has as its goal "to bring people and services into closer contact and thereby reduce alienation of the public and insulation of hospital staff."[8]

POWER SOURCES

Harriett Bartlett says:

> Participation in program planning in the hospital and in community planning is becoming increasingly important as medical social workers recognize that they can influence and improve policies and standards that affect the care of patients without themselves giving direct services.[9]

This view suggests moving out of constrictive departmental planning and launching social service into the larger sphere of organizational influence. To do so requires a commitment to change and an appreciation of the importance of conflict to the process of change.

The question of power is vital to the planning of change. Insofar as the greater goals and values of the hospital are medical and not social in nature, what power does social service have in such a setting? There exist three sources of power: expert power, value power,[10] and power derived from access to the existing power base within the institution.

Expert power refers to the expert knowledge in the area for which change is planned. Expert power implies the need to investigate problems empirically, with an analysis of the data to be presented to the administration. For example, if a physician discovered detrimental side effects of a particular medication, he would present the facts to the administration after having completed research on several patients. The medication would probably be discontinued in the hospital and a change would thus have occurred. Social service workers must establish their rights to investigate problems and be able to present a clear picture of them to the administration. In view of the constant concern about insufficient time for or lack of expertise in research, social service has a powerful tool at its disposal in the work of medical sociologists. For years medical sociology has provided valuable information about the social structure of hospital wards, the dynamics of interaction between patients and staff, normative patterns in patient and staff systems, feelings regarding illness and medical care, and community observations of hospital institutions. Social service has neglected to utilize this potent source of empirical information. Sociology has always provided much of the theoretical material and many interactional models that have been borrowed by social work. Medical sociology must be accepted as part of the social work view of the hospital community and the needs of the patients.

Value power implies the right to plan for change. This power results from social and humanitarian values and is "based on Western civilization's notion of a scientific humanism: concern for our fellow man, experimentalism, openness and honesty, flexibility, cooperation, democracy."[11] This philosophy is consonant with the values of the social work profession. The effect of value power can be heightened by the manner of presentation and involve such coercive strategies as "the utilization of moral power, playing upon the sentiments of guilt and shame."[12] Physicians are trained to be objective and distant in their relationships with patients; yet, as human beings dedicated to helping, they have emotions and values to which the normal value power of social work must be directed, and which can be mobilized through social service's use of value power for the planning of change.

Access to the power base refers to the involvement, both central and otherwise, in decision-making processes. All social service staff workers must try to gain decision-making power within their own spheres of service. This goal is equally necessary for social workers in an outpatient department, workers on other services, and administrators. The greater the combined accumulation of individual power within the organization, the more powerful the effects of the total department. The combination of planning and power can lead to change; one without the other may be futile.

PLANNING FOR CHANGE

Some of the control points that social service can use as a means of gaining power and control in the hospital must be defined. Some obvious subjects for control point planning are intake, discharge, relatives, and consumer service.

On intake a patient is generally given a full medical examination, which seems to be a crucial occasion for involving social service. The need for social assessment of psychiatric intake is obvious. The need for involvement of social workers with intake of patients with physical disorders is equally important. This service would make the physician aware of any fears or anxieties that might be relevant to the treatment of the patient. For example, a pregnant woman preparing for delivery might have a psychological problem, which the social worker can detect and communicate to the physician. Thus, intake is a source of power to the social worker who can interpret situations to the medical staff. Furthermore, the complexity of procedures in intake generally precludes the medical staff's awareness of social service in relation to problems of the general population.

Discharge planning can be used as a strategy for change and influence. Physicians are concerned with emptying the beds so that other patients can be admitted. Often the help of social service is required in finding temporary or permanent placement for the patient, even when social service has not dealt with the case during the patient's hospitalization. Discharge planning provides a good opportunity for social service to become involved with private patients and also to make physicians aware of the problems of discharge planning and the need for early and continuous social service involvement. In discharge planning the worker can have considerable control over decision-making and general planning for the patient. On a larger scale, this control can become more general and include other areas as well.

Because patients are frequently in a dependent role when they are hospitalized, their ability to be a source of power for change may be reduced. Social service must, therefore, act as a change agent for the total patient population and for the individual patient in particular. This situation could be achieved by involving the healthier, more independent members of the family who have the ego strength and concern to act on behalf of the patient. Such involvement of the relatives in social action has been much neglected as a method of intervention, but used appropriately, it can be a fruitful means of increasing power and effecting change.

Social workers in all areas of practice are becoming more cognizant of the need for partisanship. The professional must act on behalf of the client, moving all the way from a neutral position, through mediation between the client and agency, to outright partisanship on behalf of the client. The ombudsman program described earlier is an attempt to provide a consumer service within the hospital to ease the stress on the patient caused by the bureaucracy of the hospital. The revolution of the 1960s clearly indicates that the consumer is no longer prepared to accept the inequities of the past and is demanding better and more personal service. Social service must make the patient in the hospital its main concern and must change the environment to suit his needs best. If social work does not take a stand with the client, the profession will cease to be a force for social change.

PLANNING PROCESS

Robert Morris and Robert Binstock describe planning as a "relatively systematic method which men use to solve problems."[13] Seen in its most general form, planning is a method of intervention, a way of altering dissatisfaction, and a guideline to enable the completion of an assigned task. Social planning, as a mechanism for effecting social change, can be achieved through (1) altering human attitudes and behavioral patterns; (2) reforming major legal and functional systems of society; and (3) changing the policies of formal organizations in order to alter social conditions.[14] Guidelines for planning are to be examined within the framework of the first and third means.

SELECTION OF LEVEL OF PLANNING

There are various levels at which social service can develop plans for change. The basic level involves planning on a one-to-one basis, with a client or with a number of clients in a group. Such planning and the ensuing change would affect only those immediately involved in the planning. The next level for planning is within the social service department itself, with the intent of improving the methods of communication, recording systems, and staff training. These two levels of planning have been operating for some time and can generally be carried out without involvement of other departments in the hospital. As planning begins to extend beyond the department and to move up the organizational ladder outside the social service department, it becomes broader in scope and influence. The more departments that a plan influences, the more comprehensive it becomes. The emphasis here is on organizational change and the development of a comprehensive plan by the social service department to influence other departments and the administration. The phases of planning to be discussed do not necessarily take place chronologically; some parts of each can operate concurrently and influence each other.

DETERMINATION OF DISSATISFACTION

The primary step in the development of a plan is the determination of need or dissatisfaction. While this process is generally part of all social work practice, it is a prime focal point in planning. Clearly identified purposes require "an element of personal or organizational identification or causation,"[15] which social service departments have achieved through (1) interviewing individual patients with specific emphasis on their dissatisfactions; (2) developing research designs to examine the opinions of patients and staff about service; (3) examining research and programs conducted in other subjects and at other hospitals; (4) formalizing an interdepartmental workshop for determining points of dissatisfaction; and (5) organizing staff meetings, conferences, and workshops to consider the needs of patients. The last two involve other personnel, thus widening the scope for influence and interest in the hospital, lowering the possibility of threat to a particular service, and creating an increased awareness of social service. The utilization of expert power in this question is vital.

STATEMENT OF PURPOSE

Formally establishing the goals and purposes of a plan is the next step, for "when plans are expressed in terms of the results that one hopes to achieve, they may be called goals."[16] For example, the lack of patient-staff communication may be causing dissatisfaction; a specific plan for altering this situation is necessary to achieve the goal of greater participation in ward life. A concise statement of the desired goals at the beginning of planning will help to maintain consistency of purpose and reliability of action in implementing the plan.

ORGANIZING FOR PLANNING

Staffing, direction, and coordination are important in organizing for planning.[17] Division of tasks among the staff of the social service department should be based on the special skills and basis of power of the individual social workers. Responsibility should be assigned with the following initial tasks in mind: (1) examining what are feasible goals for different wards or services in the hospital; (2) examining what modifications would be necessary in the plan if it were to be used on different wards; (3) examining the cost in time and money; and (4) examining the consequences to the ward or hospital system if such a plan were implemented and whether they are desirable or not. The division of labor and delineation of tasks indicate the need for coordination, which requires communication and cooperation. Coordination also entails the involvement of other departments and the best way to achieve it. In some cases it might mean officially contacting leaders in other departments; in others it might be more on a group basis. Interdepartmental communication can be formal or informal depending on the depth of involvement of the other services. Direction, of course, is very important and should come from an individual responsible for maintaining constant communication and coordination so that all participants in the planning are aware of each other's findings and progress.

GAINING SUPPORT

There are many ways by which to acquaint the administration and hospital staff with and gain support for the functions and values of social service. The involvement of other departments in the social service activity has been dealt with above. Other means are internal hospital publications, newsletters, and talks to help the medical and paramedical services become aware of the many roles of social workers, the studies and projects of the social service department, and social work in general.

TECHNICAL MONOPOLY

Social casework as a practice method in the hospital lacks a technical monopoly, that is, a specific sphere of knowledge, theory, and practice unique to social casework in the hospital. The areas between social casework, psychiatry, and psychotherapy are large and ill-defined. As a result there is a general feeling that much of what caseworkers do can be done by professionals of other disciplines and possibly by paraprofessionals. This belief does not negate the need for and validity of social work's form of helping, but only indicates an uncertainty that is detrimental to the social worker's status in the hospital. Because the hospital is an institution in which various professional disciplines practice, the profession that is least clearly defined may be used for catchall jobs and may become the least respected discipline. Developing a technical monopoly requires expert social planning and incorporating this means of intervention as part of the total interventions on behalf of the patient.

Although it is understood that social service goals should agree with overall hospital goals, a rigid bias toward the latter could conflict with social work values. Social service should, therefore, effect change not by becoming part of the administration and making its influence felt in that way, but by retaining its present auxiliary status and becoming more specialized in the planning and implementation of change. Social service can become more autonomous through planning and through developing a technical monopoly. Furthermore, by moving toward autonomy, social service will change its method of interaction with the other subsystems or departments (for within the present status of social service a state of equilibrium exists with the other departments and the administration). Daniel Griffiths says:

> As a system operates, the subsystems develop methods of interacting in which conflict is at a minimum. Each of the subsystems has a function to perform, and each does so in such a manner as to allow it to maintain a high degree of harmony with the others. . . . Change is practically synonymous with conflict, since it means that the arrangements the subsystems have worked out no longer hold.[18]

By adopting a more autonomous position, social service can effect change more objectively and more easily. Empirical evidence has shown that "stimulus for change comes from outside the organization."[19] It is not suggested that social service leave the hospital, but that it should prepare to act as a change agent within the hospital. (Although controversy exists about whether social workers are change agents or enablers of change, the more manipulative role prescribed in planning for change in the hospital seems to indicate the acceptance of the label *change agent* because the goals for change are clear.) The client system would then consist of patients and the hospital administration and "the decision to make a change may be made by the system itself, after experiencing pain . . . or discovering the possibility of improvement, or by an outside change agent who observes the need for change in a particular system and takes the initiative in establishing a helping relationship with that system."[20]

Social service should stimulate an emphasis on the social conditions within the hospital as they affect the delivery of services and patient care. This emphasis can be achieved through the presentation of the plan developed by the department and through the use of power sources.

CONCLUSION

Social service in general hospitals must reevaluate its present functions and future directions through an awareness of the strengths and power sources inherent in its auxiliary status in the medical organization. Integration into the total departmental system of the hospital may in fact be detrimental, as social service attempts to bring about change in policy and program *within* the medical hierarchy. Future consideration must be given to the existing movements in the social work profession that are oriented toward action and change. Social service will fulfill a major gap in hospital planning by moving out of its departmental enclave and by focusing on the social policies and programs of the hospital. Social planning presents new challenges and opportunities. It should be seen not as an addition to existing services but as an incorporation into the total service offered by the department; it is a responsibility of social service and should be considered along with other priorities. As we deal with issues and policies on an individual and group level, so must we deal with them on an organizational and structural level. The action-oriented standpoint means partisanship and further translation of knowledge and values into practice.

Notes

1. Hyman J. Weiner, "The Hospital, the Ward, and the Patient as Client: Use of the Group Method," *Social Work* 4 (Oct. 1959): 57–64; and Louise A. Frey, ed., *Use of Groups in the Health Field* (New York: National Association of Social Workers, 1966).
2. *Social Work Activities in Public Health* (Boston: Department of Public Health, 1961).
3. The author gratefully acknowledges the help and guidance of Joseph W. Eaton, Ph.D., and the invaluable assistance of Mrs. Brian Segal.
4. Warren G. Bennis, Kenneth D. Benne, and Robert Chin, eds., *The Planning of Change: Readings in the Applied Behavioral Sciences* (New York: Holt, Rinehart and Winston, 1969), p. 63.
5. Ida M. Cannon, *On the Social Frontier of Medicine: Pioneering in Medical Social Service* (Cambridge, Mass.: Harvard University Press, 1952), p. 73.
6. Personal interview with Joseph W. Eaton, Professor of Social Work Research, Graduate School of Social Work, University of Pittsburgh, Pittsburgh, Pa., October 1969.
7. Raymond S. Duff and August B. Hollingshead, *Sickness and Society* (New York: Harper & Row, 1968), p. 286.
8. Ruth Ravich, Helen Rehr, and Charles H. Goodrich, "Hospital Ombudsman Smooths Flow of Services and Communication," *Hospitals* 43 (March 1969): 56–61.

9. Harriett M. Bartlett, "The Widening Scope of Hospital Social Work," *Social Casework* 44 (Jan. 1963): 3.
10. Bennis, Benne, and Chin, *The Planning of Change,* p. 74.
11. Ibid.
12. Ibid., p. 52.
13. Robert Morris and Robert H. Binstock, with the collaboration of Martin Rein, *Feasible Planning for Social Change* (New York: Columbia University Press, 1966), p. 5.
14. Ibid., p. 14.
15. Preston P. Le Breton and Dale A. Henning, *Planning Theory* (Englewood Cliffs, N.J.: Prentice-Hall, 1961), p. 7.
16. Ibid., p. 8.
17. Ibid., p. 4.
18. Daniel E. Griffiths, "Administrative Theory and Change in Organizations," in *Innovations in Education,* ed. Matthew Miles (New York: Teacher's College, Columbia University, 1964), p. 425.
19. Ibid., p. 426.
20. Ronald Lippitt, Jeanne Watson, and Bruce Westley, *The Dynamics of Planned Change* (New York: Harcourt, Brace, 1958), p. 10.

Chapter 18 Internal Advocacy and Human Service Practitioners: An Exploratory Study

Rino J. Patti

INTRODUCTION

In social welfare organizations where practitioners constitute the bulk of those at lower administrative echelons, the failure of subordinates to make their knowledge and perspectives available to decision-makers is especially critical.[1] For, without this input, executives and boards are deprived of one of the more important sources of data regarding the impact of the organizations' services on its consumers. Clients are increasingly organizing themselves to ensure that they are actively represented, but more often than not they still lack an effective means of expression. It often falls to practitioners, therefore, to see that ideas, criticisms, and recommendations growing out of the service delivery experience are advocated in the internal decision-making process.

In addition to providing data about the impact of services, practitioners are also in a unique position to alert management to those agency norms and practices that diverge from, or conflict with, professional values and ethics. From their vantage point, practitioners can serve as a countervailing force when, for example, individualization is sacrificed to proceduralism; when efficiency becomes more important than quality service; and when administrative accountability serves to stifle practitioner creativity and constrain the exercise of professional judgment. In these and other instances, human service workers can serve as advocates for standards that are too often compromised in an organization's constant struggle with inadequate resources, increasing consumer demand, and community expectations.

Although there is growing recognition of the part that practitioners can play as internal advocates in influencing the policy-program direction of their agencies,[2] there is as yet little systematic information available regarding the frequency of such efforts, the objectives sought, the methods used, or the outcomes achieved.[3] This chapter will report the findings of an exploratory study that will, we hope, provide some preliminary insights into the magnitude and nature of internal advocacy efforts[4] and thus serve as a basis for more extensive and rigorous inquiry into this much-neglected aspect of human service practice.

PURPOSE AND DESIGN OF THE STUDY

The study reported here was an attempt to explore whether human service practitioners in a variety of the agency settings had initiated and/or participated in efforts to alter or modify any aspect of their organization's policy, program, or procedures.[5] We were further interested in determining how many such efforts had been undertaken in a two-year period prior to the study, the issues and problems that had been addressed, the goals that had been sought, and whether these goals had been achieved.

Internal advocacy, for purposes of this study, was defined as efforts to alter or modify any formal aspect of the agency, where the authority to make such changes was not within the legitimate domain of the practitioner. For example, if a caseworker decided to initiate group treatment for certain of his or her clients and could do so without gaining formal approval from some administrative superior, this was not considered an instance of internal advocacy. Neither was the study concerned with change efforts aimed at altering some aspects of the informal system of an agency, such as the quality of interpersonal relationships, communication patterns, peer group norms, and the like. The nature of an informal system has important implications for how an organization operates, but no attempt was made to explore advocacy efforts in this area.

It is also important to note that our concern was with efforts initiated by practitioners, as opposed to those that an administrative superior asked a worker to become involved in. For example, if a supervisor were to ask a worker to participate on a committee charged with recommending a new intake procedure, or an administrator were to solicit a worker's recommendation regarding the desirability of extending agency services to a new population, the practitioner's subsequent activity in carrying out these requests was defined as falling outside the definition of internal advocacy. This was sometimes a difficult distinction to make, since responsibility for initiating an idea frequently became obscured in the course of committee or group deliberations. Nevertheless, an attempt was made to distinguish those situations in which, at the outset, the impetus (that is, defining the problem, formulating the objectives, and putting forth the proposal) was supplied by the practitioner.

In this study a practitioner was defined as someone in the employ of a social welfare or health agency who spent 50 percent or more of his or her time in providing social services directly to clients, or in activities directly related to the provision of such services (for example, record-keeping, staffing, collateral contacts, supervisory conferences). In so defining the population that would be the object of this inquiry, the intent was to focus on workers in the lower reaches of the administrative hierarchy whose organizational perspective derived primarily from their day-to-day experience with clients.

Since the purpose of the study was to explore an area of practitioner activity about which relatively little is known in order to generate information that might stimulate subsequent inquiry, no effort was made to ensure the representativeness of the sample. Agencies were purposely selected to reflect something of the array of organizations in which human services practitioners work (for example, fields of service, small and large agencies, public and private auspices), but even here selection was influenced by proximity and ease of gaining administrative approval. Once in the agencies, interviewers were asked to select randomly from the total complement of human service practitioners as defined above, but this was not possible in several cases, due to the unavailability of some workers or their unwillingness to be interviewed.

These limitations of the samples should caution the reader against generalizing the findings reported to all practitioners in the agencies represented, let alone to human service practitioners in similar organizations.

ANALYSIS OF DATA

A total of fifty-nine human service practitioners in nine health and welfare organizations were interviewed for the study. The agencies represented several fields of service,[6] and varied greatly in size and complexity.[7] In some settings human service practitioners constituted the primary professional staff, while in others they were ancillary to another group of professionals.

Frequency of Change Efforts

The fifty-nine practitioners were asked to enumerate and describe the efforts they had initiated, or those in which they had actively participated during the last two years, for the purpose of modifying some aspect of the policies, programs, or procedures of the organizations in which they were employed.[8] A total of 150 change efforts were reported, an average of 2.54 per respondent. Only six workers reported no involvement in attempts to alter or modify agency practices.[9]

Even these gross figures suggest that the direct service practitioners interviewed were vitally concerned about the context in which they delivered service. Although internal advocacy tends not to be given emphasis in professional education, nor is it generally encouraged by administrative superiors, it appears that these human service workers considered such efforts a part of their professional responsibility. While allowing for the fact that many change efforts were addressed to minor organizational issues, it seems clear that in the aggregate such efforts constituted a significant component of the administrative process in the nine agencies represented in this study.

Internal advocacy, then, seems to be a fairly pervasive activity among the practitioners involved in this study. Yet it is interesting to note that the frequency of such efforts varied considerably not only among practitioners in different agencies, but among those in the same agency (see Table 18-1). With this in mind, an attempt was made to identify certain

TABLE 18-1
Agencies by Mean Number of Change Efforts

Agency	Mean Number of Change Efforts
Correctional institution	1.4
District welfare office	1.7
Children's residential treatment center #1	2.0
Mental health clinic #1	2.3
General medical hospital	2.8
Children's residential treatment center #2	2.8
Child welfare agency	2.8
Medical outpatient clinic	3.3
Mental health clinic #2	4.4

organizational and personal variables that might be related to workers' decisions to become involved in change efforts.

To explore possible associations between organizational properties and the frequency of worker-initiated change activity, three variables were selected for analysis—size, vertical differentiation, and age. The three variables were selected because theoretically, at least, they are considered to have a significant impact on organizational change processes.[10]

Size was defined simply as the number of employees in an organization who were located in the one physical location where the practitioner spent most of his or her time. Vertical differentiation referred to the number of supervisory levels between the direct service staff and the agency director. The age of an organization, for purposes of this study, was defined as the number of years the agency had been in continuous operation under its current legal mandate. Scales corresponding to these variables were developed and scores for each obtained for every organization included in the study.[11] These values were then summed to derive a single score for each agency, which will be referred to as the index of organizational complexity (see Table 18-2). The possible range of scores in this index is 3 to 16, with 3 indicating the lowest complexity (few employees, flat hierarchy, and recent establishment) and 16 indicating the highest complexity (many employees, deep hierarchy, long history of operation). Organizational complexity scores are given in Table 18-2.

TABLE 18-2
Agencies by Index of Organizational Complexity

Agency	Organizational Complexity Index
Children's residential treatment center #2	3
Mental health clinic #1	4
Mental health clinic #2	4
Medical outpatient clinic	8
Children's residential treatment center #1	9
Child welfare agency	10
District welfare office	11
Correctional institution	12
General medical hospital	12

When agencies were grouped according to degree of complexity and a weighted mean of the number of practitioner-initiated projects derived for each subgroup, some interesting findings emerged (see Table 18-3). Little difference was observed in the mean number of change efforts for workers in agencies scoring low and medium in complexity (3.56 and 3.61 change efforts, respectively). In those organizations ranked high in complexity, however, the mean number of change attempts undertaken dropped markedly (2.02).

It is, of course, not possible to draw causal inferences from these data, but the findings suggest at least two plausible interpretations. The first is that the largest, most complex agencies in this study may have attracted and recruited practitioners who were less inclined to engage in efforts to modify organizational policies and practices. It is possible, in other words, that these agencies employed disproportionate numbers of workers who were predisposed to accommodate themselves to organizational arrangements, even where they found such conditions undesirable. Another interpretation of these findings is that high complexity may have contributed to the development of a normative climate in these agencies that was inhospitable to changes initiated by administrative subordinates. If nothing else, one would speculate that factors generally associated with high complexity, such as well-delineated rules and procedures, long-established programs, and little opportunity for face-to-face interaction with decision-makers, would tend to create a certain degree of organizational inertia. From the perspective of practitioners in these agencies this may have been perceived as an obstacle to successful change and thus a deterrent to their involvement.

TABLE 18-3

Degree of Organizational Complexity and
Weighted Mean Number of Change Efforts

Degree Organizational Complexity	Number of Agencies	Weighted Mean Number of Changes Efforts
Low complexity (3–6 index scores)	3	3.56
Medium complexity (7–10 index scores)	3	3.61
High complexity (11–16 index scores)	3	2.03

Since no detailed study of these organizations was done, it is impossible to say whether either of these factors was operative, or in what degree. Greater specificity about the nature of the relationship between organizational complexity and worker's motivations to undertake change efforts must await further research.

In addition to agency variables that might influence a practitioner's propensity to engage in change efforts, an attempt was also made to look at the role that personal characteristics might play. For this purpose, workers were grouped into two categories representing those who had initiated fewer than two change efforts and those who had engaged in three or more. These categories were then cross-tabulated with a number of demographic variables such as age, sex, marital status, and education.

Age, marital status, and sex seem to have little bearing on the frequency of change efforts engaged in by practitioners, although some slight differences in frequency were noted between men and women (Table 18-4). A more significant finding is the apparent association between education and frequency of change efforts (Table 18-4). In these data, workers with master's degrees, the vast majority of whom were social workers, were much more likely to engage in change efforts than those with less education. One can only speculate about the reasons for the relationship between these variables, but one possible interpretation is that workers with professional degrees were more secure in their jobs, or felt freer to take the risks associated with internal advocacy. An alternate interpretation is that professionals may have enjoyed higher status in the eyes of administrators and thus felt somewhat more confident of their ability to influence the agency's operations. Both these views would seem to be contrary to the often-repeated belief that professional education tends to promote conformity to agency practices.

TABLE 18-4
Number of Change Efforts by Sex and Education

	Number of Change Efforts	
Characteristic	0–2	3–5
Sex:		
Male	9	13
Female	21	16
Education:		
Master's Degree	11	23
B.A. or less	19	6

Nature of Change Efforts and Outcomes

Perhaps more important than the frequency of change efforts are the issues and problems practitioners seek to address and the goals they attempt to achieve. On the basis of workers' open-ended descriptions of their change efforts, an attempt was made to develop a classification scheme. The single criterion used to differentiate change efforts was the worker's stated goal or objective. Our concern was with the immediate, explicit changes the worker was hoping to achieve in the agency's policies, programs, or procedures. While it was clear that many of the change efforts would have had secondary effects, only the explicit, first-order objectives as enunciated by the practitioner were taken into consideration. No attempt was made to differentiate whether a change sought represented a major or minor departure from prevailing agency practices. The inclusion of this dimension would have been desirable, but the data available did not permit making such judgments.

The classification scheme constructed from the crude data is as follows:[12]

New or modified policies or procedures for the purpose of systematizing, coordinating, or facilitating work flow. For the most part these activities were aimed at developing more efficient mechanisms for intraagency communication and cooperation. Included here were efforts such as developing a new recording form, initiating interdisciplinary team conferences, and new procedures for interoffice or interdepartmental referral.

New or modified rules, procedures, or policies regarding client management, or the provision of service. Included here were activities aimed at altering procedures for scheduling clients or patients at intake, liberalizing furlough policy, simplifying eligibility determination, or developing new "house rules" to guide client or patient behavior.

New or modified personnel policies. This category of effort was directed at such goals as improving salaries, altering client-worker ratios, modifying leave policies, and clarifying job descriptions and responsibilities.

New or modified or expanded services or programs provided to clients or community. This type of change effort variously involved attempts to add to, or modify, a substantive dimension of a service program or extend existing services to a new client group—for example, agency outreach to a minority community, group treatment services, information and referral services, compensatory education for inmates, and volunteer services.

Modified patterns of superior-subordinate communication or decision-making processes in the organization. These efforts included, for example, attempts to obtain greater staff input in certain decisions, client involvement in staffing, unionization, and decentralization of authority.

New or additional supportive or facilitative resources to staff and/or clients. Included here were activities aimed at obtaining new equipment, expanded facilities, in-service training, and consultation for practitioners, usually in support of the provision of direct services to clients.

New or modified interagency relationships or procedures. These efforts involved modifying ways in which the practitioner's agency related to other service organizations in the community. It included, for example, developing a new referral source, changing agency policy regarding the acceptance of certain types of clients, and devising more efficient means for sharing information about clients.

Other.

Insufficient data to classify or not classified as change effort.

Table 18-5 reflects the proportion of change efforts undertaken by practitioners in each of the categories specified above. The practitioners in this study were most often involved in changing organizational conditions that most immediately affected the delivery of their services and the management of their workloads. The categories of change effort having to do with program or service changes and procedures affecting work flow, both of which have a direct bearing on how services are provided, account for nearly 40 percent of the efforts reported. If one adds to this that category of change efforts directed at obtaining new or additional facilities or resources, which were most often sought for the purpose of supporting or enhancing service delivery capability, then considerably more than half of the change efforts are accounted for. The high frequency of change efforts in these categories is not too surprising since the provision of service is the primary business of the practitioners and organizational conditions that most directly impinge on this aspect of a practitioner's functioning are likely to be a central concern. Moreover, one suspects that practitioners may be more inclined to undertake

TABLE 18-5
Type and Frequency of Change Efforts

Type of Change Effort	Number	Percent
New/modified procedures regarding work flow	28	18.7
New/modified rules regarding client management	5	10.0
New/modified personnel policies	20	13.3
New/modified services or programs	29	19.3
Modified patterns of communication or decision-making	15	10.0
New/additional facilities or resources	22	14.7
New/modified interagency procedures	6	4.0
Other	3	2.0
Insufficient data or not classified as change effort	12	8.0
TOTAL	150	100.0

change activity in these areas because they involve phenomena with which workers are intimately familiar and can speak to with authority.

Two other areas in which relatively small, but significant numbers of change efforts were reported involved personnel policy and patterns of communication with supervisors. Both of these categories concern, in different ways, the practitioner's relationship to agency administration. In the first instance, the worker is attempting to improve the conditions of his or her employment; in the second, he or she is seeking to have a greater impact on administrative decisions. Personnel policy is traditionally a concern of practitioners and one in which there is at least a quasi-legitimate right to seek changes in their own self-interests. Efforts to alter the communication and decision processes, on the other hand, involve the practitioner in an area that is more often thought to be the domain of the administrator. To the extent that this is the case, one would expect change efforts in this latter area to entail a greater risk of administrative disapproval than those in the other categories. Viewed in this context, the number of change efforts reported for this category take on added significance.

Practitioners were also asked to give their best estimate of whether they had achieved the intended goals of their change efforts. Perhaps most significant was the apparently high rate of success experienced by practitioners. Roughly three-fourths of the attempts initiated were perceived by workers as having resulted in either full or partial achievement of the objectives sought (see Table 18-6). This seems rather remarkable

TABLE 18-6
Outcomes of Change Efforts as Perceived by Practitioners

Outcomes of Change Efforts	Number	Percent
Fully achieved	62	52.1
Partially achieved	28	23.5
Not achieved	29	24.4
TOTAL*	119	100.0

*The total here does not include the 12 responses that were unclassifiable, or not classified as a change effort. Neither does it reflect 19 change efforts that were "still in process" and for which no determination of outcome was possible.

when one considers that in each case the changes proposed were initiated by practitioners in lower administrative echelons and required approval by an administrative superior.

It is, however, interesting to observe that outcomes varied significantly depending on the type of change effort being undertaken (see Table 18-7). For example, when overall outcome rates were compared with those for specific categories of change effort, considerable variation emerged. This is particularly noteworthy for efforts in categories concerning modifications in patterns of superior-subordinate communication and the acquisition of new or additional facilities or resources. In both of these categories, workers experienced higher than average rates of failure to achieve their goals. For the most part, changes in the former category involved attempts by practitioners to obtain more discretion in the exercise of their duties, or more influence in decision-making that concerned them or their clients. The latter type of change frequently required the expenditure of additional funds, or the re-allocation of funds from one area of operation to another.

That change efforts in these two categories should meet with less success does not seem surprising, since they involve questions of power and money. These, after all, are the primary resources that enable an administration to direct and control the operations of an agency. One would, therefore, expect that changes aimed at the management of these resources would be dealt with cautiously and perhaps even resisted as an incursion on administrative prerogatives.

Following this rationale, one would have expected similar outcome patterns for the category of change concerning new or modified personnel policies. Here, too, questions of money and even authority are frequently involved. It is only possible to speculate about this apparent

TABLE 18-7

Outcomes of Change Efforts as Perceived by Practitioners by Type of Change Efforts

| | Outcomes of Change Efforts | | |
| | Fully Achieved | Partially Achieved | Not Achieved |
Type of Change Effort	No. %	No. %	No. %
New/modified procedures regarding work flow	13 (59.1)	5 (22.7)	4 (18.2)
New/modified rules regarding client management	8 (53.3)	5 (33.3)	2 (13.3)
New/modified personnel policies	11 (61.1)	3 (16.7)	4 (22.2)
New/modified services or programs	16 (69.6)	2 (8.7)	5 (21.7)
Modified patterns of communication or decision making	3 (27.2)	3 (27.3)	5 (45.5)
New/additional facilities or resources	6 (30.0)	7 (35.0)	7 (35.0)
New/modified interagency procedures	3 (50.0)	1 (16.7)	2 (33.3)
Other	2 (50.0)	2 (50.0)	
TOTAL*	62	28	29

*The totals here do not include the 12 responses that were unclassifiable, or not classified as a change effort. Neither do they reflect 19 change efforts that were "still in process" and for which no determination of outcome was possible.

exception, but one possible interpretation is that administrations may view change efforts in this area as legitimate expressions of employee interests.

But what of other categories of change where practitioners experienced high rates of success—for example, new or modified procedures and new or modified programs? Analysis of the data suggests that the positive outcome rates experienced by workers involved in these efforts were at least partially attributable to the fact that in most instances they were simply asking for authorization to use their time, energy, and skills differently. The changes called for did not, by and large, require that the practitioner receive more resources (authority, time, facilities), but rather that he or she utilize already available resources differently. The most frequent example of this could be seen in the category *new/modified programs*. Here, practitioners commonly requested permission to direct more of their time to working with a special group of clients (unmarried mothers, minorities) or initiating a new treatment format (group or family therapy).

In addition, it is interesting to note that changes sought in programs or procedures were often justified on the basis of the workers' willingness to invest the time and energy necessary for implementation. In other words, practitioners were frequently prepared to absorb the costs associated with an innovation in return for administrative approval.

Thus, it would appear that high success rates in this study were more likely to occur in those categories where practitioners were seeking authority to rearrange or redirect their activities. Those change efforts that sought a redistribution of power or re-allocation of funds were, on the other hand, more likely to fail.

Outcomes of change efforts also appear to be crucially affected by the administrator's initial response to a practitioner's proposal. Workers were asked to describe the response of their administrative superior when he or she first learned of their proposal. Responses were rated on a five-point scale ranging from "strongly supportive" to "strongly opposed," with a midpoint of "neutral or indifferent." An analysis of twenty-nine change efforts, for which the most complete information was available, revealed that, in every case but one, those efforts that were fully successful were, at the outset, supported by the administrative superior. Those practitioners, on the other hand, that had partial success met with neutrality or opposition much more frequently, while those who failed were confronted with neutrality or opposition from their administrative superiors in every instance (see Table 18-8).

Based on this admittedly limited information, it seems that these advocacy efforts were virtually decided at the point of initiation. Of particular interest was the apparently determinative effect that a superior's neutral or negative initial response had on the ultimate outcome. Obviously this phenomenon requires further study, but one is tempted to speculate that this finding may reflect the inadequacies of professional preparation for internal advocacy.

CONCLUSION

While internal advocacy can potentially provide a much needed source of information and ideas to organizational decision-makers, as yet very little is known about the frequency, nature, or outcomes of such efforts. The exploratory study reported in this chapter is a preliminary attempt to generate some basic information about practitioner activity in this

TABLE 18-8
Outcomes of Change Efforts by Administrator's Initial Response to Proposal

Outcome of Change Effort	Administrator's Response		
	Strong or Mild Support	Neutral or Indifferent	Strong or Mild Opposition
Achieved	14	1	0
Partially achieved	5	3	1
Not achieved	0	2	3

area and at the same time identify certain factors that may shed light on why workers become involved in agency change efforts, the kinds of issues and problems they attempt to deal with, and whether they are successful in achieving their objectives. Like most exploratory inquiries, the data reported here raise more questions than they answer. While the findings suggest that the direct service practitioners studied were very much involved in efforts to alter or modify agency practices, we are only beginning to understand the dynamics of this activity: what motivates workers to become involved; what issues are addressed; what strategies and tactics are employed; and what factors determine success or failure. Ultimately, of course, we must be able to say whether internal advocacy makes a difference in helping to humanize organizations and increase their effectiveness as service delivery systems. Before this is possible, however, it will be necessary to know much more about the human service practitioner's activity in this vital area.

Notes

1. The literature dealing with the negative organizational effects of insufficient upward communication is vast. For a representative sample, reflecting somewhat different analytic perspectives, the following references are useful: Robert Presthus, *The Organizational Society* (New York: Vintage, 1962); Victor Thompson, *Bureaucracy and Innovation* (University, Ala.: University of Alabama Press, 1969); Anthony Downs, *Inside Bureaucracy* (Boston: Little, Brown, 1967); Warren Bennis, "Beyond Bureaucracy," in *American Bureaucracy,* ed. Bennis (Chicago: Aldine, 1970).
2. See, for example, Hyman Weiner, "Toward Techniques for Social Change," *Social Work* 6, no. 2 (April 1961): 26–35; George Brager, "Institutional Change: Perimeters of the Possible," *Social Work* 12 (Jan. 1967): 59–69; Archie Hanlan, "Counteracting Problems of Bureaucracy in Public

Welfare," *Social Work* 12 (July 1967): 88–94; Emmanuel Hallowitz, "Innovations in Hospital Social Work," *Social Work* 17 (July 1972): 88–97; John Wax, "Power and Institutional Change," *Social Service Review* 45 (Dec. 1971): 274–288; Rino Patti and Herman Resnick, "Changing the Agency from Within," *Social Work* 17 (July 1972): 48–57.

3. An exception to this is the contribution that has been made by Robert Morris and Robert H. Binstock, *Feasible Planning for Social Change* (New York: Columbia University Press, 1967).

4. Resnick and the author have elsewhere referred to this as intraorganizational change ("Changing the Agency," p. 48). Internal advocacy is employed here since it is more consistent with professional usage (Ad Hoc Committee on Advocacy, "The Social Worker as Advocate: Champion of Social Victims," *Social Work* 14 [April 1969]: 16–22).

5. The author is indebted to Dr. Herman Resnick for his assistance and support in developing this research. He also wishes to express appreciation to Professor Benson Jaffee, who made several helpful suggestions regarding modifications of an earlier draft.

6. The agencies included: one correctional institution, one general medical hospital, one public assistance district office, one voluntary child welfare agency, two children's residential treatment centers, two mental health clinics, and one outpatient medical clinic.

7. At one extreme was an agency with a total staff complement of less than ten and only two administrative levels and, at the other, an organization with over five hundred professional employees from a variety of disciplines with five levels of administrative authority.

8. The author is grateful to the following students who helped in interviewing agency practitioners: Kemp Crawford, Terry Walker, Sister Kathleen Pruitt, John Morefield, Lou Belcher, Dianne Finn, Marianne Ruehl, Joan Clements, and Barbara Penny.

9. While there is some duplication reflected in the total number of change efforts, it was not possible to determine the exact extent since the descriptions provided often made it difficult to determine whether the same efforts were being described. A liberal, albeit impressionistic, estimate is that no more than twenty change attempts were reported by more than one respondent.

10. See, for example, Jerald Hage and Michael Aiken, *Social Change in Complex Organizations* (New York: Random House, 1970); and William Starbuck, "Organizational Growth and Development," in *Handbook of Organizations,* ed. James March (Chicago: Rand-McNally, 1965), pp. 451–533.

11. The organization was given a score of 1 to 4 for size depending on whether it had: (1) fewer than 50 employees; (2) 50–100 employees; (3) 101–500 employees; (4) more than 500 employees. Vertical differentiation scores ranged from 1 to 5 depending on the number of administrative levels in the organization: (1) one level; (2) two levels; (3) three levels; (4) four levels; (5) five or more levels. Age of the organization was scored as follows: (1) 0–4 years; (2) 5–9 years; (3) 10–14 years; (4) 15–19 years; (5) 20–24 years; (6) 25 or more years.

12. The crude data were independently analyzed by both Dr. Resnick and myself. The differences in our respective classification schemes were then reconciled, and the scheme presented here resulted.

Postscript

The format of this book and the limits of space leave us with unanswered questions about the future of change from below that should be noted in conclusion. Writers frequently use a postscript to express leftover thoughts and to deal with unfinished business. Our unfinished business concerns: the potential outcomes of organizational change behavior; the effect of external social movements on organizational change; the utilization of organizational change practices and goals in non–human service enterprises; and, finally, planned change as a viable modality for the future.

OUTCOMES

One issue that receives inadequate attention in this volume is what could realistically be expected of a group of staff members engaged in an organizational change. Initially, we focused on the first-order consequences of organizational change—that is, improved delivery of service to clients. As we learned more about this mode of practice, however, its potential widened. For example, our observations of change initiated from below have suggested that workers' morale is often improved as they engage in organizational change projects, whether successfully or not. Further, there is some indication that the enhanced personal and professional efficacy that comes from being responsibly engaged in correcting or improving agency practices (what might be called organizational citizenship) may contribute to professionals' becoming more pro-actively involved in resolving community problems. Organizational change practice, then, may yield benefits to professionals and communities beyond those that accrue to clients of human service organizations. The extent to which this now occurs is a matter of conjecture, but it is our hope that future inquiries of organizational change from below will examine these potential secondary outcomes.

As yet there is little empirical research on organizational change efforts initiated from below. Most of the work reflected in this book is based on case studies, more or less systematic observations, and personal experience.[1] Work to date suggests that these efforts can have an impact on organizational policies and programs, but development of theory and practice will require that an empirical foundation be laid. There are myriad questions that require attention: What strategies, tactics, and activities seem most effective in influencing organizational decision-making? What are the short- and long-term effects of organizational change efforts on relationships between front-line workers and administrative personnel? Under what environmental conditions (for instance, crises, expansion, conflict) are proposals initiated from below most likely to be accepted? These and a host of related issues and questions require the urgent attention of the human service professions. Until there is a body of research on which to build, the practice of organizational change is likely to remain a collection of individual experiences that contribute relatively little to cumulative knowledge-building.

EFFECT OF EXTERNAL FORCES

A second issue minimally addressed in the book is the effect of external forces upon organizational change. We are not unaware that external systems have an impact on internal change efforts. For example, it is apparent that external resources such as a local newspaper or city official can be enlisted to strengthen the internal change effort. What is not sufficiently considered in the book is the explicit tie between advocacy groups (such as the women's movement or trade unions among human service workers) and organizational change effectiveness. It is becoming increasingly clear that an action system can be considerably strengthened by its linkage with a larger social movement or cause.

Recently, for example, feminist groups in organizations have systematically used the ideological rationale and, in many instances, the political resources of the women's movement in order to empower organizational change efforts aimed at more equitable personnel practices, improved services for women clients, and the like. The strategic identification with a larger movement not only appears to lend organizational legitimacy to such change efforts, but also raises the specter that the power of the movement may be enlisted by the action system. This possibility, even when not imminent, appears to increase dramatically the leverage available to internal change agents and concomitantly heighten the receptivity of decision-makers. A secondary effect of affiliation with a movement is in its impact on the action system's internal cohesion. It is our observation that, when organizational change efforts become attached to a cause, the tendency to fragmentation that characterizes so many action systems is mitigated by the shared allegiance to larger goals. In essence the action system comes to serve a larger purpose than its immediate change objective, and its persistence, therefore, has ramifications that extend beyond the organizational change project. Trade unions are another social force that change the power equation in organizational change activity. When interacting with a small action system representing themselves or, at best, a majority of the staff, administrators tend to function quite differently from when they are negotiating or discussing the same organization improvement with an action system that has linkages with a union. Although unions in social work and in other human service professions devote much of their energy to improving working benefits and pay scales for their members, their rhetoric, and at least some of their behavior, has also been directed towards improving the lot of their clients as well.[2]

Whether these social forces or institutions will dominate the goals of similarly minded organizational change agents, only the future can tell. It is clear, however, that a tension exists between the need of small action groups to increase their power through explicit alliances with a social movement and the tendency of these social movement groups to dictate the goals of the action systems for their own larger purposes. Organizational change scholars and practitioners should attend the interplay of these external forces and internal systems in the next decade.

UTILIZATION OF ORGANIZATIONAL CHANGE IN NON–HUMAN SERVICE ORGANIZATIONS

Our approach to organizational change emerged from the relatively benign organizational practices of human service workers seeking better service for their clients or a better quality of work life for themselves. We have often wondered if a model of organizational change like that presented in this book could be more effectively employed in non–human service settings such as military, governmental, or profit-making organizations. Our experience with these groups suggests that there is a good deal of organizational change from below occurring in these settings. Though not articulated as such, there is nevertheless a rich repository of experience from which human service professionals can learn. It is our hope that in the years ahead there will be more dialogue on these issues across institutional boundaries. The problems, constraints, and potentials encountered by change agents in all organizations are in many ways similar, and the sharing of these perspectives could only serve to enhance the knowledge and skill of low-power practitioners in these diverse fields.

CHANGE VERSUS NO CHANGE

In the face of increasingly large and centralized bureaucracies, influenced by political and economic forces that are often incomprehensible, many human service professionals have become discouraged about the prospects for humane and responsive organizational policies and practices. The most common expression of this despair is an unhappy accommodation with the status quo. Some few who see the policies and practices of human service organizations as a reflection of larger societal problems counsel foundamental social change as the only alternative.[3] This may ultimately prove to be true, but the approach suggested in this book is another alternative. Admittedly incremental and reformist, and perhaps unequal to the task of resolving the basic problems that confront our society, organizational change from below is nevertheless an arena in which low-power practitioners can positively influence at least a small part of the world in which they live. This modest role in social change may not equal the ambitious rhetoric of the sixties or the aspirations of those who see the human service professions as a major force in revamping social institutions. It is nonetheless a place to start. If we can be successful in humanizing our own organizations, the prospects for effectiveness in larger arenas would seem to be enhanced.

Notes

1. There has been some limited emperical work on organizational change from below that could serve as a basis for further research. See, for example, Richard Cowin, "Strategies for Organizational Innovation," in *Human Service Organizations*, ed. Yeheokel Hosenfeld and Richard English (Ann Arbor, Mich.: University of Michigan Press, 1974), pp. 698–720. See also Andre L. Delbecq, "The Social Political Process in Introducing Innovation in Human Services," in *Management of Human Services*, ed. Rosemary Saari and Yeheskel Hosenfeld (New York: Columbia University Press, 1978), pp. 309–339.

2. Milton Tambor, "Unions and Voluntary Agencies," *Social Work* 18, no. 4 (July 1973): 41–47.

3. Willard Richan and Allan Mendelsohn, *Social Work: The Unloved Profession* (New York: Franklin Watts, 1973).

Appendix   A Workshop on Organizational Change
for Supervisors and Practitioners

Herman Resnick

This appendix describes an organizational change training program for human service practitioners and/or supervisors. The objective of this program is to increase and improve organizational change activity among human service personnel. An ultimate goal, of course, is to improve service to clients as well as the quality of working life for human service workers.

Human service organizations, and others as well, are often criticized for insufficient utilization of staff ideas. Resources potentially available to these organizations are therefore not being used. Further, it has been recognized that personnel in the lower reaches of the organization often experience morale problems caused by frustration with the ineffectiveness of the organization and the tendency of administrators to ignore the expertise and potential contributions of their staff. This training pro- staff, by improving staff skills in increasing the utilization of their ideas, can be seen as an effort to improve both the effectiveness of the organization and staff morale.

DESCRIPTION OF TRAINING PROGRAM

The program is divided into three parts: pre-, during, and post-workshop phases. The agenda for the three phases is as follows:

AGENDA FOR ORGANIZATIONAL CHANGE WORKSHOP

ACTIVITY	TIME	EQUIPMENT AND MATERIALS NEEDED

Pre-Workshop: Phase 1

Letter is sent to participants asking for (1) problem they want to work on and (2) solutions they think will solve it; letter includes purpose and possible activities of the workshop as well as information about time, place, meals, and dress.	Pre-workshop	Names and addresses of participants

Workshop: Phase 2

A. *Introduction and get-acquainted*

1. During registration and coffee, participants scan their problems and solutions, which have been written on newsprint and posted on walls	8:30–9:00	Newsprint, masking tape, felt pen
2. Introduction—workshop leader restates purposes, possible activities of workshop, and details regarding meals, time, bathrooms, etc.	9:00–9:15	Chairs, flip charts, easels
3. Form trios—get acquainted and then introduce to all	9:15–10:00	Chairs

B. *Improving communication*	10:00–10:45	Chairs
1. Paraphrasing exercise		
a. Obstacles to communication—brief discussion	10:00–10:15	
b. Demonstration of paraphrasing	10:15–10:30	
c. Trio exercise—paraphrasing practice	10:30–10:45	

C. *Improving understanding of problem to be worked on*

1. Input on writing problem statements	10:45–11:00	Easel, newsprint, masking tape, felt pen
2. In above trios, discuss original problem statement, using both paraphrasing and writing problem statements input as guideline	11:00–11:30	Paper, pencils, tables, chairs
3. Alone—participants rewrite original problem statements	11:30–12:00	
Lunch	12:00–1:00	

D. *Getting the best solution for your problem*

1. Input on brainstorming from workshop leader	1:00–1:15	Newsprint
2. Trios form groups of six	1:15–2:30	
a. Each participant shares problem and has it paraphrased, then		
b. Group brainstorms suggested solutions for each participant		Pencils, paper, chairs, tables
3. Alone—individual participants review solutions, and select best solution for their particular problem and their particular agency		
Break	2:30–3:30	

E. *Developing a plan for acceptance of solution*

1. Input on strategies for and sources of resistance to organizational change	3:30–4:15	Newsprint

2. Alone—fill out Force Field Analysis Workbook (5 steps)

3. Trios—discuss work in each partici-   4:15–6:00
pant's workbook to achieve most feasible plan for acceptance of solution

4. Alone—revise plan

Dinner   6:00–7:00

F. *Back-home problem-solving*

1. Simulation design and participating in   7:00–9:00
think a situation that participants judge
would pose some problems for them in
their agencies when they are engaged in
the organizational change process
   a. Design a simulation that captures
   the essence of the situation
   b. Role-play it, with members of the
   workshop playing necessary roles
   c. Debrief

2. Workshop ends—participants confirm
next meeting date and contract to send
letter to workshop tester about progress
and problems prior to the followup
workshop

Followup Workshop: Phase 3

1. When they enter, participants scan   9:00–9:30
summaries of progress letters written
on newsprint and posted on walls

2. Workshop leader makes input on typical followup problems and suggests
design for day

3. Form teams of six—participants share
progress and problems one by one, are
paraphrased to check for understanding, and then use group as consultant

to improve their organizational change
effectiveness

Lunch	12:00–1:00
Continuation of morning meeting	1:00–2:30
4. Workshop leader summarizes major sources of resistance to organizational change projects that have emerged in followup activity	2:30–3:30
5. Individuals specify next action steps that need to be taken to complete their organizational change project.	3:30–4:30
6. Followup workshop ends—participants share their experiences with each other.	

PRE-WORKSHOP: PHASE 1

This phase, prior to the workshop itself, is intended to stimulate participants' thinking about innovations that they would wish to incorporate into their organization. To achieve that goal a letter is sent to participants informing them of the purpose, assumptions, and details of the workshop and asking that they fill out a brief questionnaire to describe an innovation that they wish to promote in their organization and the problem for which this innovation is a solution or remedy. The letters thus set the stage for the participants by orienting them to the model of problem-solving implicit in this training program—that is, the problem specification and understanding that precede solution-thinking. It also brings to the workshop itself a group of participants who, having done some advance work, are possibly more committed and involved than if they had come with little or no preparation.

The workshop begins during registration and coffee in the morning. At that time, participants are encouraged to scan the large newsprint sheets posted on the wall containing the problems and solutions they had written about. After a brief introduction by the workshop leader specifying purposes of and possible activities in the workshop, participants are asked to form trios, get acquainted, and talk briefly about their agency problems and the innovations on which they want to work. After this, members of the trios introduce each other to the rest of the workshop.

WORKSHOP: PHASE 2

The workshop has two major foci: a planning-thinking emphasis, which is the major emphasis of the program, and a back-home problem-solving focus, which comes at the end of the workshop and is of shorter duration. The planning focus engages the participants in four experiences; communication; writing problem statements; groups as a resource; and acceptance of innovations. The back-home component has two major activities: designing and participating in a simulation, and getting feedback from that experience.

Planning

COMMUNICATION

Following the warmup activities, the workshop leader begins a discussion about obstacles to effective communication and then presents a technique—paraphrasing—to reduce some of the adverse effects of these obstacles:

Exercise on Listening and Paraphrasing

In every working group, each member, at any particular time, is either (a) listening, or (b) talking, or (c) taking a vacation from the work of the group. Status leaders, generally, are expected to talk, expect to talk, do talk. Our training in communications ordinarily includes the skills of reading, writing, and speaking, but not the skills of listening. Listening carefully to the dynamic verbal interplay in a group is a difficult skill—we *assume* it. The underlying assumptions seem to be that if the message is sent in proper fashion, we need not be concerned with the receiver. This seems to be highly erroneous, however, since there is ample evidence that despite the clarity of the message, considerable distortion occurs. Some of the factors contributing to this distortion are:

1. Our attitude or feeling toward the speaker
2. Anticipating what the other person will say
3. Cultural values which cause us to screen out certain areas
4. Failure to attend to both the words and the music
5. Learned deafness in response to questions or statements which require no real answer—for instance, the greeting, "How are you?"

The practice or skill of paraphrasing when used properly should appreciably reduce the level of distortion and increase the comprehension and understanding of another person's message. *Paraphrasing is making sure you understand the ideas, information, and suggestions of others.* To check your understanding, state the other's idea in your own words or give an example that shows what you think he is talking about.

Procedure: Divide the group into subgroups of three persons each and separate as far apart as possible to reduce distraction from noise level. A topic is suggested for discussion, and group members then proceed to practice listening skills and use of paraphrase while observing the following ground rules:

1. After the initial comment, the next speaker must—*before he makes his own contribution to the discussion*—paraphase the essential meaning of the previous statement(s) to indicate that he has understood what the person was trying to say.
2. The participant making the paraphrase *must get agreement* that it is an accurate restatement from the originator before he makes his own comments.
3. If the paraphrasing does not adequately reflect what the first person was trying to say, the first person restates his point and the process is repeated.

Discussion points following the experience:

1. Repeating words verbatim does not necessarily convey understanding.
2. Silence kills us; while you're thinking, the other person starts talking again.
3. While listening and rephrasing, you forget the point you wanted to make.
4. The difficulty of listening increases with the length of the statement, the level of abstraction, and poor organization of the ideas expressed.

5. As group size increases, it becomes more difficult to participate: some feel less responsibility and sit back; some feel more responsibility to keep the group going. The tendency is toward a two- or three-person exchange, with the rest being inactive.

6. It requires special effort to really understand what people are saying to us.

A demonstration of this technique is followed by an exercise that gives participants the opportunity to practice this paraphrasing skill in groups of three. They do this by sharing with each other their original problems and solutions and then have their ideas paraphrased in these newly formed trios. This series of activities provides participants with a beginning set of skills to use in the workshop and helps form some beginning relationships as well.

WRITING PROBLEM STATEMENTS

After lunch the workshop leader provides input on "guidelines for writing problem statements" and asks participants in the same trios to discuss their original problem statements, using both their paraphrasing skills and the guidelines for writing problem statements they have just learned:

Four Guidelines for Writing a Problem Statement

Suppose that I said to you, "We have a communication problem among our faculty. What would you suggest we do about it?" You would undoubtedly want to ask many questions before hazarding an action suggestion. What is it that is not being communicated? Who feels the need for such communication? Why isn't this communication taking place? Specifically, who would need to be communicating what to whom to improve the problem situation?

A good problem statement includes answers to such questions. It is a brief, specific statement about a problem situation. A problem situation exists when there is a difference between the way things are and the way someone would like them to be. The word "problem" tends to suggest a negative meaning to most of us. The definition used here can be applied to situations that we feel negative about. It also applies to situations that are not thought of as negative ones. The situation might be generally good now and an accomplishment of a new objective might make it even better. You might have a station wagon that satisfies your family's basic needs and feel that having a sports car too would make things even better.

Using the definition of a problem situation as one where there is a discrepancy between the way things are now and the way someone would like them to be implies that there are almost always "problems" that could be worked on. There are almost always improvement goals in education that we would like to be working toward.

One of the greatest barriers to working constructively toward achieving improvement goals is lack of specificity in stating the problem. Compare the two following efforts to state a problem.

We have a communication problem among our faculty.

We use team teaching in our building. Virtually all of us involved in teams are concerned that we haven't given adequate attention to creating ways to share innovative ideas across teams. We need ways of sharing that don't take up the time of those to whom a particular idea is not relevant, but which share enough detail so that those who are interested will know how to try it out in their own setting.

The latter statement covers four points that are suggested as guidelines for writing a good problem statement. It answers each of these guideline questions:

1. *Who is affected?* Members of the teaching teams are affected: "virtually all of us involved in teams are concerned. . . ."
2. *Who is causing it?* The members of the teaching teams seem to see themselves as mainly responsible: "we haven't given adequate attention. . . ."
3. *What kind of problem is it?* Note that the reason for the problem is a lack of adequate means for doing something: "We need ways of sharing. . . ."
4. *What is the goal for improvement?* Specifically, how will things look when the goal has been achieved? In this case, it has been made clear that the goal is not simply increased communications. The goal is creation of "ways of sharing that don't take up time of those to whom a particular idea is not relevant, but which share enough detail so that those who are interested will know how to try it out in their own setting."

The most important guideline for writing a good problem statement is inclusion of a specific goal for improvement. Two kinds of confusion can arise when you are attempting to describe the goal for improvement in your statement. One relates to the fact that there may be many possible major and minor goals in the problem situation. It may require many, many pages of writing to describe the entire problem situation. Describing the problem situation is not the same as writing a problem statement. A problem statement answers the four guideline questions in focusing on one, specific improvement goal within the problem situation.

The second kind of confusion arises from needing to be specific in writing the problem statement, while at the same time being ready to change the statement any time new understandings of the problem situation indicate that you should do so. In the early stages of working on a problem, I may have quite erroneous ideas about what kind of problem it is or what the improvement goal should be. By stating specifically what I think is the case, I'll know what to explore. I will be clear about what to change in the statement any time new information shows my initial ideas were wrong. The problem statement should be as specific as possible, but always open to change in the light of new understanding.

Following are some considerations that can help you to be specific as you respond to the four guideline questions while writing a problem statement:

1. *Who is affected?* Consider these possibilities before deciding what you want to say about this. Is it you? Is it one other person? Is it a small group of people? Is it an entire organization? Is it the community or society at large?

2. *Who is causing it?* We frequently speak of problems as though they were caused by circumstances that didn't relate directly to people. This is almost never the case. There is almost always some person or persons who could influence things being different. Consider the same possibilities as above. Is it you? Is it one other person? Is it a small group of people? Is it an entire organization? Is it the community or society at large?

3. *What kind of a problem is it?* There are many ways to classify kinds of problems. The following considerations may prove helpful: There is lack of clarity or disagreement about *goals*. There is lack of clarity or disagreement about the *means* of achieving goals. There is a lack of *skill* needed to carry out a particular means. There is a lack of *material resources*. There is *inaccurate communication*. There is *too little* or *too much communication*. People have a *different understanding* of the same thing. There is *insufficient time* or *schedules* don't coincide. *Roles* are lacking or inappropriate. *Norms* are restrictive, unclear, or misinterpreted. There are conflicts of ideology. There is a lack of clarity or a conflict about *decision-making—*

for instance, power struggles. Expression of *feelings* is inappropriate or inadequate. There is conflict related to *individual differences.*

4. *What is the goal for improvement?* Ideally, this should be stated so clearly that anyone reading your statement would know how to determine when the goal had been reached. It would tell exactly who would be doing what, where, how and to what extent. Until you know where you are going, it's very difficult to make and carry out plans to get there. The more clear you are about your intended target at any given time, the more likely you will be to recognize when it is an incorrect target, should this prove to be the case.

Following this, participants spend some time alone rewriting their problem statements, making use of the critical comments from their trios. This task completes the second major set of activities in the workshop—that is, writing statements that describe as accurately as possible the problem situation as it is now and as they would like it to be.

THE GROUP AS A RESOURCE-SOLUTION

The next set of experiences is directed toward making use of the group as a resource to come up with the most creative ideas to reduce or solve each particular problem. The workshop leader makes a presentation on brainstorming as a technique for sharing ideas, and then asks that the trios form into groups of six. In this new group, each member shares his or her newly revised problem statement. The group then brainstorms all the innovations they can think of to reduce or solve each of the problems. Following this, the individuals again work alone to select, from all the ideas, that particular one that seems best. This completes the third set of exercises designed to help each participant select the best innovation to solve the problem he or she is working on.

PLAN FOR ACCEPTANCE OF INNOVATION

The fourth round of activities is designed to help participants establish a plan to increase the possibility of their innovation's being accepted by their administrators. The workshop leader presents a lecture on strategies for organizational change and asks participants to develop a strategy or plan for action that could help facilitate the acceptance of their innovations. The development of this plan is aided by the use of force field analysis workbooks, which direct participants to: (1) specify the goals of the strategy; (2) list the potential inhibiting forces in their organization vis-à-vis this goal or goals; (3) list the major potential supporting forces in this organization vis-à-vis this goal or goals; (4) specify action steps to be taken to reduce inhibiting forces and to increase the supporting forces; and (5) arrange these steps into a sequence or a plan of action.

A Problem-Solving Program for Defining a Problem and Planning Action*

This workbook is designed to help you in analyzing a problem in organization, management, or human relations—any problem which involves people working or living together. It is organized on the assumption that the participants in this course:

(1) are interested in getting a particular "innovation" utilized by their department and
(2) view this workshop as adding to their skills and knowledge to help this happen.

It is also assumed that participants have already written a brief statement: (a) identifying the problem(s) for which their innovation was seen as a "solution," and (b) describing their innovation.

The workbook is programmed. That is, it is presented in a series of separate steps or "frames" each of which contains a complete and separate idea, question, or instruction.

Be sure you understand and have completed each frame before going on to the next.

1. The first step in this process of analysis is for you to identify the problem you wish to work on in your organization (towards which your innovation is directed).

   Describe the problem as you now see it. What information do you have and how reliable or subjective is the information you have which tells you there is indeed a problem?

2. Now specify who has the problem—whom does it affect adversely? Positively?

---

*Designed by Saul Eisen. Adapted by Hy Resnick for workshops on Innovation in Organizations.

3. Briefly and specifically discuss who or what is generating the problem. What role might you be playing in generating the problem, if any?

4. What type of problem is it? Primary or secondary? Resources or allocation? Communication? Attitudes? Horizontal or vertical? Briefly discuss.

5. Most problem statements can be rephrased, so that they describe two things:
   (*a*) the situation as it is now
   (*b*) the situation as you would like it to be with your innovation accepted and used.
   Restate your problem situation in these terms.

The section of the workbook just completed was designed to help you obtain a better understanding of the problem situation.

This next section is organized to help you plan and implement strategies and action steps to:

   (*a*) increase the possibilities of the utilization of your innovation in order to
   (*b*) improve the problem situation on which you are working.

6. Now think of the person(s) who will be responsible for making the decisions affecting the achievement of your goals. Who are they? What do they typically decide on in the department? Do they have authority to do so? How will they react to your proposal?
   List these decision-makers and your responses to these questions.

Name (may be disguised) of decision-maker	Formal position in agency	Kind of decision-making done	Legitimation to do so	Support-resistance
1.				
2.				
3.				
etc.				

7. In thinking about the persons responsible for decisions affecting your proposal briefly outline your thoughts in relation to the following:

    (*a*) What are the rewards they seem to value? Financial? Professional? Organizational? Interpersonal acceptance? Other?

    (*b*) In which situations are they most receptive to new ideas? Least receptive?

    (*c*) What mode of persuasion seems to work best with them?

    (*d*) What issues are taboo with them?

    (*e*) Characterize your relationship with them—what implications might this have for acceptance of your proposal?

8. Most problem situations can be understood in terms of the forces which push toward improvement and the forces which resist improvement—in other words, *driving forces* and *restraining forces*.

Restraining Forces

Driving Forces

9. It is useful to analyze a problem by making lists of the driving and restraining forces affecting your problem situation. [See number 5(a).] Think about these now, and list them on additional pages.

    Be sure to list as many as you can, not worrying at this point about how important each one is.

10.   RESTRAINING FORCES
                 (heading for blank page)

11.   DRIVING FORCES
                 (heading for blank page)

12. Now review the two lists, and underline those forces which seem to be the most important right now, and which you think you might be able to affect constructively.

Depending on the problem, there may be one specific force which stands out, or there may be two or three driving forces and two or three restraining forces which are particularly important.

13. Now, for *each restraining force* you have underlined list some possible action steps which you might be able to plan and carry out to reduce the effect of the force or to eliminate it completely.

    Brainstorm. List as many action steps as possible, without worrying about how effective or practical they would be. You will later have a chance to decide which are the most appropriate.

    RESTRAINING FORCE A ....
    Possible action steps to reduce this factor:
    (heading for blank page)

    RESTRAINING FORCE B ....
    Possible action steps to reduce this factor:
    (heading for blank page)

    RESTRAINING FORCE C ....
    Possible action steps to reduce this factor:
    (heading for blank page)

14. Now do the same with each driving force you underlined. List all the action steps which come to mind which would increase the effect of each driving force.

    DRIVING FORCE A ....
    Possible action steps to increase this factor:
    (heading for blank page)

    DRIVING FORCE B ....
    Possible action steps to increase this factor:
    (heading for blank page)

    DRIVING FORCE C ....
    Possible action steps to increase this factor:
    (heading for blank page)

15. You have now listed possible action steps to change the key forces affecting your problem situation. Review these possible action steps and underline those which seem promising.

16. List the steps you have underlined. Then for each action step list the materials, people, and other resources which are available to you for carrying out the action.

ACTION STEPS.	RESOURCES AVAILABLE
1.	1.
2.	2.
3.	3.
etc.	etc.

17. Now review the list of action steps and resources in the previous frame, and think about how they might each fit into a comprehensive action plan. Eliminate those items which do not seem to fit into the overall plan, add any new steps and resources which will round out the plan, and think about a possible sequence of action.

18. The final step in this problem-solving process is for you to plan a way of evaluating the effectiveness of your action program as it is implemented. Think about this now, and list the evaluation procedures you will use.

Back Home Problem-Solving

Participants now have an improved understanding of the problem they are working on, they have selected an innovation to solve the problem, and they have a plan to increase the possibility of the innovation's being accepted. However, the plans need to be implemented with effective interaction if they are to receive consideration and possible acceptance by agency administration. To help participants with this aspect of the organizational change process, the last segment of the workshop focuses on those situations back home with which each participant feels he or she needs particular help. (Examples of such situations include building an action system of colleagues, meeting with administration to approve the suggested solutions, and so on.)

Each participant selects the situation they would like to work on and designs a simulation that could help them. The other workshop members participate in each simulation and observe the effectiveness or lack of it of the situation. After the simulation is run, the experience is discussed and feedback is offered to the participant conducting the simulation. As a result of this activity, the participants are now more ready to deal with some of the real-life situations they will presumably face in their organizations back home. The workshop ends with participants making specific plans for the following week to begin promoting their innovations.

POST-WORKSHOP: PHASE 3

A post-workshop phase is designed into the organizational training program because of the typical loss of momentum and energy following many workshops and the change agent's need for continued third-party help when he or she experiences reactions by colleagues and administrators to the change efforts.

A one-day followup event is held, where participants share their experiences with each other—frustrations as well as successes. The group serves as helpers for each other, as well as learners. By listening to the experience of a number of colleagues, they increase their own understanding of the organizational change process and dilemmas. Workshop leaders are used typically as information-givers. They focus on facilitating the group's using itself as a resource for its members. One unanticipated reaction was the strength drawn from each other by both the failures and successes in the organizational change process.

Index